The Politics of Heritage Management in Mali

Publications of the
Institute of Archaeology, University College London

Series Editor: Ruth Whitehouse
Director of the Institute: Stephen Shennan
Founding Series Editor: Peter J. Ucko

The Institute of Archaeology of University College London is one of the oldest, largest, and most prestigious archaeology research facilities in the world. Its extensive publications programme includes the best theory, research, pedagogy, and reference materials in archaeology and cognate disciplines, through publishing exemplary work of scholars worldwide. Through its publications, the Institute brings together key areas of theoretical and substantive knowledge, improves archaeological practice, and brings archaeological findings to the general public, researchers, and practitioners. It also publishes staff research projects, site and survey reports, and conference proceedings. The publications programme, formerly developed in-house or in conjunction with UCL Press, is now produced in partnership with Left Coast Press, Inc. The Institute can be accessed online at *www.ucl.ac.uk/archaeology*.

Critical Cultural Heritage Series, Beverley Butler (Ed.)

Charlotte Joy, *The Politics of Heritage Management in Mali*
Layla Renshaw, *Exhuming Loss*
Katharina Schramm, *African Homecoming*
Mingming Wang, *Empire and Local Worlds*
Dean Sully (ed.), *Decolonizing Conservation*
Ferdinand de Jong and Michael Rowlands (eds.), *Reclaiming Heritage*
Beverley Butler, *Return to Alexandria*

Recent Titles

Ethan E. Cochrane and Andrew Gardner, *Evolutionary and Interpretive Archaeologies*
Andrew Bevan and David Wengrow (eds.), *Cultures of Commodity Branding*
Peter Jordan (ed.), *Landscape and Culture in Northern Eurasia*
Peter Jordan and Marek Zvelebil (eds.), *Ceramics before Farming*
Marcos Martinón-Torres and Thilo Rehren (eds.), *Archaeology, History, and Science*
Miriam Davis, *Dame Kathleen Kenyon*
Elizabeth Pye (ed.), *The Power of Touch*
Russell McDougall and Iain Davidson (eds.), *The Roth Family, Anthropology, and Colonial Administration*
Eleni Asouti and Dorian Q. Fuller, *Trees and Woodlands of South India*
Tony Waldron, *Paleoepidemiology*
Janet Picton, Stephen Quirke, and Paul C. Roberts (eds.), *Living Images*
Timothy Clack and Marcus Brittain (eds.), *Archaeology and the Media*
Sue Colledge and James Conolly (eds.), *The Origins and Spread of Domestic Plants in Southwest Asia and Europe*
Gustavo Politis, *Nukak*
Sue Hamilton, Ruth Whitehouse, and Katherine I. Wright (eds.) *Archaeology and Women*
Andrew Gardner, *An Archaeology of Identity*
Barbara Bender, Sue Hamilton, and Chris Tilley, *Stone World*
James Graham-Campbell and Gareth Williams (eds.), *Silver Economy in the Viking Age*
Gabriele Puschnigg, *Ceramics of the Merv Oasis*
Joost Fontein, *The Silence of Great Zimbabwe*

The Politics of Heritage Management in Mali

From UNESCO to Djenné

Charlotte Joy

LONDON AND NEW YORK

First published 2012 by Left Coast Press, Inc.

Published 2016 by Routledge
2 Park Square, Milton Park, Abingdon, Oxon OX14 4RN
711 Third Avenue, New York, NY 10017, USA

Routledge is an imprint of the Taylor & Francis Group, an informa business

Copyright © 2012 Taylor & Francis

All rights reserved. No part of this book may be reprinted or reproduced or utilised in any form or by any electronic, mechanical, or other means, now known or hereafter invented, including photocopying and recording, or in any information storage or retrieval system, without permission in writing from the publishers.

Notice:
Product or corporate names may be trademarks or registered trademarks, and are used only for identification and explanation without intent to infringe.

Library of Congress Cataloging-in-Publication Data:

Joy, Charlotte, 1977-
The politics of heritage management in Mali : from UNESCO to Djenné / Charlotte Joy.
    p. cm.—(Publications of the Institute of Archaeology, University College London)
Includes bibliographical references and index.
ISBN 978-1-61132-094-7 (hardcover : alk. paper) — ISBN 978-1-61132-096-1 (eBook)
1. Djenné (Mali)—History. 2. Djenné (Mali)—Buildings, structures, etc. 3. Djenné (Mali)—Social conditions. 4. Cultural property—Conservation and restoration—Mali. 5. World Heritage areas—Mali. I. Title. II. Series: Publications of the Institute of Archaeology, University College London.
DT551.9.D35J69 2011
363.6'9096623–dc23
                    2011036202

ISBN 978-1-61132-094-7 hardcover

For Tom and our tiny men: Alex, Sam, and Leo.

Contents

List of Illustrations	11
Series Foreword *by Beverly Butler*	13
Acknowledgments	15
Introduction	17
Djenné: Place or People?	17
About Djenné	25
Djenné's Mosque	30
The Cultural Mission and the Heritage Elite	32
Djenné's Future	35
About This Book	36
PART I: Putting Djenné on the Map	37
1 Architecture and the "Creation" of Djenné in the West	39
Early Explorers	41
French Colonialism	43
Colonial Officials and Photographers in Djenné	45
Colonial Exhibitions	47
The Second World War and Decolonisation	48
Conclusion	49
2 Archaeology and Architecture	51
Islamic Diffusionism	51
Archaeology and Loss	53
Djenné's Architecture	59
The Dutch Housing Restoration Project	66
The Sanitation Project	70
Conclusion	73

3 UNESCO and Becoming a World Heritage Site	75
UNESCO's History	75
Working for UNESCO	77
UNESCO's Concept of Culture	80
The World Heritage List	82
Becoming a World Heritage Site	83
The Concept of World Heritage	85
UNESCO's Limits	87
Intangible Cultural Heritage and Outstanding Universal Value	88
Intangible Cultural Heritage in Mali	89
Conclusion	90
PART II: LIFE IN DJENNÉ	93
4 Islam	95
An Islamic Education in Djenné	98
The "Prayer Economy"	99
Amulets and Shoes	101
The Problem of *Garibous*	104
UNESCO and Islam	105
Conclusion	106
5 Livelihood Strategies	109
Grass Root Organisations	109
The Monday Market	110
Women	112
Material Possessions	115
Poverty	118
The 2006 Riot	120
Conclusion	125
6 Artisans, Embodied Knowledge, and Authenticity	129
Being an Embroiderer's Apprentice	130
Artisan Associations	138
Negotiating Authenticity	141
Embodied Knowledge	142
Voices of Authenticity in Djenné	144
Biennale de Ségou	145
Conclusion	146
7 Guides and the Regulation of History in Djenné	147
The Status of the Guides	149
Dramane's Story	149
The Tourist Season	154

OMATHO   157
Becoming a Guide in Djenné   159
Papa's Story   161
Djenné and Multiple Histories   162
Access to Income from Cultural Heritage   164
The Tourist   165
The Mali Circuit   168
UNESCO and Tourism   173
Conclusion   175

8 *Festival du Djennéry*   179
Festivals in Mali   182
Whose Festival?   183
Negotiations around the *crépissage* of the Mosque   185
Organising the Festival   189
The Opening Ceremony   193
Soirées Culturelles   194
The Exhibition Hall   195
Conclusion   196

9 **Conclusion**   199
The Lessons from Intangible Heritage   202
Democratising Heritage   204
Djenné's Future   204
Heritage Ethnographies   209

Appendices   211

Appendix 1: Imams of the Great Mosque in Djenné   211
Appendix 2: Chefs du Village   212
Appendix 3: Ministry of Culture *Organigram*   212
Appendix 4: Impact of Tourism Diagram   213

Notes   215

References   223

Index   231

About the Author   235

List of Illustrations

Figure I.1	House of the *Chef du Village* in Djenné	18
Figure I.2	Orange shop in Djenné	19
Figure I.3	Aga Khan Restoration Project showing collapsed part of Mosque	23
Figure I.4	Tomb of Tapama Djennépo	28
Figure I.5	Young Peul herder brings home his cows	30
Figure I.6	The Great Mosque as a backdrop on market day	31
Figure I.7	The Cultural Mission of Djenné	32
Figure 2.1	Pot fragments at Djenné-Djeno	52
Figure 2.2	European-funded museum in Djenné	58
Figure 2.3	*Djenné-Ferey* brick	60
Figure 2.4	*Toubabou-Ferey* square bricks drying in the sun	61
Figure 2.5	Tiled house in Djenné	62
Figure 2.6	House covered in tiles behind a collapsed building in Djenné	63
Figure 2.7	Mason erecting a facade of a Djenné house	65
Figure 2.8	Houses in Djenné restored by the Dutch Housing Restoration project	67
Figure 2.9	House with sanitation tank	70
Figure 2.10	A narrow street in Djenné	73
Figure 3.1	Cattle crossing at Sofara	91
Figure 4.1	Amulet or *gris-gris* commissioned by the author	103
Figure 4.2	Islamic manuscripts in Imam's museum	106

Figure 5.1	UNESCO World Heritage sign during a market day	111
Figure 5.2	Tourists buying *bogolan* at women's cooperative	116
Figure 5.3	Inside a house showing pots and chalk boards of Qu'ranic student	117
Figure 6.1	Author with Ousmane Traore, embroiderer	131
Figure 6.2	Cream thread on white bazin *grand boubou*	133
Figure 6.3	Sketch design of embroidery patterns on paper	134
Figure 6.4	Alpha Sidiki Touré, jeweler in Djenné	139
Figure 6.5	Handmade jewelry	140
Figure 7.1	Hama Lamine Traoré, guide in Djenné	148
Figure 7.2	Impromptu Djembe dance session in Djenné	155
Figure 7.3	Hotel Djenné-Djeno on the outskirts of the town	156
Figure 7.4	Blocked storm drain in Djenné	164
Figure 7.5	Dogon Country	170
Figure 8.1	*Chef de Quartier* meeting to decide on date for the *crépissage*	186
Figure 8.2	Bringing mud for the *crépissage*	188
Figure 8.3	Culture mission photos at Djenné Festival	196

Series Editor's Foreword
Critical Perspectives on Cultural Heritage

Beverly Butler

The aim of this Critical Perspectives on Cultural Heritages series is to define a new area of research and to produce a set of volumes that make a radical break with routinised accounts and definitions of cultural heritage and with the existing or "established" canon of cultural heritage texts. In a fundamental shift of perspective, the French intellectual Jacques Derrida's rallying call to "restore heritage to dignity" is to be taken as an alternative guiding metaphor by which this series critically revisits the core question—what constitutes cultural heritage?—and engages with the concerns (notably the moral-ethical issues) that shape and define the possible futures of cultural heritage studies. A key objective is that this series be of transformative value in the sense of outlining and creating new and future agendas within cultural heritage discourse using individual texts as building blocks.

This series of publications is therefore intended to provide the intellectual impetus and critical framework by which cultural heritage discourse can undergo a process of radical reflection, fundamental reconceptualisation, and engage in a subsequent reconstruction of its core heritage values, practices, and ethics. Central to this project is an alignment with a wider scholarship committed to disrupting the "Eurocentrism" that continues to underpin cultural heritage theory/practice and also with a contemporary "politics of recognition" that is bound up in articulating new, alternative, or "parallel" characterisations of heritage value. This commitment to produce a set of publications directed toward reconceptualising cultural heritage studies within these alternative intellectual, moral-ethical, and also grounded concerns is ultimately rooted in calls for the centring of cultural heritage discourse within a wider concern for the preservation of human dignity and human justice and to use these alternative discourses as a resource for future action in terms of creating a proactive (rather than reactive), responsive, and just future for a new critical cultural heritage studies.

Dr. Beverley Butler
Series Editor
Institute of Archaeology
UCL
London

Acknowledgments

I would like to thank Prof. Michael Rowlands for his constant help and enthusiasm since my first contact with Djenné in 2004. This book is the result of a dialogue between us and has been inspired by his research and philosophy.

During my research I was lucky to be hosted in Leiden by Annette Schmidt and Rogier Bedaux. I would like to thank them for their warm welcome and the access I was given to the Museum Volkenkunde archives and library. During my fieldwork I was greatly encouraged by the presence of some of my fellow students also doing their fieldwork in Mali: Laurence Douny, Alessandra Giuffrida, Bodil Olesen, and Sophie Mew. Colleagues at UCL also provided much needed support during my writing period.

Thanks to Trevor Marchand and Susan Vogel for inviting me to attend the ACASA Conference in Gainesville and to the UCL Graduate School for allowing me to attend the Terra 2008 Conference in Bamako. Thank you to Cristiana Panella for sharing her experiences with me. I would also like to thank Lazare Eloundou and Jana Weydt at the World Heritage Centre at UNESCO for their openness, interest, and feedback. At UNESCO, I also extend my gratitude to César Moreno-Triana for giving me an internship and to all the team in the Intangible Heritage Department for making my stay in Paris such an enjoyable one. I also thank my colleagues at the Museum of Archaeology and Anthropology in Cambridge, in particular Prof. Nicholas Thomas and Dr. Anita Herle. Thank you to Dr. Beverly Butler at UCL and the team at Left Coast Press: Mitch Allen, Ryan Harris, and Stacey C. Sawyer. Thank you to Peter Brick for all his help with referencing, indexing, and fact checking.

The list of people to thank in Djenné is perhaps too long to include here, but I am particularly grateful to the family at the *Tapama* and their neighbours for allowing me into their lives: Adama Boucoum, Bayere and Kadija Kouroumanse, the guides, Ousmane Traoré, Alpha Sidiki Touré, Abdullaye Sao, Morifing Traoré, the staff at the Cultural Mission, and the members of *Djenné Patrimoine*. Thank you to Prof. Phil Burnham for reading earlier drafts of some of the chapters; Dr. Donald Macleod for his feedback on the tourism chapter; the staff at the British Library for all their help; and the ESRC for funding the research.

Finally, a big thank you to my parents, friends, and family for their practical help, love, encouragement, and babysitting.

Of course, despite all this input, the book's failings remain my own.

Charlotte Joy
November 2011

Introduction

The little weighing boy just came round; he makes money by charging people the equivalent of 1 penny to stand on some broken bathroom scales. He has epilepsy and A explained that at school all the students get together to pay for his healthcare treatment. It seems that this boy's treatment has run out and now he is having the fits again as it is the summer holiday. . . . People in the streets ask if I am a doctor. In every family that I have seen in the last few weeks there is someone suffering or dying. It's hard because so many of them are children. A explained that the weighing boy's father makes terracotta tiles and his mother threads beads to make bracelets. Everyone is so desperately poor at the moment that they won't be buying either of those things. The tourist season is awaited like the one big hope. After the failed rains and the locusts the tourist season simply has to work. And there are still two months to wait.[1]

Djenné: Place or People?

This book is about a situation in a particular place and time: Djenné, a mud brick town in Mali, at the turn of the 21st century. Djenné is a city with a complex identity. At first glance, there seem to be two Djennés: the first, a timeless authentic African town of mud, declared a United Nations Educational, Scientific and Cultural Organization (UNESCO)

World Heritage Site, situated next to the ancient archaeological remains of Djenné-Djeno, to be enjoyed by tourists and celebrated by heritage practitioners and politicians; the second, a town beset by poverty, a housing crisis, with little access to the neighbouring archaeological heritage and losing population through increasing emigration. Djenné is both beautiful and poor; people are proud of their cultural heritage as well as being oppressed by it. Many young men leave Djenné in search of work and money, but many also return, finding that the world outside Djenné does not suit them.

The paradox of the two Djennés centres on an ambivalence on behalf of the town's population, who are caught between wanting to possess the heritage value of the town for their own advantage while at the same time feeling oppressed by it (see also Herzfeld, 1991; Yalouri, 2001). The paradox maps neatly on to two major, and related, debates within current Heritage Studies. First, there is a moral/philosophical question about the use of the past for current purposes. This is a well-rehearsed argument seeking to transcend an elite and exclusionary narrative of past events. In academic disciplines such as history, economics, and anthropology, the historic net has been cast more widely to encompass the experience of non-elite and previously marginalised people. Within the heritage industry,

Figure I.1 House of the *Chef du Village* in Djenné

there has been considerable difficulty in keeping up with this moral/philosophical shift—with some notable exceptions, such as the recent focus on the slave trade.[2]

The second debate is less about the representation of the past and more about its appropriation for contemporary purposes. In Djenné the past has been reified and calcified by archaeologists, anthropologists, colonial officials, architects, and travel writers. This version of the past, packaged by UNESCO and within travel guides and documentaries, is then projected back onto modern-day Djenné.

The task of finding the discrepancies between the reality and the projection is not a difficult one. However, identifying how the projection can best be used by Djenné residents to improve their living conditions is very complex. At its heart, the projection of the past on to Djenné is

Figure I.2 Orange (mobile communications) shop in Djenné

about identifying what is and what isn't authentic. Although very much a contested category, the concept of authenticity in Djenné has percolated down through different parts of Djenné's population. According to heritage officials, archaeology is authentic. Mud-brick architecture is authentic, depending on the technique and the materials used. The earliest photos of Djenné (for example, those taken by Fortier) are authentic. The masons of Djenné are authentic. For tourists, electricity pylons and conspicuous modernity is inauthentic. As is described later, local ideas about authenticity often radically differ from these outside views.

The desire to preserve an authentic Djenné for subsequent generations is at the heart of UNESCO's project in the town. At the same time, institutions such as UNESCO are struggling to realign their vision of culture within a new democratic paradigm. As discussed in Chapters 1 and 3, UNESCO's original remit was to "build peace in the minds of men" through intercultural dialogue as a response to the horrors of the Second World War. UNESCO's position is a difficult balance between universalism (we are all human, we all share the same fundamental values) and relativism (we all have different, but equally valid, ways of living our lives). UNESCO's position will therefore always be inherently contradictory—just as in the real world, where universalism repeatedly comes into conflict with relativism. Two examples of this discrepancy from Djenné are the early age of marriage of many girls and the use of child labour in the construction of Djenné's houses—both practices conflict with United Nations International Children's Emergency Fund's (UNICEF) Convention on the Rights of the Child.

Ethnographic knowledge of Djenné can throw light on the distance that exists between a professional, heritage-led approach to Djenné and local conceptions of life in the town. Ethnographic fieldwork in Djenné is inevitably concerned with poverty. To get to know a family in Djenné is to understand their struggle to meet the basic costs of food, health, education, and the upkeep of their houses. There are, of course, exceptions to this rule of poverty, and inevitably these exceptions are the "heritage elite" themselves, the outward-facing people of Djenné who overwhelmingly benefit from the heritage money that comes to the town. Unfortunately, many heritage professionals working in Djenné limit their dealings to this elite, either consciously, through time restrictions, or inadvertently through, for instance, taking up residence at the Cultural Mission during their stay. The heritage elite are very aware of the conditions of poverty faced by the majority of Djennenkés but must tread a careful path between praising the cultural heritage that provides Djenné with international attention and income and highlighting the limitations that this narrow definition of cultural heritage imposes on Djennenkés' ambitions for better futures.

Although popular with anthropologists, as Ferguson (2006: 192) states, applying the notion of "alternative modernities" to radically

INTRODUCTION

different life conditions found throughout the world can be dangerous. Instead of promoting equality, he fears that this "happy story about plurality and non-ranked cultural difference . . . risks becoming a way of avoiding talking about the non-serialized, de-temporalized political economic statuses of our time, and thus, evading the question of a rapidly worsening global inequality and its consequences."

Heritage officials working in Djenné must ask themselves some very fundamental questions about what should and should not be considered suitable living conditions for people in the 21st century. Beyond concern about the fabric of the houses themselves and the constraints they put on their occupants, there is also the wider question of livelihoods, of how people living in a World Heritage Site, intended by UNESCO to forever remain a "medieval town," can come to imagine their place in the world today and in the future.

In 1988 the Old Towns of Djenné, consisting of approximately 1,850 mud-brick houses (Bedaux et al., 2000) and its mud mosque, together with a 4 kilometre radius of surrounding archaeological sites, were judged as meeting two criteria necessary for inscription on UNESCO's World Heritage List: (1) to bear a unique or at least exceptional testimony to a cultural tradition or to a civilisation that is living or has disappeared (criterion iii) and (2) to be an outstanding example of a type of building, architectural, or technological ensemble or landscape that illustrates (a) significant stage(s) in human history (criterion iv).

Djenné's inscription on the World Heritage List has far-reaching consequences. As part of its commitment to preserving Djenné in its original state, the Malian government has set up a Cultural Mission—a body tasked with imposing strict heritage regulations—on the outskirts of the town; no unauthorised person is allowed access to the protected archaeological sites, and no visible material changes may be made to any of the houses in Djenné. Djenné must forever remain built in mud. (We must note, however, that ideas about cultural heritage are constantly evolving within UNESCO, as elsewhere, and UNESCO officials will openly state that today such a broad-brush inscription, involving an entire town and its surroundings, would not be considered appropriate.)

A review of Djenné's World Heritage status is a possibility for the future, and, as is discussed later, various plans have been put forward—a protected historic centre, a historic route through the town, representative architecture complexes—but the review risks undermining the very thing it is seeking to protect. How can some of Djenné's houses be considered more important than others? Are the monumental (elite) houses better examples than more modest homes are of a significant stage in human history?

Long-term fieldwork entails intimacy, and intimacy radically shifts the focus from the material reality of the town (the houses, the mosque, the archaeological sites) to the personal; Djenné can no longer merely be a place of architectural and archaeological wonder but becomes a place of people. Most authors dealing with Djenné to date have done so within a very broad historical span, looking to the archaeological past of Djenné-Djeno to theorise about the earliest urban settlements in Africa (McIntosh, 1998) or being concerned with its architectural future as the houses slowly decay or are altered (Bedaux et al., 2003; Maas & Mommersteeg, 1992). Through concentrating explicitly on the survival of the cultural heritage of Djenné over long periods of time, such authors discount the individual lives of people dependent on cultural heritage in different ways, such as the peasant-looters who make a living through selling archaeological objects (cf. Panella, 2002). The appropriation of cultural heritage by marginalised groups is invalidated through legal sanctions or refusal to acknowledge that such appropriation still continues.

So far, heritage professionals working in Djenné have viewed the town in a repetitive manner, without fundamentally questioning the validity of their approaches. Despite this situation, the material assistance brought to Djenné through architecture and archaeological projects has undoubtedly bolstered Djenné's status, helping it to become a UNESCO World Heritage Site and a popular tourist destination. Perhaps for many heritage practitioners this is enough. However, there is a danger in not listening to the voices of disquiet in Djenné, as was revealed in 2006 when a riot broke out after the Aga Khan Trust for Culture (AKTC) undertook restoration work on the mosque without adequately informing the population of its intentions.

In 2010 the AKTC was once again in Djenné, this time restoring the mosque to its original 1909 appearance. The restoration is being done by removing 100 years of mud from the mosque, mud that has been applied each year by hand by generations of Djennenkés. The mud is being removed for both pragmatic and aesthetic reasons. Pragmatically, there is a danger from the accumulated weight of the mud, threatening the underlying structure of the building with collapse.[3] Aesthetically, the 1909 appearance of the mosque fits within a conceptualisation of authentic Sudanese architecture. There is now talk of "professionalising" the annual process of remudding the mosque to help maintain the building's architectural and structural integrity. Such professionalisation, as will be explored, could serve to further alienate Djennenkés from their cultural heritage.

As do other studies of the imposition of a particular bureaucratic vision of the past on a population (cf. Herzfeld, 1991), this study seeks to deconstruct ideas about history, authenticity, and identity in Djenné through detailed case studies. This destabilisation is part of a growing trend within heritage studies and is beginning to be echoed by organisations such as UNESCO, who are moving their focus toward

Figure I.3 The Aga Khan Trust for Culture restoring the Great Mosque in Djenné, showing part of a collapsed tower

intangible aspects of cultural heritage and promoting the human actors that give cultural heritage its meaning. Similarly, museums across Europe and North America are rethinking their relationship with the objects held in their collections and putting "source communities" centre stage (Peers & Brown, 2003). Ideally, what would be needed would be a radical shaking out of all the categories that have come before, fundamentally questioning the tripartite relationship between people, material culture, and identity—such as the work being undertaken in material culture studies (for example, Tilley et al., 2006). In practical terms, however, organisations such as UNESCO are limited to adding categories to their possibly faulty existing projects. The political and economic imperative of many heritage projects also means that they are constrained by the expectations of politicians and the tourist industry.

The *École du Patrimoine Africain*, based in Porto Novo, Benin, has for its motto: *Un Patrimoine pour mieux se connaître et mieux se faire comprendre* ("A heritage to know ourselves better and to be better understood"). African Cultural heritage is defined and negotiated within and beyond the borders of the African continent. To date these negotiations have limited the ambition of self-knowledge and broader understanding, because they are inevitably framed within a position of Western hegemony

(Olaniyan, 2003). However, new expressions of cultural heritage are gaining recognition in Africa as elsewhere, including the recognition of intangible cultural heritage. Such cultural expressions have always been present but usually recognised in the West only by their material embodiments, such as the masks, musical instruments, and ritual objects that have found their way into Western museums and collections.

Over the last few decades, cultural heritage sites in Africa have gained increasing global recognition. UNESCO has been at the forefront of providing a successful framework for the identification and documentation of African national heritage. As part of UNESCO's work, initiatives such as "Africa 2009" have ensured the training and funding of heritage professionals across the continent.[4] Consequently, many African nation-states now have a permanent body of personnel committed to the recognition of the cultural value of their patrimony. This professionalisation of heritage has, however, not been without its casualties. In Mali, certain visions of the past have been preferred over others, and minority voices, such as that of the nomadic Tuareg, have difficulty being heard. Through the efforts of UNESCO and international archaeologists, pre-Islamic material culture has been thrust centre-stage and has been the focus of many international initiatives, although this focus is often at odds with local priorities. The professionalisation of heritage—such as the remudding of Djenné's Great Mosque—also risks alienating people from objects, buildings, and/or cultural practices they hold dear.

UNESCO's activities in Mali, which are all mediated through the Malian government, are the result of UNESCO's institutional concerns as much as a reaction to local realities. To increase its relevance and effectiveness, UNESCO needs to engage with the ethnographic reality of the World Heritage sites it brings under its jurisdiction. Furthermore, although UNESCO is officially not a development institution (Joy, 2007; Singh, 2011: 100), it is increasingly seeing its remit as one of improving people's lives through promoting their cultural heritage (see the *Mémorandum de Vienne*, adopted by UNESCO in 2005[5] and most recently the resolution adopted on Culture and Development, December 2010[6]). It is not realistic to view UNESCO's World Heritage Project as merely a labelling exercise, responding to individual government's concerns for their cultural heritage. As is later described, the process of becoming a World Heritage site is a complex partnership between UNESCO and the national government concerned (the State Party), involving repeated political and economic negotiations between the State Party and UNESCO. Furthermore, other heritage organisations working in Djenné, such as the AKTC, put development at the centre of all their cultural initiatives, since their current work in Djenné is part of the Aga Khan Development Network in Mali, which has as its aim

INTRODUCTION
25

"to contribute to poverty reduction and the improvement of the quality of life for the people of Mali."

About Djenné

Djenné is located at about 600 kilometres from Bamako, the capital of Mali. Today it is reached by way of the main tarmac surfaced road in Mali (known as *le goudron*) that runs the length of the country. Historically, Djenné provided a link between the sedentary south and the nomadic north of Mali. From the 9th century onward, Djenné played a major role as a staging post in the trans-Saharan trade and was important for the origin and growth of a succession of influential Empires. Knowledge about Mali's precolonial history is very limited. Oral history in Mali is transmitted by *griots* (Jansen & Austen, 1996; Jansen et al., 1995); however, written sources on precolonial Malian history are scarce and are predominantly written by Arabic (Levtzion, 1981) and Western visitors to the country, rather than by the indigenous population. Written sources on Djenné's history link its rise and fall to that of Timbuktu (Imperato, 1989). Both towns were centres of Islamic scholarship and became the principal trade hubs after the fall of the Empire of Ghana, founded by the Soninke, that lasted from approximately the 4th century to the 12th century C.E. (Fisher, 1982; Levtzion, 1981). The Empire of Ghana derived its wealth from the gold trade, and although the rulers of the Empire of Ghana were Animist, they accepted the presence of a large number of Muslim traders and administrators, who enabled the trans-Saharan gold trade.

The Almoravid invasions that followed effectively destroyed the Empire of Ghana and started to bring Islam to parts of modern-day Mali. Around 1230 C.E., Soundiata Keita (also known as Mari Djata), the son of a Malinke chief of the Keita clan, became the ruler of Mali, then a small vassal state of Sosso. Ibn Khaldun (1331–1382), an Arab historian residing in North Africa, provided some of the most detailed information about Soundiata and Mali, which he obtained from travellers and traders who had been to Mali. (Imperato, 1989).

Djenné first came under the control of the Kingdom of Mali, then was captured by Sonni Ali Ber (a Songhai) in 1468 and later fell to the Moroccans. Merchandise from Timbuktu was traded through Djenné, which acted as an *entrepôt* ("intermediate trade centre") during the Songhai Kingdom. In the early 19th century, Djenné fell under the rule of Cheikou Amadou Bari and was subsequently occupied by the *Tukulor* under El Hadj Omar Tall in 1862, until it was finally annexed by the French in 1893.

As is examined in Chapter 7, fixing the history of Djenné for an outside audience is a political, as well as a scholarly, aim that has been imposed on the guides of Djenné in the aim of professionalising them. The conflicting narratives found in oral tradition, as well as the large gaps in historical knowledge about Djenné, mean that the guides have always relied on colleagues, elders, and guidebooks to furnish them with "facts" and stories about the town. The process becomes circular as oral tradition makes its way into the guides' discourse, is then picked up by the writers of travel guides, and is reabsorbed by the guides as "facts."

The three pillars of the local economy in Djenné are agriculture, fishing, and pastoralism (De Jong & Harts-Broekhuis, 1985), to which can be added *maraboutage* ("prayer economy"), trade, and tourism. It is hard to get an accurate number for the population of Djenné. Reports vary from 12,000 (Schijns, 1994: 171) to as high as 30,000[7]; the actual number is probably about 16,000[8]—excluding the residents of the closest villages, considered part of the *Djénnery* (Djenné and surrounding dependent villages). Gaining an adequate understanding of the different ethnic groups that are represented in Djenné is equally challenging, because different terms are used depending on language and social status. Usually different ethnic groups are spoken about in terms of the *quartiers* ("areas") of Djenné where the groups are concentrated and their means of subsistence.

Owing to a policy of integration by the Malian government, there is little detailed published work on the ethnic distribution within the whole of Mali. Occasionally, an indirect estimate can be arrived at—for example, by a national health and demography survey carried out in 2006 (sponsored, among others, by USAID, UNICEF, the World Bank, United Nations Food Programme, and the Dutch Embassy).[9] Furthermore, fixed ethnic identities in West Africa have been criticised as being more of a product of French colonial administrators' desire to divide populations into stable groups than a reality on the ground (Amselle, 1998). However, ethnic identities are repeatedly referred to in Djenné by *Djennenkés* (Chapter 8), despite often being fluid and no longer determining people's identities and localities within Djenné as clearly as they were thought to have been in the past.

Research in the area of Mali where Djenné is located, the *Pondo*, essentially the inner delta area stretching from Timbuktu to San, reveals an ethnic mix dominated by the Peul (Maas & Mommersteeg, 1992). The Peul make up 35% of the area's population and are divided into three main groups: 1. the free Peul; 2. the group of Peul whose mode of subsistence is principally trade or artisanal; and 3. the Peul "slaves" (*Esclaves de Peul*) who are the descendants of the old Peul slaves, also known as the *Rimaïbe*. The second most important ethnic groups in the region are the Marka (17%), the Bambara (16%), the Bozo (16%), and the Bobo (7%). Also represented in the area are the Dogon, the Toucouleur, the Tuareg (named Tamachek in the national survey above), and the Songhai.

INTRODUCTION

The most recent published survey of ethnic groups in Djenné is based on research carried out between 1981 and 1983 (La Violette, 2000). However, in common with the survey mentioned above relating to the ethnic make-up of the *Pondo* region, La Violette relies on statistics published in 1967 (Gallais, 1967) and based on a 1958 census of Djenné.[10] To simplify things dramatically, ethnic groups in Djenné, like the rest of Mali, are described by people locally as correlating with subsistence activities—so the Bozo are fishermen and masons, the Peul are herders, the Bamama are farmers, and the Marka are merchants, religious elites, and rice cultivators. Gallais (1994: 20) argues that in fact the Marka are not an ethnic group but instead a cultural-historic one, defined by their Islamic religion. Additionally, these subsistence categories do not encompass other groups, such as the Bobo, who are described by many people in Djenné predominantly in relation to their practices and religion: they eat dog meat and drink millet beer, and their villages are still mainly animist and so are considered places of powerful magic. The Bobo, together with the Bozo, are considered by many in Djenné to be the earliest inhabitants of the town (*les autochtones*). It may be that the Bobo's animist views make them appear as if they belong to a pre-Islamic Djenné.

Subsistence categories also conflate diversification, subgroups or the "castes" present within ethnicities, and associations such as the *griots* (oral historians and praise singers, an inherited position traditionally attached to royal courts), blacksmiths, and hunters (Tamari, 1991). As has been noted by Maas and Mommersteeg (1992: 39), the strict correlation between ethnic groups and occupation, and ethnic group and *quartier,* in Djenné has become a trend rather than a physical reality. Owing to the precariousness of rains and harvests, many people now have a broad approach to subsistence activities, and as a result fishing, trade, and cultivation have all been appropriated by numerous ethnicities.

In terms of language, most people understand one another in Djenné by speaking *Djennenké* (a form of Songhai) as a second or third language. As well as having the *Djennenké* language (and to a large extent a *Djennenké* identity) in common, the different ethnic groups in the town get along together through formalised "joking relationships" (*cousinage*). The educated elite speaks good French, and it is still the main language taught in schools (although a new system of bilingual education, based on French being phased in gradually with the child's home language is being developed across Mali). Many people also have a basic vocabulary in other languages spoken in Djenné, such as Bamanankan (language of the Bamana) or Peul. The language used in the Monday market tends to be Bamanankan, but this varies depending on the power relationship between the transactors. Using a less familiar language can be a good way of gaining the upper hand during negotiations.

The Bozos have a special status within the town, since the founding myth of Djenné is the story of the Bozo-sacrificed virgin Tapama Djennépo (which translates as "my sister Djennépo"). Various versions of the story of Tapama can be heard, all following essentially the same narrative: when the first inhabitants of Djenné tried to build the town, malevolent spirits caused the walls of the houses to fall down. The town's elders consulted *marabouts* (Qur'anic teachers), who decreed that a virgin should be sacrificed to appease the spirits. Many people in the town refused to give up their daughters until an elderly Bozo man came forward. His daughter was gradually buried within a founding wall, and several times she shook with terror and the wall fell down. Finally, the father asked her to stay

Figure I.4 Tomb of Tapama Djennépo

INTRODUCTION

still so as not to shame him, and she obeyed, being entombed alive. The tomb of Tapama still stands in Djenné and can be visited by tourists. The present-day Djennépo family (who are said to be the kin of *Tapama*) hold special ritual offices during celebrations. For example, during *Tabay Ho* (Festival of the Rabbit), the most senior member of the Djennépo family gives the call for the hunt to start, and on the occasion of Djenné's first Festival in 2005, a young female representative of the Djennépo family was an honoured guest among the dancers.

The *Grandes Familles* (prominent families) in Djenné are often divided into *Grandes Familles maraboutiques* (Islamic teachers), *Grandes Familles notables* (nobles), and *Grandes Familles guerriers* (warriors), depending on their histories. Family names such as Konto and Masakolona are associated with past military exploits; Cissé and Touré are long-established noble names, and the imams of Djenné have over the years been drawn from a number of *Grandes Familles maraboutiques* (Appendix 1).

In Djenné, people's ethnicity can be fluid, as was the case of an elderly woman who described herself as Bozo although before coming to Djenné her family was Songhai and came from a small village near Timbuktu called Dandi. Of her grandfather's generation, five members of the family went to work in Kassina, and four came to Djenné to work as masons—that is why their family name became *Kassinantao* ("the people of Kassina"). Some clues as to the process of assimilation of subsequent migrations to Djenné could perhaps be found in the remaining *Tarikhs* kept in people's homes in Djenné and in land records and other transactions as well as scholarly writing. Overall, however, it is very difficult to put together an accurate model of power relations in Djenné based on people's multiple identities. Although it is true that some families are dominant in certain roles—for example, the Maiga family have held the post of *Chef du Village* for eight of the last eleven times when the position has changed hands (Appendix 2)—outside influences, such as decentralisation and changes in national government are having a considerable effect on some political positions.

Djennenké identity also extends to the surrounding countryside and villages that make up the *Djennéry*. Although the idea of Djenné as compact urban centre remains appealing to many tourists, the majority of whom spend only an afternoon in the town, the lived experience of many Djennenkés incorporates the surrounding countryside (talked about using the term *en brousse*, which roughly translated means "out in the bush"). Peul children tend to their cows and goats in the early mornings and evenings. Bozo women and children set small nets as traps in the many streams outside the town, and Bozo fishermen go out on expeditions at night on their pirogues. Women and children can be seen crossing the river back into Djenné on barges laden with their heavy bundles of firewood. Masons can be found moulding mud bricks on the riverbanks. However, despite

Figure I.5 Young Peul boy brings home his cows at sunset

entreaties by the guides, few tourists venture beyond the town during their visit to Djenné. Those who do are rewarded by a more rounded view of Djenné and what it means to live and make a living in the city. Tourists who take the time to watch children playing football in the fading evening light or tending to their livestock, or women working in their gardens on the outskirts of the town, become as interested in the people as they are in the archaeology and the architecture of Djenné. This humanisation of the tourist visit to Djenné points toward a new kind of possible conceptualisation of the town, one that is about people as much as it is about place.

Djenné's Mosque

The most potent symbol of Islam in Djenné is the Great Mosque, which dominates the town's cityscape. It is the emblem that makes Djenné world famous. Unlike Sénoussa, a Peul village a few kilometres from Djenné that has two mosques, Djenné now has only one mosque, and the whole town is united in its praise and protection.

In his study of the history of Djenné's three mosques, Bourgeois (1987) questions a long-held assumption that the form of the Great Mosque standing in Djenné today (built between 1906–1907) was heavily influenced by the French colonial administration at the time (Prussin, 1986: 184). To understand attitudes toward the Mosque, he explores the creation (and destruction) of Djenné's first two mosques. The first

Figure I.6 Djenné's Great Mosque with the Monday market in the foreground

mosque, built in the 13th century, was the palace of the twenty-sixth King of Djenné, Koi Konboro. He was reputedly the first king to convert to Islam and transformed his palace into a mosque. In 1818 Sékou Amadou led a Peul-dominated *jihad* against Djenné and imposed a purist form of Islam on the population. Apparently it was at this time that the small *quartiers* mosques found throughout Djenné were destroyed to stop any potential anti-Peul uprisings. Because it is prohibited in Islam to destroy a place of worship, Sékou Amadou and his followers were forced to use indirect means of destruction through blocking drains and allowing natural weathering to break down the buildings over time.

In line with his purist vision of Islam, Sékou Amadou built a new mosque in Djenné after allowing the first one to degrade against the population's wishes, in the same way as the small quartiers mosques. (Some images of the ruins of the first mosque were taken by Edmond Fortier at the turn of the 20th century and were turned into postcards.) To fit with his more severe vision of Islam, Sékou Amadou's new mosque was a simple, squat structure with room for more worshippers than provided by the original palace mosque of Koi Konboro.

Djenné's third mosque was built between 1906 and 1907 and dominates Djenné's skyline today. Bourgeois convincingly shows that although the French colonial authorities definitely authorised the Great Mosque and encouraged its construction in order to fit with their new political vision for Djenné at the time of their colonial presence, there is no written evidence to show that French engineers were in any way involved in its construction. Since contemporaneous written evidence does exist of the French authorities' involvement in the building of a Qur'anic school, a lack of records about financing the building of the Mosque leads Bourgeois to conclude that, although the French authorities actively encouraged its building in line with their support for a new imam, they did not get involved in the design and execution of the building (for Bourgeois also evidenced by the building's uneven proportions). Bourgeois maintains that the Mosque found in Djenné today is a purely African building, built and designed in an African style.

Regardless of whether the Mosque standing in Djenné today is an entirely indigenous creation or part of a colonial vision of Sudanese vernacular architecture, the whole town's population embraces it. As well as being a place of worship, the Mosque is renewed yearly in a *crépissage* (remudding) celebration whereby every member of the community physically ensures the Mosque's survival and protects the people's religious identity.

The Cultural Mission and the Heritage Elite

The Cultural Mission in Djenné was established in 1994 as part of the Malian government's commitment to protecting the cultural heritage

Figure I.7 The Cultural Mission situated on the outskirts of Djenné

INTRODUCTION   33

recognised by UNESCO in Mali and to stop the looting of archaeology material from the region. Between the 1970s and 1990s, looting in Mali had, according to experts, reached catastrophic proportions, threatening to wipe out whole chapters of African history (McIntosh et al., 1997; Renfrew, 2000, Schmidt & McIntosh, 1996).

Cultural missions were also established in the country's two other World Heritage sites at the time, Bandiagara (Dogon Country) and Timbuktu. At first, as their names indicate, the cultural missions were supposed to be temporary services put in place to help local populations to best manage their own cultural heritage. Now, the cultural missions have become permanent structures, partly because of their success but also because of the recognition that their "mission" has not yet been accomplished.

UNESCO helps the personnel of Djenné's Cultural Mission indirectly, principally through training programmes such as those put in place as part of "Africa 2009" (for example, a Cultural Mission staff member attended one of the *Professionels Africains du Patrimoine* conferences in Porto Novo). "Africa 2009" is a project for the conservation of immovable cultural heritage in Sub-Saharan Africa (see Saouma-Forero, 2006, for more details). It comprises a partnership of African cultural heritage institutions, CRATerre EAG (Centre for the Research of Earthen Architecture based at the School of Architecture in Grenoble), UNESCO's World Heritage Centre, and ICCROM (International Centre for the Study and of the Preservation and Restoration of Cultural Property).

Contrary to many people's beliefs in the town, UNESCO does not give money to the Cultural Mission directly. Indirectly, however, money is channelled through UNESCO to undertake projects such as the *Plan de Gestion de la Ville* (the management plan that was undertaken in 2008 with the help of outside consultants designated by UNESCO). UNESCO also facilitates the Cultural Mission's work with partners such as *CRATerre* and gives them access to the *Centre du Patrimoine Mondiale*, ICCROM, and ICOMOS, who can be counted on to find financial backing for projects. Necessary equipment such as computers, projectors, and digital cameras can be sourced through the Africa 2009 Project.[11] UNESCO also has a countywide presence through an office in Bamako, where they regularly organise conferences, usually for training purposes.

Along with their UNESCO-focused partners, the Cultural Mission works with the World Bank, the European Union, the Aga Khan Trust for Culture (AKTC), and the Dutch government. Day-to-day work of the Cultural Mission includes running the small museum housed in its premises on the outskirts of the town, accompanying visitors to the archaeological sites, creating inventories of the cultural goods kept in people's houses, drawing up lists of intangible cultural heritage, overseeing archaeological excavations and heritage projects coming to the town, and conducting an ongoing project of sensitisation of the local population (through work with schools, producing information leaflets for tourists and, in the past, providing mobile theatres, visiting villages, and hiring patrol officers for archaeological sites). The Cultural Mission also helps to promote Djenné's cultural heritage by entering national and international competitions, such as the *Biennale de Ségou*, held in September 2004 (described in Chapter 6). As of 2010 the Cultural Mission has become responsible for the new European Union–funded Djenné museum in the centre of town.

Politically, Djenné's Cultural Mission's status has altered with a change of president. Under Alpha Oumar Konaré (1992–2002), the cultural missions were floating structures that answered directly to the Ministry of Culture. Now all three cultural missions in Mali have become integrated into the Ministry of Culture and are consequently a couple more steps removed from power (Appendix 3). In terms of local politics, Djenné's Cultural Mission, by its own admission, is often disliked by the local population, because it has to impose legislation that comes from Central Government. It is also sometimes unfairly blamed for other people's failings, such as the misuse of the tourist tax; each tourist entering Djenné must pay 1,000 CFA (£1), intended to be invested for the purpose of tourism and related infrastructure in the town. The money is collected by the *Mairie,* who in 2004 declared 8 million CFA (£8,000), in tourist receipts. However, none of the money has been reinvested as intended in tourist infrastructure.

What is true, however, is that the Djenné Cultural Mission does benefit materially from heritage projects that come to the town, which are accompanied by cash payments for the Cultural Mission. For example, the budget for the 2006 second-phase Dutch restoration work in Djenné and the surrounding villages includes a salary for the Head of the Cultural Mission totalling 6,000 euros[12] (£4,600) over three years. This salary comes on top of the purchase of a car for the exclusive use of the Cultural Mission (budgeted at 30,000 euros [£23,000]) and an additional support budget of 3,000 euros (£2,300) for the year. The Cultural Mission staff also derives additional personal income by accompanying tourists to the archaeological sites, a fact well known by the guides in Djenné.

Somewhat in opposition to the Cultural Mission, *Djenné Patrimoine* is a heritage organisation that describes itself as indigenous to Djenné. It was founded by a Frenchman, Joseph Brunet-Jailly, and was run by the head of one of Djenné's *Grandes Familles notables,* Papa Cissé, until his death in 2008. Its founding members were mostly drawn from the educated elite or guides and largely ADEMA[13] supporters. However, this situation has changed over the years, and a broader sample of the population is now represented within the organisation. Both *Djenné Patrimoine*

INTRODUCTION

and the Cultural Mission concern themselves with the preservation of heritage within the town; however, whereas the Cultural Mission is on the outside of town and operates principally through bureaucratic measures, *Djenné Patrimoine* is located in the heart of the town and gets involved in local issues.

A small number of expatriates have built homes in Djenné.[14] They include the founder of *Djenné Patrimoine,* Joseph Brunet-Jailly; Jean-Louis Bourgeois, the author of the article about Djenné's three mosques (mentioned previously) and a book about vernacular architecture (1989); a Dutch writer and filmmaker, and a Swedish hotel owner. The presence of a handful of rich expatriates in Djenné sometimes distorts some of the local power structures, because such people have the power to change others' lives through employment and/or donations.

The rest of the "heritage elite" in Djenné consists of the *Chef du Village* and the Imam, both of whom hold powerful offices and have a strong influence over Djenné's population. Although the masons, the guides, and the artisans in Djenné benefit directly from tourism and heritage projects in Djenné, they cannot really be described as part of the heritage elite, because they tend not to be the people who negotiate directly with outside heritage agencies. Most people in Djenné are powerless to circumvent the authority and influence represented by the heritage elite.

Djenné's Future

Owing to the pivotal economic role that cultural heritage plays in Djenné, through attracting both outside sponsors and tourists, it is methodologically very difficult to disentangle people's attitudes toward their cultural heritage from the influence of the economic and political conditions of the time. This study is therefore time-bound and particular to Djenné in the first ten years of the 21st century. In 2010 Djenné seems to be facing new challenges with political instability in the north of the country (described in Chapter 4), threatening the very tourism and heritage projects that have become so important to the town's economy.[15]

It is hard to predict how the situation in West Africa will evolve, but it seems realistic to anticipate certain changes in the relationship between Europe, the United States, and Mali. Already, the United States is taking an increasing military role in the north of Mali.[16] European countries are temporarily united in their advice to tourists not to venture north of the town of Ségou, owing to the perceived threat of kidnappings from AQIM (Al-Qaeda in the Islamic Maghreb). While these travel advisories disrupt the traditional tourist routes taken around the country, they also deter some archaeologists and other heritage professionals from setting up or continuing projects in the region.[17]

The Malian government is defiant in the face of the stark travel warnings. An official press release by the organisers of the 2011 Festival in the Desert (held every January on the outskirts of Timbuktu) states that the President of Mali, Amadou Toumani Touré, will be attending the festival for the first time in 2011 to "permanently eliminate security concerns that have occupied certain quarters" and to "send a symbolic message to the world, notably to those sceptics worried about security in the sahelo-saharienne region."[18]

Other powerful changes in Mali include the increasing presence and economic clout of Chinese businesses, looking both for new markets for their export products and new natural resources. The stability of countries bordering Mali, such as the Ivory Coast, Mauritania, Niger, and Algeria, will also have a big impact on Mali's economy in the coming years.

If, as Di Giovine (2009) suggests, UNESCO's World Heritage project has successfully created a "heritage-scape," a moral community united by common values and ambitions, it may be that Djenné's World Heritage status will serve as a protective force in an uncertain future, keeping the outside world interested in its plight. Conversely, it may be that Djenné's World Heritage status will prove to be just one of many identities the town has adopted over the centuries, an identity that gives way to something very different in a new global political and economic reality.

About This Book

This study is divided into two parts. The first part concerns the creation of Djenné as a place conjured by the West—with a strong concentration on its architecture—from the early European travel writers through Colonial exhibitions to its present-day UNESCO status. The study intends to show how Djenné came to occupy a particular place in international popular imagination, and it examines the restrictions and opportunities this conceptualisation represents for the current population of Djenné.

The second part provides counter-voices to this outside vision of Djenné by looking at Islam, different livelihood strategies, and the work of the artisans and the guides in Djenné. An ethnographic approach to the study of cultural heritage in Djenné allows for a broader debate about what is and isn't important to people in the town. It also contextualises many reactions and reservations that *Djennenkés* have to heritage projects operating in Djenné.

The two parts are then brought together in an examination of Djenné's first cultural festival, held in 2005.

PART I

Putting Djenné on the Map

CHAPTER 1

Architecture and the "Creation" of Djenné in the West

Narrative about Africa is always a pretext for a comment about something else, some other place, some other people. More precisely expressed, Africa is the mediation that enables the West to accede to its own subconscious and give public account of its subjectivity (Mbembe, 2001: 3).

The historic encounter between Europe and West Africa has always been a two-way process, albeit one with a heavy power imbalance (Probst & Spittler, 2004). To understand current relationships between institutions and nation-states, such as that between UNESCO and Mali, one must document the historical precedents of such relationships: the series of past encounters that have cast agents into defined roles, some of which are very hard to move beyond.

Over the years, Europe apprehended Djenné in different ways. At first it did so through travel writing and exhibitions, part of broader imaginings about the enchantment of Africa (Hall, 2005; Leiris, 1934; Phillips & Steiner, 1999). The interest in its vernacular architecture grew from the time of the arrival in Europe of early photographs, postcards and colonial exhibitions (Gardi, 1994; Gardi et al., 1995; Morton, 2000; Prussin, 1986). These glimpses gave the impression of Djenné as a distant place, with winding streets and compact architecture. Today Djenné remains "enchanting," because it promises to be so different from people's places of origin (Hudgens & Trillo, 1999). The way in which Djenné (and its sister town of Timbuktu) has been represented by the West has to a large part been influenced by both the intellectual climate in Europe and the aims of Empire at the time.

At the end of the 18th and turn of the 19th centuries, the influential American anthropologist Lewis Henry Morgan and British anthropologist Edward Tylor postulated that culture, like nature, was subject to the power of evolution. Heavily influenced by Charles Darwin's *On the Origin of Species* (1859), Morgan argued that mankind used experimental knowledge to work its way up from savagery through barbarism to civilisation. Breaking down each stage, he includes "House Life and Architecture" as one of the milestones of civilisation:

> house architecture, which connects itself with the form of the family and the plan of domestic life, affords a tolerably complete illustration of progress from savagery to civilization. Its growth can be traced from the hut of the savage through the communal houses of the barbarians to the house of the single family of civilized nations, with all the successive links by which one extreme is connected to the other. (Morgan, 1877, reprinted in McGee & Warms, 2004: 58)

Morgan put a strong emphasis on technological progress and the ownership of private property as markers of cultural progress. In common with Morgan, Tylor (1871) believed in the psychic unity of all of mankind, so that cultural sophistication was a continuum based on knowledge and education, with "primitive" societies representing the childhood of mankind. Architectural and technological sophistication became a key materialisation of this theory. These themes were later taken up and refuted by African intellectuals (for example, Mbembe, 2001). There remains, however, a complex interaction between the West's perception of architectural sophistication and its correlation with social validation. As Mbembe states, narrative about Africa is almost always about something else: Africa is defined in opposition to the West, as, for example, by lacking the architectural sophistication of the West and therefore not being "fully human" (Mbembe, 2001: 2). However, as attitudes in the West are changed by fears of climate change and a desire for a more harmonious relationship with the natural environment, mud-brick architecture in Africa is coming to represent something new yet again: the promise of a sustainable future through low-carbon-impact technologies.[1] This promise responds to Western concerns about the preservation of cultural and natural heritage. The relationship between Europe and Africa is therefore in a state of constant dynamic evolution.

Early Explorers

The "discovery" of West Africa by Europeans began with a number of amateur enthusiasts, spurred on by legendary tales of African cities of gold and unanswered questions about the geography of the continent. The Scottish explorer Mungo Park, encouraged by the British Association for Promoting the Discovery of the Interior Parts of Africa (the African Association), set off in 1795 to find the course of the River Niger (Park, 2002). His predecessor, Daniel Houghton, had died in the Sahara desert—early European expeditions to West Africa were poorly funded and inadequately prepared. Despite suffering from severe ill health, Park managed to reach the river Niger in 1796 at Ségou (the first known European to do so) and, having been assumed dead, triumphantly returned to Scotland in 1797.

Park had failed in his aim of reaching the legendary city of Timbuktu and managed only to follow the river Niger as far as Silla, therefore falling short of both Djenné and Timbuktu. In 1805 he once again set off on an expedition to the Niger, this time as the head of a Government expedition. Of the forty Europeans accompanying him, only a handful lived to reach the Niger, and they all gradually succumbed to fever and dysentery. Park and his party regularly turned their guns on assailants, and it is clear from his account that they "killed a great number of men" (ibid: 394). Based on the testimony of one surviving expedition member (a porter), after multiple attacks by hostile parties from the riverbanks, Park lost his life in December 1805 (from Adami Fatoumi's journal, reprinted in Park, 2002) after sailing past, but never entering, Djenné (recorded as Ginne) and Timbuktu.

The story of Mungo Park's adventures, and the subsequent narrative of his travels published in 1815, captured the popular imagination in Britain and across Europe. In 1824 the French Geographical Society (*Société de Géographie*) offered a cash prize of 10,000 francs to the first person to come back alive from Timbuktu. An early contender for the prize was Alexander Gordon Laing (Kryza, 2006), a Scottish Captain in the Royal African Colonial Corps. Also encouraged by the African Association, Laing was the first European to reach Timbuktu in August 1826, but he was murdered shortly after leaving the city in September of the same year.

The first European to return alive from Timbuktu was René Caillié, a Frenchman of humble birth, orphaned while still a young child, who had long dreamed of travelling to Africa (Berque, 1996). In the account of his travels, Caillié explains his motivation: as a child, "People lent me geography books and maps: those [maps] of Africa, where I could only see desert countries or countries labeled 'unknown,' excited my attention more than any other" (Caillié, 1996: 42, my translation). In another passage, he states: "The town of Timbuktu became the continual object of all my thoughts, the aim of all my efforts; I resolved to reach it or to die" (Caillié, 1996: 41, my translation).

After a first failed expedition to Senegal in 1818 accompanying British troops who continually came under violent attack, he returned to Senegal in 1824 determined to reach Timbuktu. His innovative approach was to disguise himself as a North African Muslim traveller by first spending a long preparatory time learning Arabic and the customs of Islam in Senegal. After working for a time in Sierra Leone, he finally set off for Timbuktu in 1827, on the pretext that he was an Egyptian trying to regain his homeland. In March 1828, after a prolonged illness and numerous setbacks, he reached Djenné, where he spent two weeks. He finally reached Timbuktu on April 20, 1828.

On his return to France, Caillié was awarded the 10,000 francs prize, and accounts of his travels were published to great acclaim. Perhaps unusually, given his position, Caillié did not attempt to describe Timbuktu in romantic terms and instead painted a picture of a desert town: "Timbuktu, although one of the biggest towns I have seen in Africa, has as its only resource its trade in salt, its land being too barren for agriculture. It is from Djenné that it gets everything that is necessary for its survival: millet, rice, vegetable oil, honey, cotton, Sudanese cloth, manufactured goods, candles, soap, chillies, onions, dried fish, pistachios, etc. . . ." (Caillié, 1996: 2, my translation). Djenné and Timbuktu therefore entered popular French culture as twin towns of the trans-Saharan trade route. Although Timbuktu may not have lived up to the hopes of the enthusiasts of the African Association and the French Geographic Society, its name had forever entered into folklore, linked with adventure and hardship and the quest for unattainable riches.

Caillié's detailed description of Djenné as a thriving cosmopolitan trade centre has also had a long-term effect on the West's perception of the town. His careful attention to people's beliefs and practices, together with the recording of details including prices, hairstyles, and culinary preferences, provides a rich ethnographic account of Djenné seen through the eyes of a Frenchman in 1828.

The motivations behind Park and Caillié's journeys were both personal and economic. The French and British governments had vested interests in exploring the potential for trade and exploitation of raw materials in West Africa, and an understanding of the geography and political landscape of the territory was essential for planning further incursions. It is clear through their writings that Park and Caillié were very much aware of these concerns and sought to bring back as much information as possible for the advancement of these aims. At the same time, it is hard to adequately stress the hardship, terror, and physical discomfort suffered by both men in their quest for knowledge about the region, and what therefore must have been the depths of their personal motivation.

Park and Caillié's accounts of their adventures are considered today to be very problematic orientalist constructions (Grosz-Ngaté, 1988; Said, 2003), written within the language and prejudices of the time. They were written upon the travellers' return and, in the case of Park, with a large amount of input from a second author, Bryan Edwards, the Secretary of the African Association at the time. Caillié's account was heavily edited and based on scribbled and badly damaged notes that he secretly kept throughout his journey.

It would perhaps be easy to discount these early accounts on the basis of these limitations alone. However, despite their flaws, accounts written by the early explorers in West Africa set a particular tone for Europe's perception of towns such as Timbuktu and Djenné. The headlines of the travellers' exploits in Europe were heroic and triumphant, and to this day, travel companies advertising trips to Mali use a language of exploration and adventure in their promotional literature.

The early travel accounts are also important in two other ways. First, as will be shown, the problematic "power to represent" (Grosz-Ngaté, 1988) found in Park's and Caillié's writing is not unique to their time and continues to this day, starting with the early colonial writers and moving through the architects, archaeologists, anthropologists, heritage officials, tour guides, and filmmakers who followed. Inescapably, this book is a continuation of this tradition of the outsider looking in, albeit written within a new reflective practice of anthropology (Clifford & Marcus, 1986; James et al., 1997). As in the past, it is important to note that representations of Djenné always happen in two directions: authors are both actors and acted on (Grosz-Ngaté, 1988: 495).

The second point comes from examining the enduring power of the early European accounts of West Africa: "the fact that a counter-egemonic discourse is possible at a given point in time does not necessarily signal the end of an earlier episteme" (Grosz-Ngaté, 1988: 509). This earlier episteme can still be found in the discourses around the management of cultural heritage in Djenné today. In many ways, there has been no radical rupture with a problematic representation of West Africa by the West. Instead, much of this representation has been recast in a language of heritage more acceptable to 21st-century sensibilities.

French Colonialism

The creation of the French Sudan began in 1878 with a series of incursions under the Governor Brière de l'Isle (Robinson, 2000). Beginning from a series of posts strung along a line of advance stretching from Kayes on the Upper Senegal to Bamako on the Niger, military forays gradually extended French influence across what was to become the French Sudan. The Commandant Supérieur Archinard served between 1888 and 1893. He destroyed the last garrisons of the Umarian State, then captured Samori Touré (who had constructed a powerful state on the Upper Niger by 1880s) and installed a French military regime across the area.

Archinard was an amateur ethnographer and greatly interested in the material culture of the region. In her detailed biography of the man, Martine Cuttier (2006) traces his ambition to establish ethnographic museums in Paris and his hometown of Le Havre. The idea gradually gained ground, and in 1880 an ethnographic museum was inaugurated in the Palais du Trocadéro in Paris. The aim of the museum was to convince people of the importance and validity of the colonial project by stressing the rich trade potential of the colony. A secondary aim was to help prepare those about to travel to the French Sudan (explorers, missionaries, traders, administrators, doctors . . .) for their new lives (ibid.).

In a letter to Gautheron, the Commandant du Cercle de Djenné in 1893, Archinard urges him to send samples of all the traded items found in Djenné that may be of interest to people in France. He states that he would like "to prove in France the advantages of possessing Djenné" (quoted in Cuttier, 2006: 440, my translation). Archinard also sent back remains of African soldiers killed during his campaign to be studied by Paris museums, in the hope of furthering the case for an evolutionary model of cultural difference (Cuttier, 2006: 441). Photographs taken by Archinard and his military colleagues counted among the few images to reach France from West Africa at the time, owing to the difficulty of carrying fragile photographic equipment (see also Edwards, 2001). Photographs had to be staged given the necessary length of exposure of the glass plates, and consequently soldiers became their own journalists, largely controlling the narrative of events in the French national press (Cuttier, 2006).

An exception to this rule was the French journalist Felix Dubois, who visited Djenné in 1895. In his book *Tombouctou la Mystérieuse* (1897) he devotes two chapters to the description of Djenné and many beautifully executed drawings. According to Dubois, the Bozo fishermen accompanying him were left speechless at their first sight of Djenné, and even Dubois claims that it was the first time during his travels that he was surprised by an African-made structure. He put this down to the town's "civilised" appearance (unlike the "childlike simplicity" of other forms of habitations he had seen) and declared Djenné "the jewel of the Niger Valley" (1897: 97) and a "real town, in the European sense of the word" (1897: 99).

Dubois was so puzzled by the incongruity of the presence of a town such as Djenné in an environment he considered to be uncivilised that he postulated a theory of an Arabic/Egyptian origin for the town, based on his view that the Songhai in Djenné originated in the Nile Valley and must have been the founders of this oasis of civilisation. His observations are based on both the Songhai language and the Songhai's physical appearance, because he determined that despite their dark skin, they conformed more closely to a European physical aesthetic than did the other populations found in Djenné.

In line with mainstream thinking at the time, Dubois considered that where he identified a likeness to a European ideal (in both architecture and physical appearance), he had identified civilisation. As is shown in later chapters, although separated by time and a very different mainstream ideology, this deeply problematic view of what constitutes "culture" and "civilisation" persists in criticisms of UNESCO today, since the majority of the sites recognised by UNESCO's World Heritage List are found in Europe, leaving continents such as Africa vastly underrepresented. The cultural sites that are recognised in Africa as being worthy of World Heritage status often conform to a European ideal of monumental architecture, such as the architecture of Djenné and Timbuktu in Mali, the ruins of Great Zimbabwe, the ruins of the City of Aksum in Ethiopia, the Royal Palaces of Abomey in Benin, and the Stone Town of Zanzibar. It is only very gradually that UNESCO is embracing a broader vision of cultural heritage, as described in Chapter 3.

Colonial Officials and Photographers in Djenné

Early photographic images of Djenné include those taken by Albert Rousseau, a doctor based in Djenné between 1893 and 1894 and rediscovered by Gardi (Gardi et al., 1995). Rousseau's photographs include both ethnographic and architectural images and are regularly referred to today in relation to Djenné's cultural heritage. Other images of Djenné to reach Europe at the turn of the 20th century were the postcards of Edmond Fortier (Maas & Mommersteeg, 1992). Fortier published fifteen postcards of Djenné, and again it is the architectural nature of the town that is emphasised, since fourteen of the postcards are of buildings and only one shows boats on the river outside Djenné. The architectural images include a few people in the foreground, such as women carrying baskets or men sitting in discussion under trees.

The military officers in the French Sudan were replaced by, or became, the administrators of the Empire in the ensuing years. Charles Monteil was the French colonial administrator in Djenné between 1900 and 1903 and first published his monograph of the town in 1903 (Monteil, 1903).

Only one hundred copies of this first edition were printed, because he had to pay for the publication himself. Subsequently, in 1932 he found a publisher for his revised edition, and the book *Djenné: Métropole du Delta Central du Niger* gained a wider French audience (Monteil, 1932). By the time of Monteil's presence in Djenné, there was a strong push by the colonial authorities away from a policy of assimilation of the people of the colonies into French society toward one of governing according to local custom (Wooten, 1993). Part of Monteil's role, like that of other French colonial administrators, was to serve as a judge in "native" courts, and he therefore amassed a great deal of information about local family law and disputes. As well as discussing local customs, a large part of his book is given over to a detailed description of the geography, flora, and fauna of the area. An entire section is dedicated to painstakingly bringing together the known history of the region from a variety of sources, including early Arabic writings and oral testimonies. In a classificatory manner Monteil divides the ethnic groups in Djenné into categories based on their physical characteristics, their perceived historical role in the town, and their means of subsistence.

As well as being encouraged to write detailed ethnographic accounts of the areas under their control, the colonial administrators, or *commandants de cercles,* participated in gathering large collections of material culture for display both in France and the fledgling museums in the French Sudan. Anthropologists such as Marcel Griaule and Michel Leiris led ethnographic expeditions to the region, the most famous being the 1931 *Dakar-Djibouti* expedition sponsored by the French State, The Rockefeller Foundation, and private donors. The expedition members, drawn from many different disciplines, such as linguistics, geography, and art backgrounds, systematically collected and catalogued African material culture in the spirit of salvage ethnography (Clifford, 1988).

Distinctive fieldwork methods emerged from the *Dakar-Djibouti* expedition—for example, Griaule's "documentary system," in which objects served as reliable witnesses to the truth of other societies (Clifford, 1988: 66). The spoken word, in contrast, was considered to be mostly unreliable evidence, because Griaule regarded informants as performers, "dramatizing" their lives, both consciously and subconsciously. (Michel Leiris, however, published his account of the mission in a controversial memoir in 1934 entitled *L'Afrique Fantôme* [Leiris, 1934]), providing a much more introspective and sensitive account of the coercive nature of the collecting impulse during the expedition.)

Popular interest in France in the *Dakar-Djibouti* expedition was part of a wider movement, Surrealism, started in the 1920s in the aftermath of the trauma of the First World War by the writer André Breton (Tythacott, 2003). Non-European material culture provided surrealist artists and theorists with rich material with which to confront their own culture. Museums of ethnographic art such as the Musée du Trocadéro became the focus of the avant-garde in Paris, and African, Oceanic, and Native-American art heavily influenced such artists as Pablo Picasso and Man Ray.

Colonial Exhibitions

In 1931, while the Dakar-Djibouti mission was going on in Africa, the International Colonial Exhibition (*L'Exposition Coloniale Internationale*) was held in Vincennes in Paris. Among its prized exhibits was the recreation of a *Rue de Djenné* (Leprun, 1988: 152). The exhibition as a whole was publicised as *Le Tour du Monde en un jour* (Morton, 2000) and promised to show the general public the people, architecture, produce, and business opportunities represented by the colonies (see Coombes, 1994, for British comparisons). The aim of the exhibition was not only to bring the colonies to the French public but to do so in as contextualised a sense as possible. It was important for the organisers to "authentically" reproduce buildings, people, and performances of the colonies. This appeal to authenticity helped to create a dichotomy between the primitive "inside" of the exhibition and the civilised outside, thus justifying Europe's ongoing colonial project: "Architecture summarized the cultures of colonial people in accessible images, metonymic representations of barbarity clothed in the familiar language of exoticism" (Morton, 2000: 7).

The West-African pavilion occupied four hectares on the edge of a lake and comprised a *Grand Palais*, a scaled-down reproduction of the Djenné Great Mosque, an animist village, a restaurant, and a series of recreated streets entitled the *Rue de Djenné*. The *Livre d'Or*,[2] published in 1931 to accompany and illustrate the exhibition, recounts a visitor's route around the pavilion:

> The visitors . . . find themselves transported into the heart of Black Africa through the faithfully reconstructed narrow streets of Djenné, with their terraced two-storey houses, made of crude red "pisé," like those one comes across on the edge of the Bani. . . . In a nearby building, reproducing on an inevitably smaller scale the famous Djenné Mosque, a permanent cinema is set up where the public sees a series of films recently realised in West Africa.[3]

Morton explains that the Djenné Great Mosque and streets were intended to stand for a "primitive" stage of architectural sophistication and were juxtaposed with architecture found in other parts of the French Empire, such as Indochina. The exaggeration of certain aspects of the replica Djenné Mosque, such as the wooden beams that were made to strut out decoratively, was a conscious attempt on behalf of the architects to convey the "exoticism" of West African architecture. Leprun (1988) points out the subtle modification of the architecture, the colour (redder than the mud found in Djenné, in the style of Ségou), and the decorations used to attract the exhibition visitor.

The plans for the pavilion were based on the written and photographic sources available to the architects at the time. The architectural precursors to the 1931 exhibition include the 1889 Universal Exposition in Paris, when two small mosques were included within the creation of a Senegalese village, and the 1900 Universal Exposition, when the West-African exhibit included a Sudanese mosque based on one of the mosques at Timbuktu (probably also partly based on Dubois's [1897]) Tombouctou la Mystérieuse (Leprun, 1988: 115; Morton, 2000: 265).

The presentation of the mosque and the *Rue de Djenné* falls into the category named by MacCannell as re-presentation: "an arrangement of objects in a reconstruction of a total situation" (MacCannell, 1992: 78). Djenné's streets were recreated as bustling and prosperous, helped by the presence of traders brought over from the French Sudan to lend controlled local character to the scene.

Through attempting to recreate a total situation, the International Colonial Exhibition made the claim that what people were seeing was an authentic representation of Djenné. Authenticity and reality have been recurring themes in the debate surrounding the management of cultural heritage in Djenné ever since. As will be described, early colonial images and descriptions of Djenné remain the departure point and the locus of authenticity for heritage projects in the town. As did the recreation of the *Rue de Djenné* and the mosque in the International Colonial Exhibition of 1931, both the Dutch project and the current Aga Khan Trust for Culture restoration project in Djenné use Monteil and Dubois's sketches[4]—and, in the case of the Dutch Housing Restoration project, photographs and postcards as the "authentic image of Djenné," an ideal that must be returned to: "We took as a starting point for the inventory of houses to restore those houses that have monumental façades because they have characterised for a long time the *authentic image of the town.* This through the testimony of the old postcards and photographs of Rousseau at the end of the 19th century" (Bedaux et al., 2000, my translation, my italics).

The Second World War and Decolonisation

After the termination of their duties in Africa, administrators such as Monteil played an important part in training the next generation of colonial administrators both at the École Coloniale and at the École des

Langues Orientales in Paris. The École Coloniale was at first conceived as an institution to train both French and colonial subjects. By 1900 the education of colonial subjects was largely abandoned owing to fears of creating a generation of "agitators" within the French colonies (Cohen, 1971).

As Europe became engulfed in the Second World War, many of the young men trained for future careers in the colonial service lost their lives in the conflict. In his recollections of his feelings upon arriving at his first post in Goundam in northern Mali, Jean Clauzel, a second-generation French colonial administrator, gives us an insight into the paternalistic and romantic feelings of the French elite toward their territories by the 1950s: "Joy finally spread through me. I was truly faced with that of which I had dreamt during my year of preparation at the old lycée in the Sainte-Geneviève mountains, in the years of school and under the trees of Luxembourg [gardens], during my time in the army, faced with that which I had so hoped, and so longed for" (Clauzel, 1989: 35).[5]

Jean Clauzel talks about his time as a "Commandant" in Mali (then the French Sudan) as the apogee of his career. In part, the pride and dedication he brings to his role are linked to the memory of his friends who trained with him at the L'École Nationale de la France d'Outre Mer (known as L'École Coloniale until 1937), many of whom died as soldiers during the Second World War. He saw himself as the one person living out the life they had all imagined together during their student days. His journey to Mali therefore became a form of pilgrimage.

The Second World War brought about a radical intellectual shift in Europe, contributing to the birth of UNESCO in 1945, described shortly. Feelings about the cultural superiority of European powers gave way to self-doubt as the true horror of the holocaust was revealed to people through the media. In the face of this, UNESCO was established to be a global ambassador for the positive value of cultural difference while maintaining universal human rights. In 1959 the French Sudan and Senegal united to become the Mali Federation, which gained independence from France in 1960. Later that year Senegal withdrew from the Federation, and the modern-day Republic of Mali was born on September 22, 1960.

Conclusion

Throughout France's time of dominance in West Africa, the colonial imagination about the French Sudan altered in line with the political and intellectual climate in France at the time. The French colonial authorities' attitude toward their overseas territories depended on the nation's self-esteem, the perceived competition from other colonial powers, France's need for resources (both raw materials and financial resources collected through taxation), and the prejudices of the intellectual elite. While concentrating on a seemingly stable "reality," such as architecture, the representations of Djenné by early explorers, French colonial authorities, and journalists are often revealing narratives of the self, whereby Africa acts as a necessary "other" to an internalised identity discourse (Mbembe, 2001). At the same time, explorers and colonial officials remained both actors and acted on and were not purely able to project their visions without local military, political, and intellectual resistance.

Many of the colonial administrators in the French Sudan, such as Monteil, gained a great respect for their host culture and believed that they were able to positively influence subsequent French policies toward the colony. Others, such as Maurice Delafosse, put forward, through their teaching at L'École Coloniale, the view of fundamental equality but difference between the different races (Clifford, 1988: 61). However, understanding the historically and enduringly difficult interaction between Africa and Europe remains an important point of departure for assessing the effects and conceptualisation of cultural heritage projects in postcolonial situations. For example, when establishing the basis for cultural heritage projects in Djenné today, project managers often seek safe ground in the form of early colonial photographic images or sketches of material culture. However, these images silently index a whole host of inequalities, biases, and prejudices. Thus there is no "authentic reality" to return to, only the reality of the present.

The historic concentration on the architecture of Djenné has necessarily been a reductionist activity, with architectural representations being used in lieu of people, yet somehow still defining them. Architecture therefore becomes an object outside the social world, made to stand for the social world. Through this mechanism, ideas about authenticity become intimately linked to the material, and not to the people who inhabit the spaces in question.

CHAPTER 2

Archaeology and Architecture

Islamic Diffusionism

Early writings by westerners about Djenné's archaeology include a book written by Lieutenant Louis Desplagnes entitled *Le Plateau Central Nigérien* (Desplagnes, 1907). Lieutenant Desplagnes spent two years in the French Sudan examining archaeological material as well as architecture. As did Monteil earlier, he postulated a North African diffusionist model of culture, finding Arabic influences in the architecture he encountered in West Africa. His travels took him to Djenné, as is described in a review of his book written by H. R. P (1908: 107) in the journal *Man*:

> Lieutenant Desplagnes appears to hold that the so-called Soudanese and West African civilisations are wholly due to Phenico-Egyptian and Lyhico-Berber influences carried by successive waves of migration further and further south, a proposition which commends itself to anyone who has seen both the Soudan and North Africa.

This diffusionist model of culture was first comprehensively challenged by the excavations of Djenné-Djeno carried out by the McIntoshes in 1977 (McIntosh, 1998). If cities, long-distance trade, states, and empires had been brought to West Africa through the influence of Arabic traders, they should not have been present in the archaeological record before the 9th or 10th century C.E. However, archaeological excavations at Djenné-Djeno concluded that it had been founded around 250 B.C.E., becoming a city in the full sense in about 450 C.E., extending over an area of 33 hectares at its apogee around 900 C.E. There was not enough material culture from North Africa found during the excavation to support a theory of Islamic Diffusionism. Instead, Djenné-Djeno is the earliest excavated example of an African City (McIntosh, 1998).

A further interesting dimension to the excavations at Djenné-Djeno is that the McIntoshes cautiously concluded that they had found evidence of a heterarchical (flat) society, with no evidence of a concentration of wealth of material culture pointing to an elite or a ruler. Evidence of different centres of specialisation scattered around the site of Djenné-Djeno (comprising 69 identified "satellite" settlements) suggests that different codependent activities were undertaken (agriculture, fishing, herding, blacksmith, copper casting, pottery, and so on), each in its own separate

Figure 2.1 Pot fragments at Djenné-Djeno

location. Additionally, evidence of healthy skeletons found across the site indicates a well-fed population without a starving underclass. The widespread dispersal of elaborate decorative pottery, which would not have occurred if an elite person had exclusive access to prestigious objects, strengthens the case for a heterarchical Djenné-Djeno. Other archaeologists, however, point to deficiencies in these interpretations. First, the small size of the excavation units do not allow for the understanding of differential use of space at the site. Second, the presence of two different types of burials at the site, one in large ceramic jars, the other standard inhumations, raises the possibility of two ideologically different populations at Djenné-Djeno.[1]

The heterarchical reading of Djenné-Djeno was used by former President of Mali, Alpha Oumar Konaré, to talk about his vision for the country:

> What makes the Middle Niger urban experience so unusual—and provocative—is the apparent lack here of a state-level organization at the core of its urbanization. Provocative enough that an archaeologist Head of State (our friend, Dr. Konaré) has used presidential addresses to the nation purposefully to promulgate these cities as proof to his citizens of the deep roots of Malians' democratic instincts. (McIntosh, 2005: 12)

The abandonment of the site at Djenné-Djeno around 1400 C.E. and move to the present-day town of Djenné is considered by the McIntoshes to have been caused by the gradual Islamification of the population. Again, other archaeologists question this interpretation, suggesting that Djenné-Djeno continued to be occupied after 1400 C.E. and that the excavations undertaken in modern-day Djenné were too small and too inconclusive to confirm a theory of migration due to religion.[2]

Archaeology and Loss

In the world of archaeology, the Niger Delta is famous for looting and loss (Panella, 2002; Renfrew, 2000). Owing to the relatively small amount of information on the archaeological context of Djenné terracottas, these items have come to symbolise the most devastating aspect of global illicit excavations: the loss of all knowledge about a culture before archaeologists have had the time to study it. The extent of illicit excavations can be estimated through the number of trenches visible on the landscape in archaeological sites in Mali, as well as the large number of unprovenanced objects making their way into European and American museums. According to Renfrew: "Over the past twenty-five years, a whole chapter in the prehistory and early history of West Africa has been destroyed" (2000: 54).

For a long time, therefore, successive Malian governments' conversations with the outside world relating to the country's cultural heritage have been dominated by the fear of loss and attempts to put in place measures of protection. A 1995 special edition of *African Arts* entitled "Protecting Mali's Cultural Heritage" brings together the voices of the major figures dealing with (and in) Mali's archaeological heritage. The edition marks the United States' decision in 1993 to sign an emergency ban on importing archaeological material from the Middle Niger region. The illuminating thing about this special edition, as much as the content of the articles, is the editor's choice of authors. Each author represents a well-rehearsed position in the debate about who actually owns Mali's archaeological heritage.

An introduction by then-President of Mali Alpha Oumar Konaré (1995) begins with a plea for return and collaboration. He diplomatically praises the U.S. decision to sign the ban and finishes by hoping that a more enlightened international community may lead to the return of Mali's cultural treasures, as well as the return of many of the country's sons, scattered as they are across the world. The ex-President therefore draws a parallel between the dispersal of things and persons from their rightful place, in large part because of poverty. He says that the U.S. decision "does justice to the integrity and dignity of the cultures of the Niger Valley" (1995: 27).

Another article in the edition, by an ex–American Peace Corps volunteer turned African art dealer (Wright, 1995) purports to put forward the view of a Malian farmer, now criminalised for selling off "his" cultural property found in the ground. His position is that while poverty and a fight for survival remain the overwhelming driving forces in Mali, people should be allowed to dispose of whatever resources they have as they see fit. He is dismissive of archaeologists' claim to be able to recapture people's history through their work and sees them as using their high status to create a superior claim (while hiding the fact that they earn their livelihood through Mali's archaeological heritage).

UNESCO is represented in a short piece in *African Arts* by Etienne Clement (1995), who, although pleased with the U.S. decision to sign the ban, hopes that European countries will follow. He goes on to praise the *Vallées du Niger* exhibition, which opened at the Musée des Arts d'Afrique et d'Océanie in Paris in 1994, as a step toward valorising Middle Niger material culture. However, he does not seem aware of, or does not consider it appropriate to mention, the powerful effect such exhibitions have on the economic value of Middle Niger archaeological material available on the illicit art market.

The contradictions found throughout the *African Arts* special edition are numerous and can be seen as a microcosm of the wider complexities surrounding the protection of Malian cultural heritage today: the tension between extreme poverty and high-end tourism, the desirability of archaeological material from Mali on the international art market versus insuring its protection in situ, and the limits of a Euro-centric vision of cultural heritage in a postcolonial situation. Many of the articles are illustrated with lavish photographs of the objects they describe, thus increasing their desirability and status with collectors. The archaeologists represented in the edition, the McIntoshes and the Malian archaeologist Téréba Togola, devote their article to describing a person they call "the good collector," a person who while driven by the aesthetic beauty of the objects he or she collects maintains deep respect for the culture from which the objects originate and opens up the collections for their future use. The "bad" collector, in contrast, does not question the provenance of the objects he or she comes across and is motivated "solely for investment or for the thrill of possession" (McIntosh et al., 1995: 62).

However, nowhere within the special edition is there any fundamental questioning of the power imbalances that have led to Malian material culture being dispersed across the world, or the effect of these imbalances on people living in Mali today (for example, Rowlands & Bedaux, 2001; Schmidt & McIntosh, 1996). Samuel Sidibé (1995), the director of the National Museum in Bamako, uses his allocated space to set out the extent of the ongoing looting in Mali and to propose that a solution may lie in the dissemination of archaeological knowledge to wider local audiences. He cites the creation of cultural missions in Timbuktu, Dogon Country, and Djenné as a step toward this dissemination.

In line with the views of Mbembe (2001) discussed in Chapter 1, Olaniyan's (2003) thesis on African cultural patrimony provides a strong counterpoint to the arguments set out above. He states that "cultural patrimony is a cheap weapon of the weak to fight a battle for which it is ill-equipped: political and economic domination" (Olaniyan, 2003: 31). He also agrees with Fanon (1961) that "you will not make colonialism blush for shame by spreading out little known cultural treasures under its eyes" (quoted in Olaniyan, 2003: 31).

The validation of a country's material culture will therefore not lead to a more equitable moral, political, or economic global balance. Olaniyan contends that material culture is unable to transcend the political and economic confines in which it is created. Instead, it is used to symbolise them.

According to Olaniyan, the first reaction of African countries to political Western imperialism was political resistance. In the 1990s "culture" became Africa's favoured mode of resistance to Euro-American hegemony, a trend that is termed the "cultural turn" and was due to widespread disillusionment with post-independence politics and the nation-state.

Growing disillusionment led political leaders to resort to the promotion of "cultural pride" to divert attention away from their corruption and ineptitude. Extravagant spending on infrastructure had not led to a material improvement in people's lives.

For Olaniyan, the apogee of this trend of extravagance was the grandiose Second World Black and African Festival of Arts and Culture, held in Lagos, Nigeria, in 1977. Accompanying these great exhibitions were cultural-philosophical concepts such as "African Personality," which had evolved from such concepts as *Négritude*. These were part of what Olaniyan terms the "reclamatory" and "re-evaluative" strand of cultural politics.

The second strand is the monumentalist and conservationist one, as seen in action in Djenné. Describing UNESCO's work in Africa, he says: "Employing instruments both of persuasion and coercion, such as funding and legal statutes, the goal of such efforts is to identify, catalogue and conserve such monuments in their original locations as part of a vast network of a decentralized global museum" (Olaniyan, 2003: 28).

Pertinently for the case of Djenné, Olaniyan sees the first strand of cultural politics, the reclamatory one, as often at odds with the state, whose institutions manage cultural patrimony as monuments. He also sees the first strand of cultural politics as much the more powerful for effecting change: "The most engaging discourse of cultural patrimony, the one with profound ramifications for refashioning of subjectivities and rethinking of social relations across diverse differences, is the re-evaluative" (Olaniyan, 2003: 29).

Why is re-evaluation important? Olaniyan says that Molefi Kete Asante, the founder of Afrocentricity (Asante, 1987), puts it best: it is mental decolonisation or an "escape to sanity." Olaniyan reminds us that the interpretation and the use of cultural heritage are a political act, deployed in the present for contemporary purposes.

At the local level in Djenné, the cultural politics are such that there does not seem to be an appetite for "reclaiming" archaeological heritage. In fact, most people in Djenné do not seem to feel very emotionally involved with the pre-Islamic material culture found at Djenné-Djeno. What is present in Djenné is anger at the financial implications of their alienation from this part of their cultural heritage (Panella, 2002). In an interview, I was told that although the gathering of objects from the archaeological sites was a common occurrence before the arrival of the Cultural Mission, hostility was felt toward people from outside Djenné coming to find objects. Ownership was therefore felt as the right to exclusive access to a resource.

At a national level, however, indicated by the words of Alpha Oumar Konaré, the dispersal of Malian material culture throughout the world and the consequent loss over its interpretation are significant problems for the Malian government. However, as described earlier, the interpretation of the site of Djenné-Djeno also fulfils the "reclamatory politics" criteria set out by Olaniyan—through refuting the Islamic diffusionist model of West-African culture. Although this does not have much currency at the moment among Djenné's population, it could well take on greater meaning in the future. For example, a new library created to digitise the Islamic manuscripts in Timbuktu has had a significant effect on African-American interest in the region, because it fulfils a desire for the recognition of a distinctively African intellectual tradition.

At the moment, and despite efforts made by the Cultural Mission in local schools and with local populations, there does not seem to be a strong link in many *Djennenkés'* minds between the potential for further knowledge about their town and the archaeological sites that surround it. One man who did work with the McIntoshes over a four-year period, now a retired farmer living in Djenné, told me of his understanding of the archaeological site he excavated. He described how the team had found four different kinds of earth during the excavations: one from the time of the Prophet Mohammed, one from the time of the arrival of the Bobos in Djenné, one from the time of the arrival of the French, and one dating from modern times. He spoke warmly about his involvement in the archaeological project and explained the process of finding, washing, and entering objects into a database.

Since the departure of the McIntoshes, he has had no further involvement with archaeology and was saddened by the loss of the one document given to him by the McIntoshes relating to Djenné-Djeno. His understanding of the work of the Cultural Mission is that by protecting the archaeological sites, it is protecting the objects found at the site. However, he believes that this is done because the state wants to sell the objects itself and keep the money, and it is for this reason that the site cannot be looted. He thinks that the money raised by the Malian state in this way could be used to help Djenné's population. As things stand, he feels that Djenné has not benefited materially from the surrounding archaeological sites, despite hearing claims that a museum would be built to attract tourists and increase visitor income. When asked about the wider population's attitudes toward Djenné-Djeno, he reported that many people thought that the site had been sold to the "whites" for the economic benefit of the government, which had become the broker of Djenné's cultural heritage.

In 2009 a European-funded museum was finally built in the centre of Djenné, with an opening ceremony planned for January of 2010. At the time of this writing, however, in the autumn of 2010, the museum remains empty and closed, and part of the building has collapsed owing to heavy rains. It is still unclear what the museum will eventually contain, and, after some negotiation, it seems that the Cultural Mission will be responsible for its management.

Owing to a lack of access to the archaeological sites (*Djennenkés* can visit Djenné-Djeno only if accompanied by a Cultural Mission guide) as well as education about archaeology, many people in Djenné are left disenfranchised from a process that they could enrich with their own knowledge and experience.

Before the arrival of the Cultural Mission, the discovery of archaeological objects at Djenné-Djeno sometimes had a transformative effect on people's fortunes. Stories of remarkable finds are still circulating in Djenné. One such story involved a man who was out walking with his dog. His dog ran after a rabbit and followed it to a hole, where the dog started digging. The owner saw something in the ground and on further inspection found that it was a bronze statue of a man mounted on a horse. Not knowing the value of the object, the man made sure that a local *antiquaire* ("antiques dealer") heard about it and came to see it in his home. Thinking that he may get a few thousand CFA for the object but not wanting to open the bartering, the man was surprised when the *antiquaire's* first offer was 100,000 CFA (£100). The story was told humorously, with the incredulous owner of the statue finding the *antiquaire*

Figure 2.2 The European Union–funded Djenné Museum, shortly before completion

bidding ever higher until the owner was finally paid 900,000 CFA (£900) for his find. The *Djennenké* telling the story thought that the *antiquaire* would then have been able to go on and sell such an object for about 8 million CFA (£8,000) in Bamako. Given the lack of evidence about such finds in the region, we might suspect that the story is not true; however, the important point is that it is still being retold, long after sensitisations projects are supposed to have had an enlightening effect on local populations. As is described later in relation to the riot in Djenné in September 2006, preventing access to the money represented by the town's cultural heritage is a dangerous flash point between *Djennenkés* and the local authorities in charge of Djenné's architecture.

Djenné's Architecture

Maas and Mommersteeg's (1992) thorough survey of Djenné's architecture categorises houses into those with interior courtyards (*maisons à cour intérieure*) and those built around an enclosure (*maisons à enclos*). The houses with interior courtyards are again divided into two categories: the older ones, characteristically compact, built on several floors and constructed in *Djenné-Ferey*; and the newer ones, usually more spacious and constructed in *Toubabou-Ferey*. The houses built around an enclosure are characterised by their fragmentation (because of being built in stages or some parts of the house falling into ruin). Some of these houses will eventually become houses with interior courtyards.

Of most interest to the tourists visiting Djenné are the façades of the houses. There are three styles of façade in Djenné: la *Façade Marocaine*, la *Façade Toucouleur*, and the undecorated *façade*. The undecorated *façade* may be so by design or may have become so through lack of upkeep. The *Façade Toucouleur* is differentiated from the *Façade Marocaine* through the overhanging "screen" on the front door. A technical description of the meaning of the façades can be found in the literature (Bedaux & van der Waals, 1994; Maas & Mommersteeg, 1992; Marchand, 2003), contrasting with a lay interpretation that can be heard when speaking to the guides in Djenné. The guides now include the houses restored by the Dutch project (discussed shortly) in their itinerary around the town.

The architecture of Djenné, like everything else in the town, is constantly changing. Most notably in the last few hundred years, the masons of Djenné have changed the technology they use to build mud bricks from the precolonial *Djenné-Ferey* to the current use of *Toubabou-Ferey*. Before colonial times, the masons of Djenné built using hand-moulded cylindrical bricks called *Djenné-Ferey*. In an interview with a retired mason, I was told that these old bricks were ideally made from a mixture of mud, rice husks, *beurre de karité* (a powder made from the fruit of the *Néré* tree), and a powder made from the fruit of the Baobab tree. This mixture was broken down with the use of animal urine and dung until it was ready to be moulded and "baked" in the sun.

Djenné-Ferey bricks are remembered by today's masons as more hard-wearing than contemporary *Toubabou-Ferey* bricks. *Toubabou-Ferey* are square bricks, made using wooden moulds and, owing to their shape, easier to manufacture and build with. They are usually made only of mud and rice stalks, because the other ingredients are now too expensive—such as

Figure 2.3 Cylindrical *Djenné-Ferey* brick

the *beurre de karité*, which has a high commercial value as the base for beauty products and other manufactured goods. In addition to the technological change, a second fundamental change has therefore been the choice of materials used for making bricks. While some materials are becoming increasingly unaffordable, other materials, such as the wood needed for the construction of the roofs (*bois de ronier*), are becoming increasingly rare.

Furthermore, a change in agricultural practice that has led to the degradation of the quality of the bricks used in Djenné has been the introduction of mechanical rice dehuskers. These machines, that can be seen working at the river's edge, reduce the rice husks to powder, a far less appropriate ingredient for bricks than the manually extracted husk. The husks are used to bind the mud in a way that the powder does not achieve. Masons are reduced to expensively importing rice husks from outside Djenné and substituting, in part or in whole, the stalks of the plants for the rice husks. Additionally, the exposed stalks prove to be irresistible meals for the animals living in the compound, so some accessible parts of people's homes are simply nibbled away. Today, the only occasion when houses in Djenné are built with traditional ingredients such as the *beurre de karité* is when rich expatriates in the town commission them. Building to such high standards is beyond the means of the ordinary *Djennenké*.

Figure 2.4 *Toubabou-Ferey* square bricks drying in the sun

Many masons in Djenné believe that the bricks they build with today are of lesser quality than those used in the past not only for the reasons stated but also because of the nature of the mud. Decreased rainfall and river levels and the subsequent depletion of fish stocks has led to a weaker concentration of calcified fish bones that reputedly made the mud resistant. Additionally, pollution in the river in the form of strands of plastic bags and bottle tops are now found in the mud and simply applied to the façades of the houses during the annual protective relayering of mud.

Figure 2.5 Tiles applied to the walls of a house in Djenné

These factors have led to the increasingly common practice of using fired clay tiles to protect the outside of Djenné houses. The tiles are fixed to the house with the use of cement, a practice that many heritage experts warn can fundamentally undermine the entire structure of the building. An often cited example of mud and cement not mixing is the mosque in the nearby town of Mopti that was partly covered in cement to reduce the cost of its upkeep. The cement part of the building began to degrade the banco underneath, and an Aga Khan Trust for Culture–funded restoration project had to be brought in to rip off the cement and restore the mosque back to its original form.

The practice of using tiles on Djenné's houses is condemned by the Cultural Mission and UNESCO, yet it is gaining in popularity among residents, because it promises to solve the regular problem of finding the funds to remud houses. Despite the initial high outlay, tiled houses can last for years without needing maintenance, providing peace of mind for their occupants. Schijns (1994: 173) suggests that the use of tiles is also linked to local notions of prestige and modernity.

As mentioned, in the past the use of tiles had been reserved for the rich people of Djenné (such as the owners of *Millionso* in the quartier of Kanafa, which is entirely covered in tiles) or only for use on the floors of houses. Now, even less well-off residents tile the outside of their houses, because they believe that in the long term it makes more financial sense to do so. At the end of 2005 one tile cost 20 CFA (£0.02). The cost of a mason's labour

Figure 2.6 House covered in tiles stands behind a collapsed building in Djenné

is higher for tiling than for remudding, because tiling takes more time, but year on year, the peripheral costs associated with remudding are rising. For example, in 2005 a bag of rice husks cost 1,500 CFA (£1.50), and preparing the mud by the river cost 500 CFA (£0.50), with an additional 250 CFA (£0.25) per cart used to transport the mud. However, a study undertaken by a French architect in conjunction with *Djenné Patrimoine* in 2006 revealed that tiling houses was fourteen times more expensive than using banco with added *beurre de karité,* and eighteen times more expensive than using ordinary banco (2,800 CFA [£2.80] per square metre for tiles as opposed to 196 CFA [£0.19] for banco with *beurre de karité* and 152 CFA [£0.15] for simple banco).[3] The evidence therefore suggests that despite an intuitive feeling among some *Djennenkés* that the use of tiles is a good long-term investment, the reality may be very different.

When asked about the practice of using tiles, many masons felt uncomfortable about their use yet unable to refuse the requests of the owners of the houses that are their moral responsibility. I was told on numerous occasions that if they did not give in to the request of tiling someone's house, then another mason would do the job, leading to the breakdown of their relationship with the house. Tiles can crack and let in water, but masons are skilled in their repair, and, provided that the repair is done quickly, no damage should be done to the mud bricks beneath.[4] I was also told that it was very important to use the best-quality tiles available, meaning those that have been fired correctly. A blackened tile usually has not been fired correctly and may be brittle.

An added dimension to the debate surrounding the upkeep of houses is the fact that local authorities in the area, operating with restricted budgets, cannot meet the costs of upkeep on banco buildings and therefore build their administrative buildings, on the outskirts of town, in cement. Similarly, administrative buildings within the town are undermining the conservation message. In one instance, the house of the *Sous-Préfet* near the Campement Hotel in Djenné was covered in tiles, leading to the intervention of the Cultural Mission, who insisted on their removal.[5] As a compromise, the Cultural Mission has agreed to pay for the ongoing annual upkeep of the house.

Among Djenné residents, there is a high level of awareness that the attraction of the town to tourists is primarily because of its architecture. The masons themselves are somewhat resentful that they do not derive more direct benefit from tourism for their labour, and in the past they have demanded a share of the tourist tax to better reflect the importance of their role within the tourist equation. One mason told me: "That's why tourists come. To see the houses, built one or two hundred years ago, in banco, still standing. Well, that is what fascinates [people], that is what attracts them. It's what gives us our value."[6]

Figure 2.7 Djenné mason erecting a façade of a Djenné house at the National Museum in Bamako in 2008

With the increasing cost of living in the town and new technologies (such as the mechanical rice dehuskers), all parts of the population are updating and changing their subsistence practices. For example, although in the past fishermen used to use string nets costing 50,000 CFA (£50) for 100 meters of net. The majority now opt for a cheaper plastic version costing only 15,000 CFA (£15). Not only is the plastic version cheaper, but it is also more efficient at catching fish.[7] However, unlike changes in architectural practices, the changes in fishing practices go uncommented on by heritage officials in the town. A frame of reference for what can and cannot change within the town is therefore inconsistent and sometimes contradictory.

The arguably arbitrary nature of the heritage interventions in the town has led to some frustrations. Joseph Brunet-Jailly (founder of *Djenné Patrimoine*) believes that for there to be true "restoration" or "protection" of houses, there should be a revival of architectural techniques, such as the production and use of *Djenné-Ferey*. (For a response to this opinion see Bedaux et al., 2003: 58.) He feels that the houses restored during the Dutch Housing Restoration project would have benefited from using the old technology when appropriate: "If you take an ambiguous position towards the restoration of heritage, people find it hard to understand, if we say that architecture is the masons' knowledge, the embodiment of this knowledge, and their relationship with house owners, why is it that not more is made of the technique that these masons use?"[8]

In a round-table discussion about Djenné's architecture broadcast by Djenné's local Radio Jamana in June 1999, a representative of *Djenné Patrimoine* and the ex-director of the Cultural Mission put forward their respective positions.[9] *Djenné Patrimoine* advocated the declassifying of some parts of the town to allow for development and change. They believed that when restoration took place, as in the case of the Dutch Housing Restoration project, it should be done following the strictest criteria set out in the Venice Charter,[10] which for them meant using the old technique of *Djenné-Ferey* when appropriate. At the same time, *Djenné Patrimoine* would like to see parts of the town built *en dur* ("in cement") using the expertise of international architects to help replicate the traditional appearance of Djenné. The Cultural Mission felt that this position was contradictory and referred to the masons as the locus of authenticity.

During the Dutch Housing Restoration project, it was the masons who felt unable to restore the houses using *Djenné-Ferey* technology, and so the use of *Toubabou-Ferey* was considered appropriate. The Cultural Mission also largely rejected declassifying part of the town or bringing in international architectural experts to find new realistic solutions to Djenné's housing problems. Again, this action was in part in reference to the town's masons, who would perhaps become alienated from the town's architecture if international architects replaced traditional expertise.

The Dutch Housing Restoration Project

The Housing Restoration project undertaken and funded by the Dutch government between 1994 and 2004[11] encountered many of the issues faced by Western Heritage interventions described throughout this book. The Dutch have a long-standing interest in Djenné, beginning in 1975 when a team from the University of Utrecht undertook archaeological excavations in Djenné and Mopti (Bedaux et al., 2003: 9).[12] They were followed to Mali by many other Dutch researchers including geographers, anthropologists, architects, and archaeologists (for example, Mommersteeg, 2009). A group of architects at the University of Eindhoven have been undertaking detailed documentation of Djenné's architecture since the beginning of the 1980s (Maas & Mommersteeg, 1992: 7). It is through this long-term involvement with Djenné that the Dutch Housing Restoration project was born.

The aim of the project was to restore a core number of representative houses that would stand as an inspiration for the rest of the town.[13] The project also undertook a thorough survey of a significant proportion of houses in Djenné and catalogued their state of repair. The choice of houses to be restored was from the outset explicitly Eurocentric,[14] with houses with monumental facades represented in early photographs and postcards of the town being given priority. The project proper was launched after an exhibition was held at the Rijksmuseum voor Volkenkunde in Leiden entitled *Djenné, the Most Beautiful Town in Africa* in 1994. The exhibition was also shown in Bamako and Djenné (Bedaux et al., 2003: 46). The original project team was made up of archaeologists from the Rijksmuseum voor Volkenkunde in Leiden and an architect from Breda, who worked with Malian heritage professionals, the National Museum in

Figure 2.8 Houses in Djenné restored by the Dutch Housing Restoration project

Bamako, local officials in Djenné, including the Cultural Mission, and the masons. A Scientific Committee that met annually to discuss the project's progress oversaw the project. Inevitably, the project ran into some difficulties, and the number of restored houses had to be scaled down from the original goal of two hundred. The restoration work started in 1996 and ended with somewhat fewer than one hundred restored houses and the publication of a book on the architecture of Djenné in February 2003 (Bedaux et al., 2003).

Some of the unexpected consequences of the project can be contextualised through ethnographic knowledge of Djenné. For example, at the outset house owners feared that consenting to restoration work on their houses would threaten their ownership rights. A rumour of houses being "sold" to the Dutch in some ways echoed similar rumours of the archaeological sites being sold. The Cultural Mission's involvement with the project also led to some resentment and mistrust. Another issue that inevitably came up was the issue of change, as noted by Marchand: "Households that agree to participate in the project are expected to make no further structural or planning modifications to their houses. . . . In my view, the house takes on the status of protected monument above and beyond its function as a home" (Marchand, 2001: 150).

There was a strong desire among many house owners to use the project as an opportunity to improve their houses. Changes in family structure and consequently in accommodation needs, a desire for a more open social space in which to welcome guests, and a desire for brighter, more airy spaces led to some clashes between the restoration project and home owners (Rowlands, 2003). As much as possible, the Dutch team tried to find mutually agreeable solutions. Additionally, while the project intended to promote and "re-launch" an enthusiasm for the architecture of Djenné among residents, in some ways it also served to set up expectations of help from house owners, who believed that the Dutch relationship with the houses, once established, would continue indefinitely. The Dutch team had made provisions for handing over the ongoing remudding (*crépissage*) costs of the restored houses to the Malian government (it was agreed that this would take place every two years); however, the funds needed for ongoing maintenance (10 million CFA, promised by the Ministry of Culture) have taken many years to materialise.[15]

Throughout the restoration project, there appeared to be two positions: first, that of the Dutch, which focused on the architecture of Djenné and its promotion (and had as a subsidiary focus the alleviation of poverty); second, that of many of the residents, who inevitably considered their houses in more practical and immediate terms. Those who had their houses restored tended to speak about the benefits of the project primarily in economic and practical terms and wanted to maintain a relationship with the Dutch, who were regarded as patrons. Pride in owning a newly restored house was important but mostly came second to the alleviation of economic burden that the restored house represented.[16] For those in Djenné who did not have their houses restored, the project served less, as had been intended, as inspiration but instead seemed to reinforce the view that help should, and would, come from the outside—and in time more such projects would come to Djenné.

The Dutch Housing Restoration project can be seen as an attempt to create a physical archive of Djenné's houses for posterity. It also led to the direct employment of masons, workmen, carpenters, tile-makers, and wood merchants, among many others, for a period of seven years. However, from the outset the project was beset by the problems of Djenné's political and economic realities. To summarise: First, the choice of houses to restore caused consternation among the *Djennenkés* who were excluded. Inevitably, many of the houses chosen for restoration belonged to the *Grandes Familles* in Djenné[17] (houses with monumental façades), and therefore the situation looked like a case of the elite serving themselves. Second, *Djenné Patrimoine* did not believe that the true spirit of restoration had been respected in the choice of material used, and therefore further local political turmoil ensued.[18] A third problem encountered by the project was one of ownership: questions arose as to what rights householders were passing on to the Dutch when allowing them access to their houses. Fourth, householders resented the fact that the project did not allow them a greater degree of self-determination and an opportunity to improve their living conditions by, for example, extending their homes or adding windows. The themes that emerge from the experience of the Dutch Housing Restoration project are therefore lack of trust owing to the circulation of rumours (many started by rival heritage factions in Djenné), a need for further clarity in objectives, insufficient financial incentives, and a lack of self-determination. These themes come out time and time again when one examines the impact of outside cultural heritage projects coming to Djenné and could be considered to have reached their logical conclusion during the riot of September 2006.

Another dimension to the problems is that despite the Housing Restoration project's concern with the "authentic image of the town" and *Djenné Patrimoine's* concentration on authentic materials, there does not seem to be matching concern about authenticity among *Djennenkés* themselves. As is discussed in relation to the work of artisans in Djenné in Chapter 6, authenticity is a negotiated practice. Marchand describes the masons in Djenné as having an "expert discourse" made up of transmitted technical, magical, and ritual knowledge, as well as claims to ancestry (Marchand, 2001: 155). The client-audience invests faith in their practices, and thus their built environment is reproduced. "Authenticity" in a built heritage sense is therefore for the majority of the population an invisible concern. It is made visible only through the work of heritage officials in the town who use the concept to claim authority over the way cultural heritage should be managed.

The Sanitation Project

The sanitation project, begun in 2002, responded to one of the most pressing needs in Djenné. The pilot phase was as add-on to the Dutch Housing Restoration project. After the pilot phase, the German government

Figure 2.9 Sanitation tank built on the outside of a house in Djenné

financially supported the roll-out of the project across Djenné. One of the main threats to both people and architecture in Djenné is the accumulation of wastewater in the small alleys between the houses. This wastewater, which remains stagnant in the heat for days, soon poses a public health threat as children play in it, people are forced to walk through it, and mosquitoes and other insects use it as their breeding grounds. Historically, Djenné was free of wastewater as people had to collect water from the river. However, ever since the Canadian government built a water tower in the 1980s, providing many *Djennenkés* with running water in or near their homes, the accumulation of wastewater in the streets has been a major challenge for the town. The water tower project had not made any provisions for the removal of wastewater.

Like all the other projects involving external funding, the sanitation project ran into a number of difficulties that provide insights into the local political economic landscape of Djenné. The pilot phase of the sanitation project was broadly successful; however, a few seeds of dissent were planted from the outset, leading to difficulties with rolling out the project across the whole town. The masons taking part in the sanitation project were asked to train for five days to learn how to build the drainage tanks. This training was without remuneration, since their training would ensure them future paid work on the project. The lack of payment for training led to a number of masons not taking part in the project, which in turn led to bitter resentment later, when masons who had not been trained saw those who had been build the sanitation tanks in houses that were traditionally the untrained masons' responsibility. Additionally, the masons chosen to run the project did not fit with local conceptions of hierarchy within the masons' association (*the barey-ton*). Soon rumours began to circulate that the sanitation project was fundamentally flawed, that the wastewater, now channelled into individual tanks at the side of houses, would accumulate and undermine the foundation of the buildings.

A sensitisation project was launched to support the implementation of the sanitation project. An artist from Timbuktu was employed to illustrate the problems linked to the wastewater in Djenné and the proposed solutions brought by the project. Three men and one woman then had the job of going to speak to house owners and explain their illustrations. The sanitation project undertook to fund half of the cost of the tanks (28,000 CFA per tank [£28]), and the house owners were required to pay back the cost of the other half (27,000 CFA [£27]) over twenty-seven months, providing ongoing funding for the project. They were also asked to pay an ongoing 200 CFA (£0.20) per month for maintenance costs, a charge that was deeply unpopular, because it was permanent. The resistance of some householders to the project was in part due to rumours started by the disenfranchised masons but was also due to the financial burden the systems represented and the fact that some technical difficulties led to blockages and problems (for example, metal filters had to be replaced with cement filters, which degraded too rapidly). There was also an administrative problem with billing that led to some house owners not being billed for months and then suddenly being presented with a demand for 4,000 CFA (£4) or 5,000 CFA (£5). People consequently refused or were unable to pay, putting in jeopardy the rolling out of the project across the whole of Djenné.

Understanding the resistance of many *Djennenkés* to the sanitation project is important when one considers broader attitudes toward the preservation of cultural heritage in Djenné. Sanitation had been identified as the most important priority for the town by residents, local authorities, and the national tourist office (OMATHO). *Djennenkés* regularly complained about the stench of wastewater, the health threat it posed to their families, and the fact that they often trailed their clothes in the festering drains. Before the sanitation project, drains from rooftop bathrooms opened straight onto the narrow streets below. This project therefore marks a considerable improvement in living conditions for the majority of *Djennenkés*.

However, like any other project coming from the outside, it represented financial resources and therefore became the focus of a struggle for access and influence. The project's limited success was due to its encroachment on a complex political economic scene. A brief summary of the factors that frustrated the project's progress would include the encroaching on the masons *barey-ton* hierarchy, not including the traditional authorities such as the *Chef du Village* in early negotiations about setting the cost for the ongoing running of the project, underestimating the cost of communicating the project to the population, misunderstanding the conceptual importance of evacuating wastewater out of the compound (not in a tank attached to it), running into difficulties with the lack of technical expertise of a decentralised local administration, and coinciding the project with bitter local elections and the subsequent replacement of the Water Users' Board,[19] the body chosen to oversee the ongoing running of the project. The consequence of these difficulties is that the project incurred a direct loss of 50 million CFA (£50,000).[20] However, despite these difficulties, three-quarters of the town was finally covered by the project. A report written in 2007 evaluating its success concluded that despite residual worries, 85% of the people surveyed declared themselves to be in favour of the system.[21] But the ongoing success of the sanitation initiative is undermined by the fact that the majority of homeowners do not pay their sanitation bill; 80% of those surveyed declared that they couldn't afford it. Additionally, many homeowners are simply passing on the cost to their tenants, the poorest people in Djenné, who see their monthly bills rising.

Figure 2.10 A narrow street in Djenné with pipes opening straight onto the street below

Conclusion

Like the colonial administrators and early French explorers before it, UNESCO's concentration on the archaeology and architecture of Djenné has led to a distinctive way of apprehending the town, prioritising the material over the immaterial in an effort at stabilisation. Heritage organisations working in Djenné have respected UNESCO's classification of Djenné as a World Heritage site and worked within a philosophy of conservation and protection, sometimes in difficult circumstances. A detailed examination of the Dutch Housing Restoration project or the sanitation project starts to shed light on where a largely static model of preservation comes into conflict with social changes, economic imperatives, and political struggles over power in the town.

It would be wrong, however, to assume that because its instrument and objectives seem fixed and have as their goal a certain stabilisation of a situation, UNESCO itself is a rigid institution. Instead, it is an institution in a constant state of flux, with a complex internal dynamic dictated by political and economic concerns. As is described in the following chapter, the machinations of life within UNESCO in Paris are as complex as the political machinations found in Djenné, where different factions vie for political and economic influence.

CHAPTER 3

UNESCO and Becoming a World Heritage Site

UNESCO's History

UNESCO was established on November 16, 1945, as a response to the Second World War. It was partly founded on the model of the former *Conference of Allied Ministers of Education* (CAME), which had been established in London in 1942 (Imber, 1989: 98) and had brought together the interests of the Paris based *International Institute for Intellectual Cooperation* and the Geneva based *International Bureau of Education*. At the heart of UNESCO lies the belief that the promotion of different global "cultures" is key to global peace. UNESCO's constitution today still declares that its ambition is to "build peace in the minds of men,"[1] words first pronounced by the British Prime Minister Attlee addressing the new UNESCO conference in 1945.

As well as its cultural initiatives, UNESCO's remit includes projects concerning education (for example, teacher training, literacy projects, the production of school textbooks) and social and natural sciences (for instance, press freedom, women's rights, climate change, international cooperation, and dissemination of research). UNESCO works toward its overarching mission together with a series of shorter-term targets and initiatives, such as the 2015 UN Millennium Development Goals.[2] UNESCO is therefore a combination of a visionary body and a practical institution. In the domain of culture, it has the dual task of setting a future agenda as well as responding to the immediate needs of its member states.

The power balance between UNESCO and its member states is a complicated one. Turtinen emphasises UNESCO's influence on nation-states: "UNESCO is indeed a powerful producer of culture, and a highly influential actor, capable of defining and framing conditions, problems, and solutions, and thus framing the interests and desired actions of others, especially those of the world's nation-states" (2000: 6). However, nation-states also have an influence on UNESCO. For example, in 1984 the United States withdrew its membership from the organisation, followed by United Kingdom's withdrawal in 1985 and Singapore withdrawal in 1986. The United Kingdom returned to UNESCO in 1997, the United States in 2003, and Singapore in 2007. The U.S. withdrawal in 1986 was officially due to a critique of the agency's programme, budget, managerial style, and competence (Imber, 1989: 96).

However, many contemporary observers thought that the U.S. threat to withdraw was merely a political ploy to gain greater influence within the organisation (Finn, 1986). Off the record, the United States was becoming increasingly concerned with what it perceived as UNESCO's pro-Palestinian position. It was also concerned with a proposal entitled the *New World Information and Communication Order* (emerging as a recommendation of the UNESCO commissioned *MacBride Report*). This order was a series of proposals to help developing countries gain more control over the way they were represented in the global media. The United States considered this a potential attack on press freedom.

Within UNESCO at the time therefore, the balance of power was seen to be shifting away from Western countries towards non-Western concerns. Furthermore, the United States detected a politicisation of the institution toward areas that it did not consider to be within its remit, such as disarmament and issues of "collective rights" eroding individual rights and freedoms recognised in the *Universal Declaration of Human Rights* (Imber, 1989: 109).

Despite its withdrawal, the United States remained involved with UNESCO throughout the 1990s by making extra-budgetary financial contributions. Now it has returned to the UNESCO fold, the United States is once again the single biggest contributor to the UNESCO budget (22% in 2007, followed by Japan's 16.7%). In contrast, Mali contributes only 0.001% of the annual budget[3]). In 1995 U.S. President Clinton stated that substantial progress had been made in addressing the reasons for the U.S. withdrawal, but owing to budgetary constraints it took until 2003 for the United States to officially rejoin UNESCO. Another significant reason for the United States' re-appraisal of its position toward UNESCO was the perceived progress made by the institution under the two Director Generals who succeeded Amadou-Mahtar M'bow of Senegal, the director general at the helm at the time of U.S. withdrawal (1974–1987). The first was the Spanish Frederico Mayor Zaragosa (1987–1999), followed by the Japanese Director General, Koïchiro Matsuura (1999–2009).

These early struggles between UNESCO and its member states are important, because they highlight some of the tensions still present in the institution today: the extent to which UNESCO is biased toward Western concerns, the economic clout of the richer member states and their consequent ability to change the institution's focus, and the marginalisation of non-Western concerns, such as the *New World Information and Communication Order*. The fact that the United States and the United Kingdom withdrawals happened under an African Director General is also of enduring symbolic significance.[4]

Furthermore, the power balance within UNESCO is illustrated by the fact that richer Western member states are more likely than poorer non-Western ones to opt out of any initiative that they see as a threat to their national sovereignty such as the *Convention for the Safeguarding of the Intangible Cultural Heritage*, described below. The United States and Australia have refused to be signatories to the Convention, and it can be suggested that this is due to the Convention's promotion of the collective rights of indigenous people. The United Kingdom has also refused to be a signatory, as it does not think that is it useful to separate tangible and intangible heritage when seeking to protect cultural heritage.[5] The United States, Australia, and the United Kingdom are all at liberty to opt out of the Convention, since they are not in any way dependent on the funds that the Convention has put in place for participating poorer member states. UNESCO is therefore a global institution and contains within it all the economic, political and social power imbalances existing on the outside. It is also an ideological institution and much of its founding ideology has come from Western intellectual concerns, as described later.

Working for UNESCO

In June 2004 I arrived outside the UNESCO buildings in Rue Miollis in Paris to begin my two-month internship in the Intangible Heritage

Department of the organisation. All the interns had been gathered the day before in UNESCO's imposing headquarters on Place de Fontenoy and issued with our contracts (we were nominally paid $1 for the duration of the internship) and our security passes. The Place de Fontenoy headquarters is an unusually shaped three-pronged building, flanked by large railing and flags fluttering in the wind, situated in Paris's prestigious 7th Arrondissement. The building has a direct view on to the Parc du Champs de Mars, and many employees and interns gather there after work for drinks and picnics under the shadow of the Eiffel Tower. The Rue Miollis building, although less aesthetically striking than the official headquarters, is a very large building, with tight airport-like security to enter and exit and the feeling of grandeur in the lobby and throughout its halls. As well as countless offices, the building houses a canteen, a duty free shop, a café, a bank, and a travel agency and has beautiful views over the Parisian cityscape. I shared my office with two other members of the Intangible Heritage Department, sitting at a desk with a direct view of the Eiffel Tower.

It is hard not to be enchanted by life at UNESCO. At once you feel that you are working in a Noah's Ark of different nations, from the great variety of languages spoken in the lifts to the different forms of dress and customs displayed everywhere you turn. It is UNESCO policy to keep a balance of employees from each Member State belonging to UNESCO so each country is "represented," "under-represented," or "over-represented" at each level of the organisation. Consequently, a person from an over-represented country may find it very hard to progress within the organisation, whereas someone from an under-represented country may be fast-tracked through the ranks.

Although outwardly concerned with education, science, and culture, UNESCO is in fact an organisation necessarily concerned with politics. Decisions, initiatives, programmes, and proclamation that may cause offence (even in a very indirect manner) to a member state are wholeheartedly avoided. UNESCO is a place of diplomacy, even if it is sometimes at the expense of efficiency. Unfortunately, this diplomacy combined with the organisation's doctrinal idealism often leads to platitudes and over-generalisations in its output: watered-down versions of less palatable truths.

UNESCO's bureaucratic structure has a direct impact on its output. As an institution, UNESCO echoes other UN institutions in its operational set-up:

> It operates on the basis of one state, one vote with the supreme governing body being the General Conference of Member States, which meets every two years to elect the Executive Board, appoint the Director General, and admit new Member States. The day to day running of the organization

is done by the Director General and his staff, the Secretariat. The basic structure of UNESCO can be seen to exist as a tension between a permanent Secretariat of professional international bureaucrats, and the Member States in the National Commissions and National Delegates; a tension that can also be framed in terms of State Parties and UNESCO bureaucrats, or even in terms of the sovereignty of the Member States versus the influence of the "international community" represented through UNESCO. (Fontein, 2000: 22)

The position of Director General is one of particular influence and can change the focus of the institution for the duration of the post and beyond. Koïchiro Matsuura (Director General between 1999 and 2009) was instrumental in driving forward the promotion of intangible cultural heritage and putting in place Japanese Funds in Trust to financially support his vision. The current Director General is the Bulgarian Irina Bokova, the first woman to hold the position.

UNESCO's work is dependent on a network of experts, working in centres across the world. This makes the study of UNESCO as an organisation particularly difficult:

The UNESCO headquarters are located in Paris. There are three expert bodies. One is based in Paris, France, one in Gland, Switzerland, and one in Rome, Italy. In addition, many other organisations are involved in World Heritage, and the network is constantly expanding. When a state ratifies the convention, state institutions, organisations, and individuals locally, regionally and nationally are drawn in. Moreover, meetings and conferences regarding World Heritage take place in different places in all parts of the world. Both people and ideas travel across national and organisational borders. All these conditions make a qualitative study of World Heritage a complicated and challenging endeavour. (Turtinen, 2000: 8)

The World Heritage Centre was created in 1992 and is housed in its own building at the heart of the Place de Fontenoy complex. UNESCO's cultural division is divided into different sectors, which are fairly fluid and often change name or focus or are re-deployed or absorbed into each other. In 2007 the sectors were Cultural Diversity, World Heritage, Tangible Heritage, Intangible Heritage, Normative Action, Intercultural Dialogue, Cultural Industries, Arts and Creativity, Copyright, Museums, and Cultural Tourism. Different sectors within the cultural division may grow and gain prestige, as was the case for the World Heritage sector, which was once housed within the Tangible Heritage sector. From its inception, the World Heritage List has been a great success as governments have responded enthusiastically to UNESCO's call for candidates and the programme has received high profile media attention. This success has meant that not only did the sector gain its autonomy and acquire its own building but also the Tangible Heritage sector is now being absorbed into the World Heritage sector, in a case of the child eclipsing the parent. Each sector therefore has a vested interest in its own promotion to ensure its survival and attract the institution's funds to its cause.

As well as its permanent staff, UNESCO relies on a large number of external experts (for example ICOMOS, the International Council on Monuments and Sites, an independent body of experts that acts as judge for the Candidature Files, or *Dossiers de Candidatures*, for inclusion the World Heritage List) and also always employs a large number of unpaid interns. Despite the official rhetoric that internships do not lead to jobs within the organisation, many of the employees I came across had started life in the organisation as interns and had been kept on, sometimes for many years, on a series of short-term contracts.

UNESCO's Concept of Culture

Working within UNESCO gave me first-hand experience of how instruments to measure and define *culture* are created. The concept of culture is necessarily fluid within an institution such as UNESCO, and fixing its meaning becomes a political negotiation. It is therefore not surprising that the early foundational texts for UNESCO's concept of culture were in part based on writings commissioned by two leading French intellectuals at the time: Claude Lévi-Strauss and Michel Leiris (discussed in Chapter 1). In an interview with Didier Eribon to mark Lévi-Strauss's eightieth birthday (Eribon, 1988), Lévi-Strauss describes the central theme of his commissioned work *Race et Histoire*:

> D. E.: In 1952 with the text *Race et Histoire*, you left the perspective of pure social anthropology to position yourself at the level that can be called "political," which touched in any case directly on contemporary problems.
>
> C. L.-S.: It was a commission. I don't think I would have written the work myself on my own initiative.
>
> D. E.: How did this commission arise?
>
> C. L.-S.: UNESCO asked a number of authors to write a series of booklets on the racial question: Michel Leiris was one, I was another . . .
>
> D. E.: There you affirm the diversity of cultures, you put into question the idea of progress, and you proclaim the necessity of "coalition" between cultures.
>
> C. L.-S.: In general, I was seeking to reconcile the notion of progress with cultural relativism. The notion of progress implies the idea that certain cultures, at given times or in given places, are superior to others, because they have produced works which those others have shown themselves incapable of. And cultural relativism, which is one of the basis of anthropological

thought. . . contends that there can be no absolute criterion for judging one culture as superior to another. I tried to shift the problem's centre of gravity.

Claude Lévi-Strauss[6] was one of a few key people consulted in the early days of UNESCO to define the institution's remit and focus concerning culture. He identified a tension between universalism and relativism, one that continues to provoke lively debate today (Eriksen, 2001).

In terms of working definitions, UNESCO has defined cultural heritage in its Convention Concerning the Protection of the World's Cultural and Natural Heritage (World Heritage Convention[7]) as

> Monuments: architectural works, works of monumental sculpture and painting, elements or structures of an archaeological nature, inscriptions, cave dwellings and combinations of features, which are of *outstanding universal value* from the point of view of history, art or science; groups of buildings: groups of separate or connected buildings which, because of their architecture, their homogeneity or their place in the landscape, are of *outstanding universal value* from the point of view of history, art or science; sites: works of man or the combined works of nature and man, and areas including archaeological sites which are of *outstanding universal value* from the historical, aesthetic, ethnological or anthropological point of view. (my italics)

More recently, it has defined intangible cultural heritage in the Convention for the Safeguarding of the Intangible Cultural Heritage[8] as:

> The "intangible cultural heritage" means the practices, representations, expressions, knowledge, skills—as well as the instruments, objects, artefacts and cultural spaces associated therewith—that communities, groups and, in some cases, individuals recognize as part of their cultural heritage. This intangible cultural heritage, *transmitted* from generation to generation, is constantly recreated by communities and groups in response to their environment, their interaction with nature and their history, and provides them with a *sense of identity and continuity*, thus promoting respect for cultural diversity and human creativity. (my italics)

In the case of the World Heritage Convention, therefore, the emphasis is on "outstanding universal value." In the case of intangible heritage, however, the emphasis is on transmission, identity and continuity.

UNESCO's most complete recent statement on its vision of culture comes in the form of a publication entitled *Our Creative Diversity* (World Commission on Culture and Development 1996). The document deals with the issue of culture and development and advocates that culture should not be seen as a facilitator of development but instead development should be seen as part of culture. It also champions "cultural freedom," which it sees as a collective, and not an individual right.

Eriksen (2001: 133) broadly welcomes the statement, while noting that in reference to cultural rights, *Our Creative Diversity* falls short of what could be expected from UNESCO as it avoids the question of how cultural rights are balanced within the broader framework of individual human rights. Similarly, Susan Wright (1998: 13) does not believe that the document adequately deals with the potential contradictions between human rights and cultural diversity by pointing out that there may be such things as acceptable and unacceptable diversity.

UNESCO's World Heritage Project at first glance may seem somewhat removed from these direct ethical considerations, yet these considerations exist at the heart of the project. *Our Creative Diversity*: "Finally, freedom is central to culture, and in particular the freedom to decide what we have reason to value, and what lives we have reason to seek. One of the most basic needs is to be left free to define our own basic needs" (World Commission on Culture and Development 1996: 4).

If freedom is central to culture, then the protection of Djenné as a World Heritage site may need radical re-thinking. In Djenné, the tension between self-definition and the protection of cultural heritage imposed by its World Heritage status is palpable and leading to a "UNESCO debate" within the town. This debate takes on many forms and happens at different levels. For those educated *Djennenkés* (teachers, civil servants. . .) who have a good understanding of UNESCO's global activities, it often leads to resentment as they feel that UNESCO should either get more directly involved with the protection of Djenné's cultural heritage or not have a say in the matter. For many *Djennenkés* who have a lesser understanding of UNESCO's remit, there is the general feeling of being let down after the initial excitement of having being declared a World Heritage site in 1988. Rightly or wrongly, people in Djenné expected to see positive changes (in practice meaning better economic conditions) occurring in Djenné after its inclusion on the World Heritage List. Many *Djennenkés* therefore question the wisdom of being on the World Heritage List if the consequences are a curtailment of their rights to self-definition without visible economic benefits.

The World Heritage List

Following UNESCO's adoption in 1972 of the *Convention Concerning the Protection of the World's Cultural and Natural Heritage* (widely known as the World Heritage Convention), a World Heritage List was begun in 1978 to identify and protect sites of "outstanding universal value" throughout the world. To date the convention has been signed by more than 150 states known as "state parties" (Hitchcock, 2005). The decision was taken to adopt a common approach to both natural and cultural heritage: "The *World Heritage List* links the concept of nature conservation with site preservation. For the purposes of the Convention, these are treated as complementary ideas relating cultural identity associated with sites to the natural environment in which they occur" (Magness-Gardiner, 2004: 29).

In July 2007 there were 851 properties inscribed on the list, of which 660 are cultural, 166 are natural, and 25 are mixed sites.[9] Only 71 of these sites can be found in sub-Saharan Africa, leading to the launch in 2006 of an Africa Fund to help African State Parties prepare national inventories and nomination dossiers (known as Candidature Files, or *Dossier de Candidature*). A World Heritage Committee, consisting of 21 elected members of the State Parties to the convention is responsible for the day-to-day running and assessment of the programme (Turtinen, 2000: 11). The 1972 World Heritage Convention was the first convention to enshrine into international legislation the concept of "common heritage of humanity," yet it has to respect national sovereignty, and comes second to property rights provided by national legislation. Consequently, as will be described shortly, the World Heritage Convention is unable to protect the common heritage of humanity through direct intervention.

The Euro-centricity of the World Heritage project has been widely commented upon (see, for example, Cleere [2001] and Eriksen [2001] for a discussion). The list has so far favoured monumental buildings and seems to articulate the cultural superiority of Europe through its archaeological and architectural heritage, leaving big parts of the world under-represented. The criterion of "outstanding universal value" is the one criterion that unites all the World Heritage sites found on UNESCO's World Heritage List. It has long been problematic and subject to different and changing interpretations as its definition cannot be found in the World Heritage Convention itself but in its operational guidelines and is thus subject to constant review (Titchen, 1996).

Becoming a World Heritage Site

World Heritage sites are chosen by UNESCO and a panel of experts drawn from international heritage organisations:

> ICOMOS is named in the 1972 UNESCO World Heritage Convention as one of the three formal advisory bodies to the World Heritage Committee, along with the World Conservation Union (IUCN), based at Gland (Switzerland), and the International Centre for the Study of the Preservation and Restoration of Cultural Property (ICCROM), based in Rome (Italy). It is the professional and scientific advisor to the World Heritage Committee on all aspects of the cultural heritage. It takes part in the work of the World Heritage Committee and in the implementation of the Convention.[10]

The inscription of a site on the World Heritage List is therefore given authority through the judgement of international expert bodies. It is not enough for a national government (State Party) to put forward a site of national importance for inscription, it must be judged against an international standard of heritage value, embodied by a network of experts:

> All new nominations are to be sent by States Parties to the World Heritage Centre of UNESCO, in Paris by 1st February each year. UNESCO officials check the elaborate nomination dossiers for completeness and deliver them to ICOMOS by 15 March, where they are handled by the officials of ICOMOS International Secretariat, who deal with World Heritage. At ICOMOS International Secretariat, the world heritage team studies the dossiers, in order to ascertain the nature of the property that is proposed, and the first action involved is the choice of the experts who are to be consulted. The process of selecting experts makes full use of the ICOMOS networking potential.[11]

The candidature files are then examined through two different processes, the first involves judging the file against the criteria of "outstanding universal value," the second involves a visit to the site by a regional expert who liaises with local heritage experts to discuss site management, tourism and development plans. Each examination process leads to a separate report, and the two reports are presented in September for final evaluation together with the original candidature file. Through a series of meetings with further international experts, recommendations are produced for each nominated site by ICOMOS to be put before the UNESCO World Heritage Committee in the April of the following year. Final decisions are made in June when summaries of each nominated site are presented to the full World Heritage Committee.

It is clear therefore that even before a site becomes included on the World Heritage List, it is subject to scrutiny and a "professionalizing" gaze. The aspects of the site that are most likely to appeal to the World Heritage Committee are emphasised, while others aspects may well be played down. In this sense, UNESCO acts as a "global cultural broker" (Butler, 2007: 273). At the end of the process, the site is reduced to a simplified dossier, justifying its "outstanding universal value" as well as making a case for inscription, often couched in terms of threats to its future survival. Although it is the State Party that officially puts forward the candidature file, in practice by the time of the decision of the World Heritage Committee, a large number of heritage professionals have become invested in the successful outcome of the dossier, and, if successful, many of them will be employed in the future to devise and oversee management plans of the various sites. Even at the very first stage of putting the original candidature file together, UNESCO officials will be involved in helping state parties, as was the case for the *Yaaral and Dégal* in Mali, discussed below. It is therefore hard to argue that the primary relationship is that between a World Heritage site and its national government, and that UNESCO merely acts as a "labelling" institution. Particularly in cases where the national governments lack economic and political power, World Heritage sites within their territories are subject to a high level of intervention (through UNESCO delegations visiting the site, management plans put in place by international experts, outside funding for the sites promotion).

The Concept of World Heritage

When considering the validity of the World Heritage project in Djenné, one must address two broader aspects of the World Heritage Convention: first, the problems surrounding the term *outstanding universal value* and, second, the concrete consequences of World Heritage status on a site it claims to protect. In the afterword to his edited volume *The Politics of World Heritage*, Michael Hitchcock states in reference to UNESCO's 1972 World Heritage Convention that "looking back over 30 years, it has become clear that the Convention lacked an important provision from the outset, the need to conduct research on how well the Convention was fulfilling its brief in scientific terms" (Hitchcock, 2005: 181).

Owing to political sensitivities and its bureaucratic nature, it is very difficult for UNESCO as an institution to question its practices. It is also difficult for UNESCO to define its "scientific brief" when dealing with cultures, since outcomes are not as measurable as some of its other work, for example that concerning the protection of natural World Heritage sites. There is consequently, in the cultural sector at least, little impetus to put in place feedback mechanisms that would change the way in which UNESCO operates throughout the world. During my internship I witnessed that the bureaucratic nature of working practices within UNESCO meant that the speed at which it could respond to events or new challenges was inevitably greatly reduced. As a way of circumventing the bureaucracy, new initiatives are constantly launched leading to the addition of new categories and programmes instead of a more pragmatic revising and streamlining approach to its past activities.

Recently, new programmes within UNESCO have included intangible heritage and heritage landscapes (Fontein, 2000). This shift in focus away from the tangible toward a broader definition of culture may be thought of as one in a long line of reactions UNESCO has had to the changing political climates it finds itself in. Taking the long view on UNESCO's protection of heritage, Blake (2000: 62) states that:

> It is worth noting that the three Conventions so far adopted by UNESCO reflect the political and/or intellectual concerns of the time at which they were developed: the 1954 Convention expressed the powerful post–World

War II desire to reduce potential sources of international conflict; the 1970 Convention embodied an approach to cultural property which might be characterised as "nationalist" or "statist." . . . And the 1972 Convention reflected both the growing concern in environmentalist issues in its integration of the cultural with the natural heritage as well as the concept of "common heritage of mankind" which had been developing at this time in relation to seabed mineral resources.

The concept of the 'Common Heritage of Mankind' (CHM) has allowed for the development of a framework within which to discuss ownership rights to previously unclaimed, and potentially valuable resources, such as the ocean bed, outer space, the moon or Antarctica. In a discussion of the legal consequences of the concept, Joyner (1986) concludes that despite treaties emerging based on the concept, it remains a philosophical notion with only the potential to crystallise into a legal norm. Joyner attributes five characteristics to the concept of CHM as applied to common space areas: (1) They would be regarded as regions owned by no one but hypothetically managed by everyone; (2) all people would be expected to share in the management of a common space area and universal popular interest would assume priority over national interests; (3) any economic benefit derived from extraction from the common space area would be shared internationally; (4) use of the area must be limited to peaceful purposes; (5) any research in the area would be freely and openly permissible on the condition that it posed no physical threat to the environment. It goes without saying that the concept of CHM in these cases is being applied to spaces devoid of people.

Applying the CHM concept to UNESCO's work on cultural heritage is problematic yet the idea of the CHM is implicit within the World Heritage List. In fact, the idea of CHM has percolated down to some people in Djenné who logically conclude that CHM entails common responsibility and should mean a sharing of the financial burden of preservation. The CHM concept "globalises" human identity by stating that there are places of importance to all of mankind that must be preserved for all of our futures. Building on the Universal Declaration of Human Rights, the CHM discourse makes claims on behalf of our shared humanity and as such, distances itself from localised dissenting discourses (Niec, 1998). The CHM's universal vision justifies the fact that it sometimes ignores relativist realities.

The concept of CHM is useful, because it clarifies the World Heritage Convention's *raison d'être*: to pass on to future generations its true *héritage*, in the French sense, meaning "inheritance." No part of the "global family" may unilaterally decide to do away with that which has been recognised as important by the whole. That said, World Heritage sites remain under the jurisdiction of individual nation states who may appeal to the global community for help in their protection but who may also, as was the case in Afghanistan, destroy them.

UNESCO's Limits

O'Keefe (2004) describes the World Heritage Convention as a treaty with no third-party effects on third parties unwilling to be drawn in. He explores this statement in relation to the actions undertaken by the Taliban at Bamiyan in Afghanistan. At the time of the destruction, Bamiyan was not yet a World Heritage site. Somewhat controversially, UNESCO declared Bamiyan a World Heritage site in July 2003 in an "emergency inscription" after the destruction of the Buddhas in March 2001.

Although the destructions of the Buddhas at Bamiyan[12] were described by United Nations state parties as a "grave wrong," an "act of cultural vandalism," and a "sacrilege to humanity" (O'Keefe, 2004: 200), no legal intervention could be mounted against the Taliban regime, because the statues were not destroyed during warfare but deliberately, during a time of peace. As a response to the destruction, UNESCO adopted a resolution concerning "*Acts constituting a crime against common heritage of humanity*" (Manhart, 2001). In defiance the Taliban passed an edict in 2001 ordering the destruction of all statues and non-Islamic shrines. This met with overwhelming international condemnation, but again no reference was made to violation of the World Heritage Convention obligations. The Convention does not set out a law but behavioural guidelines:

> All in all, the relevant State practice attests to a remarkable universal consensus that the destruction of the Buddhas at Bamiyan was condemnable as a matter of policy, being harmful to the interests of the Afghan people and to humanity as a whole. But none of it supports the conclusion that a State is presently under a customary legal obligation, in times of peace, to protect, conserve and transmit to future generations cultural heritage situated on its territory either straightforwardly or as a function of a human right. (O'Keefe, 2004: 205)

In other cases, such as in Cambridge, England, the invitation to apply for World Heritage status was turned down, because the town was already considered adequately protected by the University (van der Aa et al., 2005). Similarly, the resistance of many stakeholders to putting forward a candidature file for World Heritage status for the Dutch part of the Wadden Sea is described by the authors as "World Heritage as NIMBY" (not in my back yard) (van der Aa et al., 2005). The resistance was based on fears over loss of independence and uncertainty around what World Heritage status would entail. As the authors put it: "Wherever 'heritage' exists, pressure to share it with outsiders and higher status outsiders at that, is likely to be present" (2005: 18).

In Djenné, the cultural heritage is invariably shared with higher status outsiders, and most residents will not have the opportunity to visit, or have any influence on cultural heritage in other parts of the world, or even in their own country. There is therefore a radical asymmetry to the way in which people participate in the World Heritage Project. Furthermore, the impact of World Heritage status on local populations can actually be negative. Wall and Black (2005) describe how local populations have been displaced from sites such as Borobudur and Prambanan near the city of Yogyakarta in Indonesia to make way for archaeological parks. To gain access to the tourists and the money they bring, local people now have to pay for access to the sites. In this case, the placing of a *cordon sanitaire* around the sites effectively excludes local people from their own cultural heritage and potential income it represents.

Ambivalence toward UNESCO's World Heritage project may therefore include its perceived powerlessness in times of real crisis, the consequences of allowing one's heritage to be considered the "heritage of humanity" (especially if much of that humanity has a higher status and more power than the local population) and fears over access to heritage. However, in Djenné the situation is further complicated by the fact that much of the population has not heard of, or does not accurately understand who or what UNESCO is. Furthermore, as will be discussed later, *Djennenkés* understand outside intervention within a paradigm of poverty and expectations of development, leaving many people who are aware of UNESCO's labelling of the town perplexed as to UNESCO's lack of helpful practical intervention. Although it cannot be seen as UNESCO's original intention, the fact that Djenné has been declared a World Heritage site has set-up a number of expectations amongst some *Djennenkés* who do not understand the complexities of the World Heritage inscription process. For them, if the town is to be protected in the name of UNESCO and "World Heritage," then money should flow to the town in an attempt to help them preserve that heritage.

Intangible Cultural Heritage and Outstanding Universal Value

In recognition of the importance of intangible heritage, and in part because of the enthusiasm of the Japanese Director General at the time, UNESCO launched the Proclamations of Masterpieces of the Oral and Intangible Heritage of Humanity (henceforth the Proclamations) in 1997. The Proclamations reflect concerns about the validation of non-monumental, non-elitist heritage and are the logical next step in UNESCO's portfolio of measures to validate and protect global cultural heritage. However, the Proclamations have inadvertently shed new light on the difficulty of defining the term *outstanding universal value.*

The Proclamations were at first intended to do for Intangible Cultural Heritage (ICH) what the World Heritage List did for tangible cultural and natural heritage. Three Proclamations, taking place between 2001 and 2005, saw the inscription of 90 "Masterpieces" on a new global list drawn up by UNESCO.[13] In each case, the inscription procedure for the Proclamations echoed that of the World Heritage List, with member states submitting candidature files to be considered by an international panel of experts. However, in 2006 UNESCO decided to discontinue any further Proclamations and instead set up a Representative List drawn from member state's own inventories of ICH. Officially, this decision was due to the coming into force of the Convention for the Safeguarding of the Intangible Cultural Heritage in April 2006. UNESCO states that the Proclamations were only ever intended to be an awareness-raising exercise and were never to be an on-going list like the World Heritage List. Yet it can be argued that behind the decision to abandon the criterion of "outstanding universal value" in relation to ICH (and consequently any further Proclamation) lie a number of practical difficulties confronted by UNESCO.

Partly, there was a realisation within UNESCO of the difficulty of assigning a static cultural value to changing expressions of cultural life, such as those expressed through ICH. There was an awareness that the approach chosen to protect ICH had to be different from that used to protect tangible cultural heritage and that the usual exercises of documentation would not suffice. Additionally, the criterion of "outstanding universal value" proved problematic in relation to ICH since the ICH that lends meaning to people's lives is rarely "outstanding" or "universal" and most often is commonplace, such as language or regular cultural performances. This lack of definition led to a huge diversity in the kinds of candidature files put forward by member states, ranging from national cuisine to singing, specialised craft, festivals, and minority activities.

A concrete measurement of "value" could therefore not be achieved by UNESCO in relation to ICH because the value they were trying to protect was that embodied by the human actors themselves and therefore highly personal. Performances, cultural spaces and endangered languages proved to be moving targets and, as cultural expressions rather than cultural artefacts, much harder for UNESCO to archive. This reassessment in relation to ICH can be used to identify the difficulties encountered by UNESCO's original World Heritage Project, especially in cases where the restrictions imposed by World Heritage status directly affect people's everyday lives.

Intangible Cultural Heritage in Mali

The leadership of President Alpha Oumar Konaré strongly focussed attention on Mali's tangible cultural heritage. Since Konaré's Presidency, Mali has had great success with the promotion of its tangible cultural heritage (now having four World Heritage sites: The Tomb of the Askias, in Gao, being inscribed in 2005). In 2006 this success was complemented by UNESCO's declaration of the Festival of the *Yaaral et Dégal* (a Peul Festival marking the annual transhumance of cattle) as a Masterpiece of the Oral and Intangible Heritage in UNESCO's third, and final Proclamation.

The *Dégal* marks the descent of the cattle into the pastures of *Walodo Débo*, where they will stay until the rainy season begins and they make their journey once again back to the north. During their transhumance the cattle make their journey from the inner delta region all the way to Niger. The Festival is said to date back to 1821, when Sékou Amadou sedentarised the Peuls, and it is an opportunity for the returning herders to reunite with their families and for people to be reunited with their cattle. Herders display their cattle to local dignitaries in a form of "beauty contest" and music, poetry recitals and dances are performed. The dramatic crossings of the river by the cattle on different days are arranged after a negotiation between farmers (who must have had enough time to cultivate) and the herders (who need new pastures for their cattle). A calendar is then drawn up indicating when local river crossing will take place and consequently the dates and places of celebrations.

Cultural officials in Mali, as in other parts of the world, are now been asked to draw up detailed inventories of their intangible cultural heritage. This broader approach to cultural heritage should have the effect of redressing some of the imbalances found in UNESCO's original World Heritage project. However, UNESCO's approach to the protection of intangible cultural heritage is still fundamentally informed by its approach to tangible cultural heritage, so the *Yaaral and Degal* celebrations are now subject to detailed documentation, a Management Plan and an effort to bring them into line with a predictable tourist calendar, in order to increase financial revenue. Complex negotiations between herders and farmers now have an added political dimension, the "heritage dimension," with the expectation of money and the privileging of the performative element of the festival over the social relationships it mediates.

Conclusion

In 2010 UNESCO launched a Priority Africa mission following a regional review of all UNESCO (educational, scientific, and cultural) activities in Africa between 2008 and 2009. It is "a collective and concerted action geared to bring peace and development to the continent."[14] More broadly, on December 20, 2010, UNESCO adopted a resolution putting development at the centre of its cultural programme, for the first time linking cultural initiatives explicitly to its Millennium Development Goals. Culture is

Figure 3.1 Cattle crossing at Sofara

therefore now seen as central to the fight against poverty, and UNESCO wants to be at the centre of things by providing sustainable development through capacity building, establishing local markets for cultural goods and developing tourist networks.

Singh (2011: 83) quotes Laurent Lévi-Strauss, the Chief of Section for Tangible Heritage at UNESCO (and son of Claude Lévi-Strauss), as saying that UNESCO's World Heritage project has been moving from a "monumentalist" vision toward a more "anthropological" one. In order to fulfil this new mandate, UNESCO's World Heritage project is having to come to terms with the lives of people it inevitably brings under its jurisdiction (even if UNESCO claims that the relationship between itself and the people who live in World Heritage sites is only ever indirect, through the mediation of the State Party). As Singh states, many of UNESCO's reports and initiative are "eloquent on philosophic principles but laconic on practical measures" (2011: 108). As in many other countries where resources are scarce, it is the practical measures taken by UNESCO in the next few years that will determine how *Djennenkés* feel about their inclusion on the World Heritage List.

PART II

Life in Djenné

CHAPTER 4

Islam

In Djenné, a move away from a monumentalist vision of cultural heritage toward an anthropological one is not straightforward. To begin, the parameters of the town's internationally acclaimed cultural heritage have to a large part been set by the outside vision of the town, as explored in Part I. These parameters, internalised by many Djenné residents, are also the material reality of life in Djenné: people's home, the cityscape, the surrounding topography. They are therefore both real for the people living in Djenné and to a certain extent "imagined" for those outside who are projecting their ideas about Djenné onto the town.

An ethnographic approach to the study of cultural heritage in Djenné allows for the contextualisation of cultural heritage within the political, social, religious, and economic realities of the town. Focussing on issues relating to cultural heritage often means focussing on areas of conflict, misunderstanding, or absence. Simple questions such as "who is implicated in UNESCO's World Heritage Project in Djenné?" raise a number of complex issues. The aim of the ethnographic approach is to draw out local conceptualisation of Djenné and its cultural heritage as a counterpoint to an external, somewhat imposed version.

Life in Djenné is synonymous with poverty. Despite initial impressions, it seems that people's unique cultural heritage is often not redemptive and can in some cases be seen to hinder their ambitions. UNESCO is acting in concrete ways in Djenné while a majority of the population remain disenfranchised from UNESCO's World Heritage Project. What emerges from fieldwork is a complex picture of a population negotiating access to its material culture while attempting to maintain its dignity and autonomy— and at the same time navigating traditional power structures and the new realities brought by tourism.

If asked about Djenné, many Malians in the rest of the country first mention the town's link with Islam before commenting on its architecture. Djenné, like Timbuktu, remains an important centre for Islamic learning in West Africa and the Qur'anic "vestibule" schools found in the courtyards of many homes; the high number of students brought together from other parts of Mali, the large number of Islamic teachers (*marabouts*), and the Great Mosque are all a testimony to this ongoing status.

Louis Brenner and Benjamin Soares have written extensively about Islam in Mali. Brenner (2001) stresses the need to avoid normative notions of Islam. The history of Islam in Mali, from the *jihad*s onward, has been about claim and counter-claim to power, with adherents often invoking and refuting different interpretations of Islam along the way. Material remains of this struggle are present throughout Mali—such as the Great Mosque in Djenné, the third to be built in the town and only 100 years old, as described in Part I. Soares (2005a) rejects the distinction between "orthodox" and "unorthodox" Islam, a distinction he sees as rising out of Orientalist scholarship. Instead, he sees Islam as a "discursive tradition"—but he warns that it is theologically questionable to many Muslims to treat Islam as a plural phenomenon. Saul (2006) claims that West-African anthropologists have for too long ignored the impact of the historical influences of Islam on West-African societies, creating a schism between a "great hall" exhibiting ethnographically interesting material, on one hand, and a small room reserved for the study of Islam, on the other. Islam and traditional Africa are in this way kept apart.

Le Vine (2007) states that although Islam was brought to Mali during the 7th century through the Arab conquest of North Africa, it did not become the majority religion in the country until the 20th century. Following the French model of separation between church and state, Mali is a secular state; however, Soares (2005b) explains that every post-Independence Malian government has associated itself in one way or another with Islam. After Independence in 1960 Mobido Keita avoided antagonising religious leaders, many of whom were from the *Malinké* ethnic area that made up his key constituency. After Moussa Traoré's coup in 1968, ever-closer links were sought between the government and Muslim leaders until the regime became more oppressive and a number of religious leaders fled the country.

Amadou Toumani Touré's accession to power on March 26th, 1991, and the subsequent democratic election of Alpha Oumar Konaré in 1992 saw the rise of Islam in Mali through the flourishing of civic associations, a significant number of which had Islamist agendas. Gradually, the Islamic agenda in Mali took on more formal incarnations, such as the opening of a privately owned Islamic radio station in Bamako in 1992 and the creation of a High Islamic Council, a body that was intended to represent the views of the Islamic Associations and the mosques. In 2002 and again in 2007 Amadou Toumani Touré won the presidential elections as an Independent candidate and represents the religious views of the Malian people, owing to a pragmatic political culture closely affiliated to Islam. In terms of actual government, however, Muslim religious specialists have as a rule not been involved in the making of public policy decisions, owing to an overarching paradigm of development needing technical and administrative experts (Soares, 2005b). This situation is somewhat changing with the rise of Islamic civil societies, many of which stress the link between Islam and development.

The challenge for the Malian government today is identified by Le Vine (2007) as dealing with the rise of Wahhabism (Sunni), a part of the Salafiyya movement of Muslims that promotes a return to original beliefs and practices of the *Salaf*—the founding fathers of Islam. The activities of militant groups in the east and north of Mali have led the Malian government to obtain international help with antiterrorist training after the Salafi Group for Preaching and Combat (also known as GSPC) broke away from the Algerian *Groupe Islamiste Armée* in 1998 and was reported to be involved in kidnapping of 32 tourists in 2003 on the Malian/Algerian border. In 2007 the group was renamed Al-Qaeda in the Islamic Maghreb (AQIM) and came to the international community's attention in January 2009, when it kidnapped two Swiss nationals, one German, and one Briton near the Mali/Niger border. The Briton, Edwin Dyer, was subsequently murdered; the other three hostages were released.

The international community, more specifically the Americans, are becoming concerned with the rise of radical Islam in Mali and now have a military presence in northern Mali as part of U.S. AFRICOM (United States Africa Command). Whereas Mali was historically regarded as a bulwark against radical Islam, especially because of its strategic borders with Mauritania and Algeria, it is now being described as a potential breeding ground for Islamic fundamentalists (Soares, 2005b). This view is disputed by many Malians, as well as the anthropologist Jeremy Keenan (2009), who argues that there is little material evidence for many of the reported minor terrorist incidents in the north of Mali and suspects state collusion in fabricating false information. He suggests that the militarisation of the previously hard-to-control regions of the Sahara would be to the advantage of Western governments seeking to exploit the vast mineral wealth in the area, particularly uranium. The British government is keen to strengthen ties with Mali and established an embassy in Mali in April 2010.

An Islamic Education in Djenné

Djenné and Timbuktu are powerful Islamic centres in Mali owing to their historically important positions on the trans-Saharan trade routes. The religious scholars of both cities have enjoyed fame across the country and beyond and have attracted a large number of students and followers. Islamic scholars in Djenné describe themselves as conservative, in opposition to radical forms of Islam that are gaining ground in big cities such as Bamako (Soares, 2005b). They are also conservative in terms of preserving their particular traditions and autonomy. In the past, a large number of older *Djennenkés* had avoided going to colonial school as resistance to the colonial regime. *L'École des blancs* ("the white man's school") was considered by many, until about twenty years ago, to be an agent for indoctrinating Djenné's children against traditional Islamic values. Now, most children who go to school in Djenné attend Qur'anic school in the mornings for an hour and then attend French school (now known by the less derogatory name of *l'école classique*) for the rest of the day. Some children exclusively attend French school, although it is rare to find a student who has never been to a Qur'anic school, if only as a young child for a few years.

Qur'anic schools, or vestibule schools, in Djenné are distinguished from *médersas* schools, where an exclusively Arabic curriculum is taught. There are only a handful of *médersas* schools in Djenné, owing in large part to the resistance of the elders to such an education. In interviews, older men told me that because children learn Arabic at *médersas* and can therefore read and understand the Qur'an, they can question their elders' religious interpretations and would inevitably become "impolite." Belonging in Djenné, I was told, meant participating in religious life through prayer, and this you could learn adequately at the vestibule schools, where the Qur'an is memorised but not understood (Diakite, 1999). Both boys and girls attend these schools early in the morning, which were often described as a sort of kindergarten where young children learn to concentrate and sit still. Teachers at the *écoles classiques* therefore see no contradiction in pupils having both kinds of education. Some pupils who prove themselves to be very capable at the vestibule schools will continue to attend until they are much older, and some may do so to the exclusion of French education to become *marabouts* themselves. Only at this stage will the whole meaning of the Qur'an be revealed to them.

A desire for more *médersas* schools, usually funded by Arabic countries, is present among some of the population in Djenné, such as certain *marabouts,* the Imam, and the *Chef du Village.* However, these schools remain very much in the minority. Brenner (2001) explores the rise of *médersas* schools (and their *Salafi* doctrine) across Mali and sees their growing popularity outside Djenné as part of a rise of a rationalist *episteme,* in part brought about by the French colonial schooling experience. He goes on to state that so-called Islamic fundamentalism therefore can be understood "as an effort to combine Muslim doctrine with contemporary technologies of power, most of which have their origins in European culture. . . . However, many Islamists seem to be unaware of indebtedness of some of their ideas to the very culture from which they seek to distance themselves" (Brenner, 2001: 308). Islamic education, politics, and power are therefore, as elsewhere, inextricably linked in Mali.

Islamic morality and values in Djenné are maintained by the presence of the *marabouts.* Even people who may seem to align themselves with Western traditions and dress, such as the owner of the American Shop on the main market square, are critical of overtly un-Islamic behaviour and dress among tourists. The American Shop owner explained that this behaviour was not appropriate in Djenné: *Ici, c'est un coin de marabouts* ("This is a *marabouts'* town"). There is complete respect for the *marabouts* in Djenné, and many parents, especially from the poorer sectors of Djenné's society, confided their ambitions that their child would one day become a *marabout.* Because of the poverty in Djenné, *marabouts* are seen as some of the more affluent members of Djenné's society through their links with the wealth of the outside world. However, many *marabouts* in Djenné remain very poor and rely on the little money earned on their behalf by their *garibous* students ("child-students") to survive. Students attending the vestibule schools in the morning will also pay a small amount to the *marabout* each week if they are able to. In 2005 that amount was as little as 50 CFA (5 pence).

The "Prayer Economy"

Like other towns in Mali, Djenné has a very strong "prayer economy," a term coined by Benjamin Soares (2005a). He describes the prayer economy present in a Malian town, *Nioro du Sahel.* The economy is created by the use of "esoteric sciences" by (Sufi) religious leaders, such as petitionary prayer and the creation of amulets. Usually, the more extravagant the gift, the more important the intervention via the esoteric sciences is on behalf of the giver. Similarly in Djenné there is a religious economy based on petitionary prayer and amulets.

The *marabouts* in Djenné make a living from the town's historic reputation as a powerful Islamic centre. Some are paid to pray on behalf of their rich patrons in other towns. For example, in 2005 I interviewed Amadou, who was a recently married *marabout* in his early thirties. He had contracted polio at an early age, probably around two (he has no memories of walking). He now got around Djenné with the help of an adapted bicycle, and his main income came from a rich businessman in Bamako who paid him monthly to say benedictions on his behalf. The businessman did not have the time to properly attend to the spiritual dimension of his life, because he regularly worked until the early hours of the morning. He also did not have Amadou's knowledge of the Qur'an. Perhaps paradoxically, the more problems the businessman had, the more money he paid Amadou.

Before becoming a *marabout*, Amadou trained to be a teacher and successfully studied in Bamako. But because of his disability, he found it impossible to work and so had been officially unemployed since 1990. He tried unsuccessfully to get a job with Handicap International and finally decided to become a *marabout*. He felt very lucky that his occupation provides him with a regular income, because many disabled people in Mali are destined for a life of begging. His income allowed him to get married, despite the original scepticism of the bride's family.

Amadou comes from one of over thirty big *marabout* families in Djenné (*Familles Maraboutiques*). He said that in Djenné, everyone is *un peu marabout* ("a bit *marabout*"), since everyone learns the Qur'an. However, there are gradations of *marabouts*, starting as a student and going on to become a *Grand Marabout* and finally, Imam. (One cannot become an Imam without first being a *Grand Marabout*.) A few of the *marabouts* in Djenné are "sponsored" by rich Saudi Arabians who see them as worthy recipients of the *Zakah* (alms-giving relating to a fixed proportion of income, the Third Pillar of Islam). In Djenné, the understanding of the *Zakah* is that you should give 25 out of every 1,000 CFA (£1) you earn once you earn over 400,000 CFA (£400) annually. *Marabouts* are also paid for other ritual offices they perform, such as benedictions for the dead and marriage officiation (Sanankoua, 1985).

Traditional readings of the Qur'an are accompanied in Djenné by more synchretic practices, such as the use of holy water, or *eau bénite*. Qur'anic writings on rolled-up paper, contained within *gris-gris*, or amulets (described shortly), are ubiquitous in Djenné. The practice of sacrificing a chicken with the blessing of a *marabout* to ensure luck during a football match or other event is also common. This happens both when people are themselves playing and when they are supporting a favourite international team whose match is broadcast on television. When people are ill, they often turn to traditional healers. One remedy I witnessed involved mixing the dissolved Qur'anic chalk writing from a little blackboard with chicken and cooking it to give relief from malaria.

Mommersteeg (2000) distinguishes between the different uses of Qur'anic writing employed to undertake *maraboutage* in Djenné. The *tira* is the use of Qur'anic writing and symbols on paper made into *gris-gris*. The *nesi* is the "water amulet," the use of dissolved Qur'anic writing as just described; and the *dugu* is a "fire amulet," which entails burning either a piece of Qur'anic writing or throwing a water amulet on burning embers. When anger erupts in Djenné, some people resort to threats of witchcraft, which they term *maudire* ("to curse"). Powerful spirits are said to inhabit Djenné, and grown men will not walk through certain parts of the town at night because of fear of provoking bad luck.

Amadou is aware that Muslims in other parts of the world do not approve of what he refers to as their "traditional" or "conservative" practices. He says their forefathers passed down these practices to the *marabouts* in Djenné today, and they were the first converts to Islam in Djenné. He describes their differences in the approach to Islam as being like the differences in the Christian Church between Catholicism and the Church of England and does not see any contradictions in his syncretic practices. He does, however, believe that there is un-Islamic behaviour in Djenné, particularly in the dress and attitude of young women.

The attitudes of Djenné's *marabouts* toward outside criticism of their syncretic practices demonstrates a fundamentally secure Islamic identity, based on the practices passed on from the earliest *marabouts* in Djenné. Djenné's resistance to *médersas* can similarly be seen to be a resistance to outside destabilising forces.

Amulets and Shoes

Leather amulets (*gris-gris*) are ubiquitous in Djenné. They are given to children at birth and commissioned throughout people's lives to protect against illness, malevolent spirits, theft, and injury and to bring good luck in work, love, childbearing, and economic fortunes.

To understand how amulets are created, I commissioned one from a local leatherworker. There are four principle leatherworking families in Djenné, all with slightly different specialties—two named *Koné*, one named *Kassé* (the biggest), and my commissioned leatherworker's family, *Gakou*. His family specialty is sandals, but he also makes bags and belts, as well as *gris-gris*. All the leatherworkers also carry out repairs and alterations to leather objects.

The leatherworker whom I hired was happy for me to video the whole process from start to finish and ask questions as he worked. The day of the interview I went to find him in his usual place at the daily market. Next to him, his apprentice was working on a large order of leather sandals. Sitting crossed-legged, and wearing an opulent blue *bazin* tailored shirt and trousers, he placed a wooden board before him (of the type used by *garibou* children, when copying out parts of the Qur'an). He started by placing a small piece of un-dyed sheep's leather on the board and blackened it with the use of a homemade black dye (contained within a recycled tomato puree tin) applied with an old toothbrush. The recipe for the dye is a secret and is passed on within leatherworking families.

He took a thin strip of leather and repeated the dying process with his toothbrush. Then he clasped the first piece of leather, black side down, against the board with his big toe and used a knife, held by fingers at each end, to repeatedly scrape the leather until it was supple. At this point he showed me a plain white piece of paper and explained that usually it would have an extract from the Qur'an written on it, either copied out by him or written by a commissioned *marabout*. Since I am not a Muslim, we agreed that the paper should remain blank, thus removing the potency of the *gris-gris* and making it a purely decorative object. As he folded the paper into a smaller and smaller package, he explained how he had learned his trade from his uncle.

At this point, two children came over to ask for some money, and he gave them 100 CFA (10 pence). I asked him whether they were his children, and he said, no, they were his friend's children. His children had been sitting by his side when I first arrived but had since left for school. Such interruptions were continuous throughout the process of making the *gris-gris*, with friends calling greetings, other clients enquiring about their orders, and the general hustle and bustle of the busy daily market all around.

The next step was preparing some traditional glue using some powder made from the fruit of the Baobab tree (*n'zira* in Bamanankan) mixed with water in a hollow cow's horn. The glue was applied to a small strip of material (an off-cut from some Dutch wax cloth) using a blunt knife. The piece of folded paper was then carefully wrapped within it to form a small square. He explained that the cloth is used to protect the paper. Then, after scraping the first piece of dyed leather again with the blunt knife, he encased the little material square package within it, using a large blunt metal instrument shaped like a rounded arrowhead to firmly close the leather around the package. The excess leather was trimmed off with a knife, and the blunt instrument used to push the remaining leather into a neat parcel.

The parcel was then sewn shut with two stitches, using thin strips of leather as thread. The leatherworker first bored holes with a sharp spike to allow the leather through. Then, the whole package was once again covered in black dye using the toothbrush. The long thin strips were made into a necklace by spinning them together with repeated hand motions. The leather package was then threaded on to the necklace and secured with small strips of orange leather, and a geometric design was etched onto the front of the package with a knife.

According to the leatherworker, *gris-gris* were being made in Djenné before the arrival of Islam. He explained that some people in Mali do not consider the use of *gris-gris* to be in accordance with true Islam, but most people in Djenné, whom he describes as "traditional" Muslims, embrace the use of *gris-gris*. Despite Djenné's reputation as a pious city, he believed that leatherworkers were as likely to make *gris-gris* in other parts of Mali as they were in Djenné; it was simply a part of their work. In fact, he went on to say, the creation of *gris-gris* is a pan-West-African phenomenon. The only difference between leatherworkers in Djenné and those farther to the north of the country, such as Gao and Timbuktu, is that occasionally women can become leatherworkers in the north.

Figure 4.1 Amulet, or *gris-gris*, commissioned by the author (photo by Roberto Garagarza)

At the time of the interview with Amadou in 2005, a *gris-gris* cost anything from 2,000 CFA (£2) to 50,000 CFA (£50), depending on its potency. A *gris-gris* to protect from gunshot wounds would be expensive, whereas one that is simply used to protect personal possessions in the home would be cheaper and less elaborate. My *gris-gris* took about 15 minutes to create and cost me 2,000 CFA, the price of the simplest form of protection. Unlike *gris-gris* found in other part of Africa that may contain animal bone or plants, the *gris-gris* in Mali derive their potency from the power of the Islamic text they contain. Any error in the writing will lead to the *gris-gris* being ineffective (Mommersteeg, 2009).

The Problem of *Garibous*

One association in Djenné that is working to preach moderate Islam is the *Association Malienne pour le Soutien de l'Islam* (AMSI), an apolitical, pan-African association. It calls for people to respect other religions and find true Islam. It rejects terrorism and works to protects Islam's good name as a religion of peace. In Djenné it is trying to find solutions to the problem of begging *garibous* (or *talibés*), the child-students of *marabouts*, usually recruited from the villages in the surrounding countryside. The system of recruiting *garibous* is a pan-West-African phenomenon with recent international attention focussing on the phenomenon in Senegal.[1]

The problem of the begging *garibous* in Djenné is both a shocking and a very sensitive issue for discussion, owing to its close association with Islam. Throughout numerous interviews I was told that the way in which *garibous* live in Djenné today is a distortion of a system that used to promote their well-being and provide them with an Islamic education. In the past, *marabouts* would have owned land and would have exchanged the children's labour on the land for assured food and an Islamic education. Today, these *garibous*, as young as 5 or 6, have no access to non-Qur'anic education, have little or no access to healthcare, and are in an incredibly vulnerable position, since they are a long way from their families. They have to beg for food by going from one house to the next in the evenings and rely on the scraps they are given, tipped into their little plastic buckets. They are consequently very vulnerable to diseases—food is heated, eaten communally with hands often not washed by soap, and then left to cool before being given to the *garibous* and animals.

Owing to the poverty of the *marabouts*, very few of these children sleep under mosquito nets, and if they do develop malaria or cholera there is very rarely any money to treat them. They tend to be dressed in rags, and many of them have troubling skin conditions, such as scabies, and infected eyes. The *garibous* in Djenné, as in other parts of Mali, are used by their *marabouts* to earn money through begging, fetching firewood from the surrounding countryside, and commonly as labourers on Djenné's building sites or for tasks that others in Djenné may not accept to do, such as emptying sewage tanks.

UNICEF and other international organisations are working with the Malian government to try to find solutions to the problem of *garibous*.[2] In large part, the problem is one of poverty, but the sensitivity of the issue lies in the fact that the children are acquiring a Qur'anic education and that many of their parents give them up willingly, believing that their children are acquiring a valuable *apprentissage*. People in Djenné are, however, very aware of the way in which the *garibous* system is viewed by the outside world, and associations such as *Djenné Patrimoine* are actively trying to find local solutions to the problem.

UNESCO and Islam

Djenné's Islamic heritage could be seen to be at odds with UNESCO's vision of the town—for example, in relation to the relevance of pre-Islamic archaeological material for *Djennenkés* today. Occasionally, the Cultural Mission has come into conflict with religious authorities in Djenné, when it has been powerless to stop some material changes being made to the Great Mosque (for example, fans paid for by the U.S. Ambassador and the door installed at the front of the Mosque to prevent animals from entering).[3] In line with a UNESCO doctrine of preservation, the Cultural Mission maintains that no new dimensions should be added to classified monuments. However, the staff at the Cultural Mission, being Muslim themselves, are not in ideological conflict with Djenné's population; they merely have a slightly different emphasis owing to their background as heritage professionals.

In 2007 the Imam set up a new library near the Great Mosque in Djenné to house Djenné's *Tarikhs* (Islamic manuscripts). However, to date only a small proportion of *Tarikhs* have been handed over for safekeeping to the library (in contrast with the very successful archiving project taking place in Timbuktu,[4] which concentrates on the archiving of clerical treaties). One of the Cultural Mission's staff explained that it was very hard to convince people to entrust their manuscripts to the library. This is in part because of distrust of the financial motives behind the setting up of the library but also because there is as yet no money in place to preserve the documents, all of which are in a very fragile condition. The library is built in banco, and two of its ceilings have already fallen in as the result of heavy rains. Perhaps most surprisingly, one of its outside walls has been covered in tiles to prevent further rain damage. To see the use of

Figure 4.2 *Tarikhs* in the museum set up by the Imam in Djenné

tiles on a building so near the Mosque is a new development in Djenné, but in this instance the emphasis is on the protection of the manuscripts inside, not the aesthetic of the building outside.

Conclusion

Djenné's status as a powerful Islamic centre within both Mali and West Africa seems to be assured through the continuing fame of its mud Great Mosque as well as the vibrant scholarship in the town. However, like other parts of Djenné's cultural heritage, traditional practices such as the *garibous* system of apprenticeship is threatened by poverty. Conversely, the international prayer economy in Djenné seems set to continue to thrive as richer Islamic countries such as Saudi Arabia increasingly take an interest and invest in the town. In some ways, Djenné can be seen to have a dual identity—one given by UNESCO (with a monumental focus) and a local identity (with a religious focus). The two identities are in fact inextricably linked, and it would make little sense locally to try to conceptually separate the two.

Concern about the radicalisation of young men in Mali seems far removed from the current situation in Djenné, since there are powerful conservative forces operating against such moves. *Djennenkés*, even those who may appear distant from a conservative stance owing to their appearance or habits, are united in their praise for Djenné's Islamic identity and in their respect for the *marabouts* in the town. They actively participate in the prayer economy through the consumption of amulets, seeking the services and advice of *marabouts* in times of need and ensuring that their children receive the appropriate Islamic education that allows them to fully participate in the town's religious life.

CHAPTER 5

Livelihood Strategies

Grass Root Organisations

In Djenné there seemed to be a *Groupe d'Intérêt Economique* (GIE) for every conceivable cause: the women working in cleaning associations, the masons running the housing restoration project, young *garibous* maintaining the tanks for the sanitation project, the guides who formed an association named *Yérédeme* (literally, "help yourself"), the hotels and restaurants (who formed the *Association pour le Développement de l'Activité Touristique, Culturelle et Artisanale de Djenné*), and the artisans.

GIEs are corporate bodies that collect and manage funds on behalf of their members. Some of the GIEs are more successful than others in mobilising their members and accumulating wealth. For example, the tourism GIE had little difficulty in raising money from its rich members (restaurant/hotel owners) to put on activities such as a *lutte traditionelle* ("traditional wrestling") to attract tourists in 2005. Others have been less successful, such as the women's cleaning GIE, which acquired equipment through the intermediary of a Peace Corps volunteer (buckets, brushes, a few carts) only to see their equipment being redistributed by the authorities before it reached them.

The presence of numerous GIEs in Djenné attests to the fact that people know they must organise themselves into corporate bodies to lend legitimacy to their demands for help from the outside. The success of the GIEs in Djenné and the fact that they are regularly created and disbanded demonstrates how people are trying numerous strategies to elevate themselves out of poverty in a dignified manner. People are aware that in Djenné you need a cause to raise money, and the causes that seem to bring in money are health, education, women, sanitation, and, increasingly, cultural heritage projects.

Most people in Djenné depend on money and resources coming from the outside. This happens in a myriad of ways beyond GIEs. For example in 2005 sources of outside help included, among many others: a government rice distribution project, a privately funded rice distribution project (Jean-Louis Bourgeois), the housing restoration project, the sanitation project, a UNICEF baby milk project, the Cuban doctor scheme, money sent from migrant workers, money from Arabic countries, Peace Corps–funded volunteers, tourism, and sponsorship for the First Djenné Festival. Resources coming to Djenné are primarily judged on their potential economic benefit and UNESCO's more opaque proposition is therefore harder for *Djennenkés* to understand.

The Monday Market

The Monday market is the economic engine of the town. It is the marker of time and the day when people from the wider village communities, the Djennéry, flood into Djenné. It is therefore a day of celebration and of trade and the day on which the tourists descend on Djenné, arriving like the market traders on Sunday evening and leaving on Monday evening or Tuesday morning. For the rest of the week, Djenné is a quiet town, and few tourists can be seen in the streets. Mondays bring not only buyers to the markets but also patients to the hospital and maternity clinic. It is the most important day of the week for everyone in the town, including the children who attend school from Tuesday to Saturday, so that they are free to help buy and sell produce in the market.

The market stallholders start to set up on Sunday evenings amid a carnival atmosphere, as trucks, carts, and people invade the square in front of the Great Mosque. Despite a continuous stream of people arriving until early on Monday morning, it is not until about 10 A.M. that the market is in full swing:

Figure 5.1 UNESCO World Heritage sign during a market day

Another market day, there are so many people everywhere. The market is a mass of colourful chaos. You walk past mounds of fruit and then seconds later you are overwhelmed by the stench of fish. There are people wielding baskets, fishnets, buckets and radios. On the way to the see Ousmane, I had to walk through what I now recognise as the dried fish section. I hadn't noticed before that it is divided into sections – clothes as you first arrive on the wall in front of the Mosque, then fruit and vegetables a bit further forward. The pharmacy type stuff is at the front near the bead sellers and the material sellers are in the middle.[1]

Each week, the market traders all resume their positions from the previous week, and in this way the market itself leaves a presence in its absence. However, there have been subtle changes in the market's physical distribution over the years. Compared to a sketch of the market drawn in 1982 and reproduced in 1992 (Maas & Mommersteeg, 1992: 48), certain products, such as second-hand clothing, seemed to have gained in presence.

Produce that cannot be found during the rest of the week, such as eggs, potatoes, honey, and certain fruits, can all be purchased on a Monday. It is also the day on which people can buy dried fish and rice (the basis of the Djenné diet) in bulk. A large selection of second-hand clothes is on offer, as well as plastic buckets, pots, pans, radios, torches, shoes, and most of the things needed for everyday life in Djenné. Despite the large tourist presence, the produce in the Monday market is not aimed at them; only the women selling their bead jewellery particularly solicit the tourists. There are also some itinerant jewellery traders (often Tuareg) who come to encounter tourists. Because of the market's density and the very strong smells and heat, most tourists quickly visit the market with their guide and then look on from the more comfortable vantage point of a bench, rooftop, or café. The tourist presence, however, ensures that the artisan shops are busy, as well as the restaurants and hotels that are often full to capacity during high season.

For many of the tourists visiting Djenné, the market serves as dramatic foreground activity in their photographs of the Mosque. The travel guides to Mali are united in their advice to visit Djenné on Monday, creating a challenge for local guides, who are presented with a glut of tourists on Mondays, with little or no activity for the rest of the week. Djenné's intangible heritage in the form of the market is a major draw for tourists and tour companies alike, who schedule their itineraries around it. Developing tourism beyond Mondays was one of the *Office Malienne du Tourisme et de l'Hôtellerie* (OMATHO) key challenges (discussed in Chapter 7). Therefore, Djenné, in terms of tourism, is heavily defined by its intangible heritage (its Monday market) as well as its tangible heritage.

Women

I met Aminata through working with her in one of the public women's gardens on the outskirts of Djenné. She told me that the garden was started a long time ago. At the beginning, it was simply surrounded by

5 · LIVELIHOOD STRATEGIES

straw, but the sheep ate it and destroyed the garden. Then, the women planted trees to protect the garden, but the sheep still got in. A mud brick wall was then built but fell down because of the rain, so in the end they found foreign financial help to build the fence that successfully protects the garden today. The garden is situated around a well and provides food and additional income for dozens of families. Similar gardens can be found all around the outskirts of Djenné, and they stand out for large parts of the year as the only little patches of irrigation in an otherwise dry landscape.

Learning a bit about Aminata allows us to consider the extent to which she is affected by UNESCO's World Heritage Project. She is in her forties, although her thinness makes her appear older. Aminata agreed that in return for allowing me to use some of her land in the garden, I would pay for my own seeds and share my harvest with her. I also provided her with a new watering can (made from recycled oil cans and bought at the Djenné market) and a rubber bucket and rope to get water from the well.

Aminata talks about her life in terms of the activities she does to provide for her family. She taught me how to plant carrots, tomatoes, and lettuce, each requiring different soil balances and care. She has specialist horticultural knowledge that she is passing on to her children and relatives. Despite our limited communication during our work in the garden (Aminata spoke only *Bozo* and *Djennenké*), I managed to find out more about her through regular interviews with my research assistant. She is fairly representative of many women in Djenné. She divides her time between working in the garden, fishing, housekeeping, and jewellery making. Her days start early and end late and involve a lot of physical labour. She usually wakes at 6 A.M. and after her prayers starts work in the garden. The only duty she does not do is cooking, which is done by her husband's first wife. Many women in Djenné supplement the household income by selling goods or produce at the daily women's market. Excess produce can also be bartered in times of need.

Aminata lives in a compound with her children, her sister's orphaned children, and some female adult relatives. Having lost her first husband, she remarried an older man who already had a wife and who lives in a compound a few minutes' walk away. He visits her regularly, but he is very poor, too old to work, and therefore not able to contribute much financially to her household. It was explained to me that it was important for women in Djenné to be married; so, unless very elderly, a woman will usually be found another husband through an intermediary of her family.

For Djenné 2005 was a very bad year owing to the lack of the rain. Aminata explained to me in an interview in October that she was unable to do the things that she would usually do, such as go and visit her relatives in nearby towns, because of a total lack of money. Minimal rain for the second year running meant that people had no reserves to fall back on, and many had to content themselves with one meal a day and go to bed hungry. Despite the government food-distribution programme, numerous families in Djenné at the end of 2005 were not able to eat properly, and therefore rates of illnesses soared. This was true for Aminata and her family, who had regular bouts of malaria and typhoid and who, weakened by their poor diets, were ill for a long time.

In between the end of a normal rainy season and December, the women's gardens are flooded, so there is a four-month wait until planting can begin again. Aminata told me that she did not have the money to buy beads and make bracelets that would have contributed to her income. Usually, she would use the money she made from selling fish to buy the beads. She would sell a kilo of dried fish for 800 CFA (£0.80), but the fishing was poor owing to low water in the river. A bag of beads costs 2,000 CFA (£2) and so is a considerable outlay, since at least three colours, therefore three bags, are needed to make the bracelets. Usually, she could make five bracelets in a day and sell them to a market trader for 75 CFA (£0.075) each. When unable to buy the beads for herself, she makes bracelets for another woman who pays her 500 CFA (£0.50) per week for her labour. Therefore, as a means to make additional income through tourism, jewellery making is not very lucrative and even less so when it is an indirect relationship between the producer and the tourist. Bracelets and necklaces are usually sold for a few hundred CFA to the tourists, the price depending on the nature of the design and how much the tourist is willing to pay.

When she was a child, Aminata used to make a type of basket called *foutou* in Songhai. These baskets no longer exist; bags have replaced them. She has long since lost the knowledge she would need to make these traditional baskets.

Like many people her age in Djenné, Aminata feels that life used to be better. She thinks that children today are arrogant and no longer respect their parents. However, I saw her children watering the garden every day, selling straw in the market, helping with household chores—and, for a few of them, balancing all this with the demands of school. She remembers a time when there was plenty of water and consequently good harvests and fishing in Djenné. Aminata worries about the future of her children, although she has a strong religious belief that they will be taken care of. She would be happy for them to leave Djenné if it meant that they could make money. She fears, however, that her son will become a mason like his uncle. She would prefer him to use his education to get a better job, because, despite UNESCO's promotion of the masons in Djenné through the protection of the town's architecture, the job of a

5 • LIVELIHOOD STRATEGIES   115

mason remains that of a skilled manual labourer and consequently does not have in many people's minds the prestige of less physically difficult occupations.

Aminata's situation is typical of that of many women in Djenné who have the responsibility of the majority of the domestic labour while also needing to supplement their small family income with bartering and low-level trade. In most households in Djenné, one if not more of the women is involved in producing jewellery that is sold locally and also on Mondays to the tourists at the market. Despite variations in style and colour, women produce very similar products throughout Djenné, and there does not seem to be an interest in diversifying their work. The creation of a women's co-operative of artisans at the entrance of the town has to some extent brought women's domestic production of *artisanat* (principally *bogolan* production) to the attention of tourists. However, the barriers that lie between the women and the tourists' money include the guides working in Djenné, who carefully regulate their clients spending to ensure a commission.

Although Aminata lives in one of the houses protected by Djenné's World Heritage status, she does not know who or what UNESCO is. The concept of World Heritage is alien to her, since she has never travelled farther than the capital city, Bamako. The tourists that come to Djenné, in part because of its UNESCO status, do provide her with some income from the sale of her bracelets and thus help her with the precarious work of providing for her family. Owing to the Canadian-built water tower in the town, many of the residents in Djenné now have access to clean running water in their homes; Aminata and her family have access to a tap outside the entrance to their home that saves them the daily journeys to the river. However, Aminata lacks knowledge of the correct discourse (Smith, 2006) to gain direct access to the money coming to Djenné in the form of cultural heritage projects.

Material Possessions

Aminata has no surplus of goods of any kind in her home. Her house is fairly typical of the poorer houses I saw in Djenné. Entering a house is usually done through a vestibule, which is where old men making tea, and women making jewellery and looking after young children, sit and talk during the day and are able to interact with passers-by. Once through the vestibule, one enters into the courtyard, where most of the household activities take place (see also Van Gijn, 1994). The courtyard is usually bare apart from a few low wooden stools and cooking utensils, pots, and pans stored in an area marked off as a kitchen, sometimes by low mud-brick walls. Increasingly, people have plastic chairs or metal chair frames

Figure 5.2 Tourists buying *bogolan* at women's cooperative

woven with plastic rope to offer to their visitors. More traditionally, mats are arranged on the ground, and shelter from the sun is provided by a porch made from material or plastic sheeting hung between two poles and one of the walls.

The courtyards of the houses in Djenné are alive with the activity of women, children, and animals. When the men are present, they sit a little

Figure 5.3 Inside a house showing pots and chalk boards of a Qu'ranic student

away from the domestic activity, usually with a small coal fire at their sides to make tea. At meal times, the whole family gathers around communal bowls to eat, the men usually eating apart from the women and children. The different rooms in the house lead off from the courtyard.

Except in the richest households, bedrooms are bare rooms with mattresses and blankets on the floor, and clothing is hung across from one wall to another to keep it off the ground. Prayers mats are often kept in the bedrooms and brought out for use. Most houses have a storeroom where grain and equipment is kept. The poorer houses in Djenné are scaled-down versions of the richer houses. They are usually arranged on one floor and often lack salons, adequate room in the courtyard to make a clear kitchen space, and separate rooms for the parents and children. The poorest families rent a few rooms around a communal courtyard and live in cramped conditions.

The rooms in Djenné houses are small and let in little light. Most houses, however, have a flat-roof living space, some with views across the town. Many of the older and richer houses are two storeys high, with the roof space providing a third storey where people sleep and spend time during the hot season. The washing is usually hung out to dry on the roof, and the bathroom (including a drop toilet), a mud-brick ceilingless bare room, is also found on the roof.

Poverty

Being a Westerner in Djenné offers you privileged and often-uncomfortable access to people's private lives. One of the most extreme examples of suffering I came across in Djenné was through my involvement with a small child, Miriam. I first came into contact with her when I was interviewing one of her neighbours, who lived in a tiny cramped compound and was showing me part of the top floor of his house that had fallen to ruins, meaning that his children no longer had a place to sleep. When it rained he would send his children to sleep at his brother's house for shelter. At other times the children would simply sleep outside. His wife was ill and was coughing up phlegm throughout our interview, which she then wiped on the wall behind her while her children clambered about her person. I saw Miriam in her courtyard, a painfully malnourished baby, cradled in her sister's arms.

Miriam's first hospital visit resulted in a diagnosis of malaria and typhoid together with severe malnutrition; Miriam weighed only 5.5 kilograms, less than half the weight she should have been at her age. I did not intend to get more involved with Miriam than with any other child in Djenné, but I found out that she was particularly vulnerable, because her family had fairly recently arrived in Djenné from a neighbouring village. It was clear that the little family unit had completely run out of resources. Her brothers, in threadbare clothes, could often be seen begging at the market. Through a woman living in my compound, I heard about a UNICEF-run programme in Djenné intended to help malnourished children. After much negotiation, I managed to get Miriam enrolled in the feeding programme, which meant that each week she was given three little bags of fortified flour.

Over the following weeks, despite Miriam putting on weight on her new regime, it was clear that the rest of the family was struggling badly. Miriam's father left for Burkina Faso to become a migrant labourer. Their government-distributed food[2] was fast running out, and, like many other poor families in Djenné at the time, they were reduced to eating one meal a day. Through a friend in the Peace Corps, I found out that one of the expatriates who has a home in Djenné was funding his own rice-distribution project intended to help the poorest families at this time of crisis. Miriam's family qualified for this help, so I delivered a 10-kilogram rice bag to them on Independence Day in September 2005. This allowed them to survive until the return of Miriam's father four months later.

In an interview after his return from Burkina Faso, Miriam's father explained to me that he brought his family to Djenné in the year 2000 so that his children could go to school. He showed me an old and battered copy of a magazine about the problem of farming in Mali. He had unsuccessfully tried to start an association for Peul herders, hoping that together they could raise the money to buy a few animals that they could then breed. He had been born in Djenné, but his family moved out to a village when he was young. They used to have cattle, but his father lost his cattle during the 1985–1986 droughts.

Miriam's father used a multiple-approach strategy in trying to provide for his family. As well as being a migrant labourer, in 2005 he had been a *marabout* for nine years and was providing Qur'anic education for local children, who came to him for instruction in the mornings.

Miriam's father was renting two rooms for his family in a shared compound for 1,000 CFA (£1) a month and liked living in Djenné. Ideally though, he wanted to own his own home. When asked about Djenné, he said that he could not describe Djenné as beautiful, because it is such a poor town. He explained to me that poverty was the reason I found his daughter so ill and that he would have liked to have been able to pay for her treatment. He hoped his wife could start making a bit of money by setting up a small shop in the entrance of the courtyard from which she could sell tea, sugar, and cigarettes. Despite having to leave his family every year to go and work in Burkina Faso, he considered the sacrifice worthwhile if it meant his children received a good education (by which he meant sending them to the local French-speaking school). On a visit to Djenné in 2008, I found Miriam well and happy. However, her new baby sister was ill with typhoid fever. Her elder sister Awa had been married the previous year at just 15 to a man many years older than she and was already pregnant. Awa's husband, a wealthy man by Djenné standards, had taken her as his second wife and to a certain extent could provide a new layer of financial security for the rest of the family, especially since Miriam's father was once again away in Burkina Faso. Life for Awa, however, had changed dramatically, because she had had to abandon all her academic ambitions, despite having previously done very well at school.

My involvement with Miriam was just one of many relationships that ran through my time in Djenné. She was one of the poorest children I came across, but I saw her experience reproduced in many ways: through the adults in Djenné who bear the scars of childhood malnutrition, the young *garibous* who are reliant on *marabouts* in turn too poor to care for them, and in constant conversation with people preoccupied with the rains and harvests. As a starting point for talking about cultural heritage in Djenné, Miriam's experience is illuminating. In Djenné, UNESCO is carrying out its World Heritage Project in a context of extreme poverty. It is not an exaggeration to suggest that the success or failure of UNESCO's promotion of Djenné and the subsequent impact this has on tourism and other income is sometimes a matter of life or death for people. Money that comes to the town through heritage projects and tourism helps to make life in Djenné viable, especially in times of drought. However, the World Heritage Project is not a development project, and it is not within UNESCO's remit to save lives through heritage. Instead, it is the material heritage in Djenné that is considered in danger, the mud-brick architecture and the surrounding archaeological sites.

According to the United Nations 2010 Human Development Index, Mali ranks 160th out of 169 countries and is therefore one of the poorest countries in the world.[3] The Index is arrived at by combining measures of life expectancy, educational attainment, and adjusted real income and is a standard way of measuring wellbeing, especially child welfare. Describing the consequences of poverty on people's attitudes toward their cultural heritage is important to identify the reason for the schism between UNESCO's view of Djenné and the views of people living within the town.

Ferguson (2006) argues that "modernity" (in spite of all the problems with the term) is something that many people in Africa feel that they lack. Advocating a new rational approach to talking about the continent's problems, Ferguson is trying to rebalance the discourse of Africa's place in the world within a more realistic (and humane) global reality. His thesis can usefully be applied to discussions about cultural heritage, because the radical inequalities, poverty, and life conditions he describes are the reality that cultural heritage projects encounter when they encounter many parts of Africa. In Djenné, advocating a detemporalised architectural status for the town is often locally read as the advocating of a detemporalised economic status. Additionally, it is the town's very architecture (for example, the cramped conditions, drop toilets, leaks, and collapsed ceilings in the rainy season) that is contributing to the health epidemics of malaria, typhoid, and cholera in Djenné.

The 2006 Riot

Heritage projects brought to Djenné are seen by much of the population as "cash cows" for those who have the legitimacy to benefit from them. The resentment this causes within the population cannot be underestimated, as was witnessed during the riot that broke out in September 2006 over what the population saw as "unauthorised" restoration work on the Great Mosque carried out by the Aga Khan Trust for Culture (AKTC). According to *Djenné Patrimoine*,[4] the riot broke out because the population and the masons had not been informed about the project, although the Imam and the *Chef du Village* had given their consent. In anger and frustration, young people stormed into the Mosque and pulled down the fans and sound system (that had been paid for by the American Ambassador), then went on to vandalise the Imam's three cars and the

5 • LIVELIHOOD STRATEGIES

Cultural Mission, where the buildings and some archaeological objects were badly damaged. The *Chef du Village* and his wives' houses were also attacked. Police were called in from Mopti, and tyres were burnt on the bridge at the entrance of the town to prevent their entry. There followed violent clashes between the police and Djenné's population and the death of one young man of 22, who drowned while trying to escape from the police. Many young people were arrested and held in prison in Djenné. The prison was so full that the soldiers who had come as police back-up were forced to use the *Maison du Peuple* as a temporary holding place for people they had arrested.

It is difficult to gain an adequate picture of the events of September 20, 2006. However, in an interview in February 2008 with the person thought in Djenné to be responsible for provoking the riot, one version of the story was put to me. Adama, in his early forties, disputes the charge of provoking the riot. As well as his oral narrative, he had kept a diary of events from the time of the riot, which he showed me. His version of events is that he had been to the Mosque on the morning of September 20 to see the work he had heard the AKTC was undertaking to deal with the problem of bats in the Mosque. However, when he got there he found that the Aga Khan staff, accompanied by a representative from the Cultural Mission and a member of AMUPI,[5] were on the roof and that they had dug a large hole, covered in a plastic sheet, in the most "sensitive" part of the Mosque, near the Imam's place of prayer.

In my conversations with others about the riot these few "facts" kept recurring: that the Aga Khan staff dug a hole on the roof,[6] that they had obscured the hole with a cover, and that their actions were very suspicious given that they were supposed to be dealing with bats inside the Mosque. Some of the more fanciful stories told include suspicions that the Aga Khan staff were trying to take some of the earth away (by putting it in a box), that they were digging up something sacred they knew was there (especially considering the location of the hole), and that somehow they were intending to do harm to the Mosque.

Adama claims to have asked the representative of AMUPI what was going on and was told that it had been announced during the Friday prayers. A discussion then ensued between Adama and a representative of the Cultural Mission. (Adama is a guide and resents the fact that he is not authorised to take white people into the Mosque when the Cultural Mission do so with impunity.) The son of the Mosque guard was then said to have started fighting with the man from AMUPI, because he felt that they had no right to be digging a hole without authorisation. Adama then left the Mosque, since things were beginning to get out of control.

Downstairs, lots of young people had started to swarm into the Mosque, and some began to destroy the technical equipment brought by the Aga Khan staff and rip the fans from the ceilings. Adama says that he had no further role in the riot and in fact intentionally avoided the scene until the next day, when he found out that the *militaires* ("soldiers") who had come to Djenné to quieten the riot were looking for him. He fled *en brousse* ("to the surrounding countryside") and waited for things to calm down. After a week, he turned himself in to the police and was locked up in Djenné's prison for three months, together with eleven other young men. Although over forty people had been arrested on the day of the riot, most were let free after a payment from their families. Adama was, however, not able to afford this and consequently had to serve his sentence. After two weeks detention he was seen by a judge in Djenné, who questioned him about the riot. Adama claims to have had no legal representation, and to his knowledge no formal judgement was made against him. He was finally released from prison on the December 26, 2007.

Another person present during the riot, Lassina, lives in a house very near the Mosque. He is a retired *fonctionnaire* ("civil servant") in his early sixties. He claims that on the day before the riot, the AKTC were working on the Mosque and people began to become suspicious of a hole they were digging on the roof. He describes it as being 60 cm x 40 cm deep and, crucially, covered in a plastic sheet. Suspicions were confirmed when the head of the *barey-ton,* the masons' association, denied any knowledge of the work. Rumours began to circulate about what was really being done, especially since people were unfamiliar with the equipment used by the AKTC; they wondered whether the AKTC was trying to put some kind of device, such as a computer, in the hole or somehow damage the Mosque (rumours of even a bomb circulated). The next day, the Wednesday of the riot, the rumours had gained momentum, and many people had come to see what was going on in the Mosque. They felt that they needed to tell the authorities that an unauthorised hole was being dug on the roof, and so some people went off to find the Imam. Other young people went in to the Mosque and started ripping down the fans in anger, because they symbolised "white" intervention (having been given by the U.S. Ambassador).

The AKTC staff fled together with the Cultural Mission staff, and the police arrived on the scene. However, as the violence escalated, police reinforcements were sent from Mopti (and had a lot of trouble crossing the river, owing to the slow cooperation of the people at the *bac,* the boat operators). Finally an army presence arrived on Thursday to restore order. There followed a period of violence, described by everyone I spoke to in Djenné as surprising and indiscriminate. Lassina's son was pulled from his bed where he was lying sick from malaria and beaten in front of his father. Lassina tried to interfere and was himself threatened with a beating. He fled to the *gendarmerie,* but they said they couldn't help him. For a few weeks after the event, many people could not leave their houses for fear of being beaten. The Minister of Culture at the time came to Djenné and together with the town's *Député* declared that all those responsible for the riot would be found and held to account. This stance led the *Député* to lose his job in the elections of 2007, when Sékou Abdul Kabri Cissé won with the help of his brother, a local *marabout*, whose gesture of replacing the fans in the Mosque with *Djennenkés* fans was met with widespread approval.

The reasons for the riot and the subsequent destruction of property belonging to people one could call the "heritage elite" in Djenné are, in my view, tied up in perceptions of corruption and an elite continually benefiting from scarce heritage resources. The Imam in Djenné is accused in private of numerous counts of profiting from money brought to the Mosque in the town's name. Additionally, the Cultural Mission continues to flout the *Interdit aux non-Musulmans* ("forbidden to non-Muslims") sign on the outside of the Mosque by taking white visitors inside, and it has lost—owing to rumours of corruption—some of the trust it had fostered with *Djennenkés* during their early archaeological sensitisation work (Panella, 2002: 200).

The tensions from the riot are still present. However, in February 2008, non-Muslim delegates of the *Terra 2008* Getty Foundation Conference visiting Djenné were ushered into the Mosque by Cultural Mission representatives in front of many angry residents. Residual anger after the riot also led to the cancellation of Independence Day celebrations in September 2007, because they coincided with the anniversary of the riot. The failure to celebrate the centenary of the Mosque in 2007 with a festival was also described by many *Djennenkés* as being due to residual tensions and fears of further violence.

There are many rumours of corruption constantly circulating in Djenné. In her ethnography of the building of the great library at Alexandria, Butler describes similar rumours as forming a "critical chorus," a form of subversive "echo" (Butler, 2007: 187). Heritage projects, like any other outside project bringing money to the town of Djenné, are invariably subject to suspicion by those who see themselves as excluded from their benefits. In his study of corruption in Africa, Olivier de Sardan (1999) identifies a "corruption complex," a continuum that encompasses a great many corruption practices from minor *délits,* such as bribing an official, to government misappropriation of funds. He states: "Corruption in Africa today is embedded in collective norms, collective logics and collective identities, and that is the reason for its pervasiveness on a continental level, i.e., its regionalization" (De Sardan, 1999: 248).

The commonalities found in all corruption in Africa are described by Olivier de Sardan as (1) routinisation—corruption is commonplace and part of the ordinary functioning of African bureaucracies; (2) stigmatisation—despite seemingly accepting corruption, most Africans experience it as a calamity and attribute many of the current problems of African society to it; and (3) lack of sanctions—people are protected by the social relationships that bind them. The embeddedness of corruption practices in Africa is located in cultural norms such as the act of gift giving (*prix du kola*[7]) and the stranglehold that solidarity networks have (such as age groups) on individuals who cannot operate outside them.

The nature of corruption in Djenné cannot therefore be viewed as a local phenomenon but instead must be viewed as a pan-African one (see also Amselle, 1992, for a comparison with the situation in Eastern Europe). What is, however, specific about Djenné is that since its inclusion on the World Heritage List and the increased international attention paid to it, some of the alleged corruption is operating within discourses of cultural heritage and identity, and therefore it stirs up feelings of anger and resentment that sometimes even the social norms of solidarity networks cannot contain.

Djenné Patrimoine accuses the authorities in Djenné, in their attempts to preserve the town's cultural heritage, of preferring to access easily sourced foreign money rather than dealing with the reality of the living population. However, both donors and authorities in the town are using cultural heritage in Djenné as a symbol of a legitimate cry for help. Contrary to donations concerning economic development, health, and education, heritage projects carry with them a perceived degree of dignity and autonomy that makes them especially attractive to foreign donors. The projects deal in measurable outcomes, they are time-bound, and they often pay only lip service to the involvement of local populations. What the projects have so far failed to deal with is the reality of Djenné as an inhabited space.

Since the riot, efforts have been made to reconcile the population with the authorities, in part through the creation in 2007 of a management committee of the Mosque. Despite their experiences during the riot, Adama (in his liaison role with the guides) and Lassina are both part of this management committee, as are masons and representatives of the Cultural Mission and *Djenné Patrimoine*. To some extent, the authorities in Djenné—such as the Cultural Mission, the Imam, and the *Chef du Village*—cannot be blamed if, when they are seeking external funding for their projects, the projects come in a form not easily inclusive of local concerns. The reality is that Djenné is crying out for economic development, health, and education projects. Helping people out of poverty and supporting their traditional livelihood strategies could preserve Djenné's cultural heritage. Although not directly dealing with cultural heritage, newly created wealth would have a ripple effect, allowing people to pay for the upkeep on their houses and stay in the town.

People in Djenné need employment and opportunities for young people. These opportunities are in some measure created by the tourists, who are motivated by the cultural heritage, which is in turn supported by the heritage projects. However, this link is not made explicit to many people in Djenné, who simply see the authorities profiting from projects brought to the town in their name. As was the case for the Dutch Housing Restoration project, the key elements of trust, clarity in objectives, financial incentives, and self-determination must be present to ensure local consent.

Conclusion

The long-term survival of the architecture of Djenné is intimately linked to people's ability to pay for the regular upkeep of their houses. An ethnographic approach to heritage shows how "cultural heritage" (in a UNESCO sense) is dealt with within the context of broader social and economic pressures. For example, poor harvests due to a lack of rains lead to an increase in the incidence of illness within families. The cost of healthcare and an inability to work lead the family to decide not to pay for their house to be remudded that year.

A less direct example would be one of a family who considers it more important to spend money on dressing correctly for festive occasions than paying for the upkeep of their house. Again, in this instance a lack of resources is at the heart of the decision not to remud the house. The immediate need of acquiring new clothes for a festival takes precedence over the long-term need of spending money on the house. Money is therefore spent on the production and reproduction of culture in different ways. Money is found to send children to school, to see traditional healers, and on the production of *gris-gris* (amulets). However, large sums of money, such as those needed to pay for the remudding of houses, are rarely found from a combination of small economies. In part, this is due to the inability to hold on to money over time, described in Chapter 7, but it is also due to the multiple demands of everyday life.

An analysis of *Djennenkés'* attitudes toward their universally recognised cultural heritage should therefore begin with a bottom-up approach. People in Djenné live within their political, economic, and religious affiliations. Houses in Djenné are first and foremost individual homes that shelter and leak, welcome and exclude, and they are part of people's economic responsibilities. It would be wrong to describe peoples' inability to find the funds to pay for the upkeep of their houses as a short-termist outlook, because that would not explain, for example, people sending their children to school.

It could be argued that paying for upkeep is a difficult emotional decision, because in many ways it is paying for what you already own. The practice of using tiles, described in Chapter 2, allows a *Djennenké* not only to buy peace of mind into the future but also to aesthetically transform the house. Despite the belief in some quarters that people in Djenné, given the choice, "will express themselves in mud,"[8] it is clear that in reality people are choosing to turn to new materials to maintain their homes.

Unlike the *crépissage* of the Great Mosque in Djenné, which is a time for celebration, the yearly (or biennial) remudding of individual houses in Djenné is becoming an increasing burden. This situation, combined with the fact that people do not reject the aesthetic appearance of the tiles or particularly care about the "patina" and rounded shapes so often eulogised, especially by Western observers, could lead to more and more of Djenné's houses being covered in the reddish fired clay tiles. This trend could have a radical effect on tourism and on the future of Djenné as a World Heritage site. However, for the inhabitants of Djenné it could increasingly be seen as the most cost-effective solution to the problem of their current housing crisis.

Part of the reason for my choosing to do an ethnography of heritage was the desire to approach the question of cultural transmission from the basis of local knowledge. In Djenné, as everywhere else, there proved to be far too many variables when talking about people's identity (temporary, permanent, long or short term, passive, active, political, economic, and so on) to be able to reach any satisfactory general conclusions about how people position themselves *vis-à-vis* their cultural heritage. However, what became clear in Djenné is that what unites people is poverty and the fact that the long-term preservation of Djenné's architectural and archaeological heritage is dependent on the way in which this heritage can be made to "work for" local populations, both politically and economically.

Perhaps the important point to consider is that any legal or political instrument concerning cultural heritage in Djenné is based on a series of assumptions, some of which anthropologists have helped to create, as has been argued in the case of UNESCO. An anthropological approach to cultural heritage in Djenné therefore suffers from the anthropologist being implicated in his or her own project of demystification. In Djenné, UNESCO has identified the two most conspicuous aspects of the town's cultural heritage for special note: the archaeology and the architecture—this is a long way from saying that these represent the material things people consider important to them in Djenné. In fact, the very notion of "outstanding universal value" is a quest for the unique; however, the experience that UNESCO has had with intangible heritage is that it is often the "mundane," the everyday, that lends meaning to people's lives. In this Djenné is no different from any other place in the world, and material possessions such as clothing, jewellery, and status symbols (mobile phones, televisions, motorbikes) all have enormous importance for people. *Djennenkés* also describe Djenné in terms of its intangible heritage: its Monday market, its festivals, and the social relationships that hold people together and lend Djenné its sense of place and identity.

Perhaps UNESCO's quest for the unique ("outstanding universal value") means that through its World Heritage List it is undertaking a project concerned with difference, not similarity, across all cultures. It is this very difference that is capitalised on to attract tourists. However, this difference may not necessarily be experienced by *Djennenkés* as a positive thing.

CHAPTER 6

Artisans, Embodied Knowledge, and Authenticity

The artisans in Djenné specialise in the production of many of the textiles, jewellery, and leather products found throughout Mali. In fact, at first glance, there is nothing particularly *Djennenké* for tourists' consumption, despite calls by *Djenné Patrimoine* for artisans to return to the basic crafts of the town (namely, embroidery and leatherwork). Djenné, like other places in the Mopti region, most famously San, is well known for its production of *bogolan* ("mud cloth"). The production of pottery is also widespread (La Violette, 2000). The restrictions of technology in Djenné, such as the lack of a machine to mechanically produce flat sheets or long strands of silver, does mean that the production of jewellery in Djenné is done entirely by hand, unlike other centres of production such as Mopti and Bamako. Djenné is famous for embroidery, yet embroiderers in the town, no longer able to compete with mechanically produced material, have long since had to orientate their craft toward tourist consumption and rich Malian officials. Instead of being portable forms of wealth, *grands boubous* (traditional long robes worn by both men and women) are

129

now becoming artefacts that are making their way into museums or are being worn by Malian politicians on special occasions.

Artisans in Djenné are negotiating their own authenticity while seeking to diversify their production for an ever-changing tourist market. A strong theme that emerges from the study of artisans in Djenné is that the authentic production of crafts not only combines the embodied knowledge of the artisan but is also negotiated through the choice of materials used for production. Innovation in production is constant and strongly encouraged within a sometimes contradictory framework of success and failure. The artisans in Djenné are first and foremost shrewd businessmen and -women who see the outside world as a potential market for their products. Unfortunately, access to these new markets is very hard to negotiate and predict, and the creation of long-term trade relationships is very rare.

The embodied knowledge of the artisans allows their work to remain "authentic" while constantly changing. This embodied knowledge (conceived of by UNESCO as intangible cultural heritage) is firmly located within Djenné, the artisans, and their families and is similar to the knowledge of the masons, who find themselves at the centre of UNESCO's project in Djenné (Marchand, 2006). Unlike the masons, the artisans constantly have to adapt to an external tourist market. However, a discussion of the negotiation of authenticity through practice is relevant to the work of the masons who also have to adapt to new economic realities and international interest while maintaining their integrity as masons.

Being an Embroiderer's Apprentice

Although the history of Djenné embroiderers remains little documented (Gardi et al., 1995), it is still possible to learn the art of embroidery in Djenné today. A detailed description of the techniques and styles of embroidery of Djenné can be found in a book entitled *Djenné d'Hier à Demain*, edited by Joseph Brunet-Jailly (Brunet-Jailly, 1999), the founder of *Djenné Patrimoine*. The descriptions include the cataloguing of the Songhai names and photographs of each stitch as well as the different kinds of traditional garments produced.

My relationship with Ousmane, a famous Djenné embroiderer, lasted throughout my time in the town. Ousmane is an elderly man who works in a small *atelier* with one of his sons and a jeweller, named Alpha Sidiki Touré. When I first arrived in Djenné, the *atelier* was situated down a side street that links the main market square to the other main road in Djenné, which runs down past the school to join the main road leaving the town. It was strategically placed very near Chez Baba, a hotel and restaurant popular with backpackers. The atelier was flanked by a tailor's shop on one side and a grocer/hardware shop on other. The two metal doors opening on to the street were draped with *bogolan* and embroidered cloth for sale within the *atelier*. Ousmane worked sitting on the floor on a mat within the *atelier*, with a view straight onto the road outside, which allowed him to greet friends and acquaintances passing by. Opposite him, and separated from him by a glass cabinet displaying his wares, sat Alpha, the jeweller. He also sat on a mat, surrounded by the things he needed to make his jewellery: tools, I learned later, that had been passed on to him by his father. At the back of the *atelier* sat another man who worked on a sewing machine, as well as Ousmane's son. A radio was on all day long, tuned into the local radio station, combining news and music.

Ousmane had had experience of teaching a Western woman once before, when a Belgian artist had spent some time with him. I was quickly accepted into the workshop and from my daily attendance developed a friendship with Alpha, the jeweller. Alpha, being younger than Ousmane and speaking better French, was able to talk to me more openly about life in Djenné and later, through our involvement together in the Djenné Festival, became a good friend. Unlike many people in Djenné, he spoke to me about politics, about which other people were more circumspect. This openness was partly due to his keen interest in politics and international

Figure 6.1 Author with Ousmane Traore, embroiderer in Djenné

affairs and his frequent questioning of the state of politics in the United Kingdom and the comparisons he drew with Mali.

To pay my way with Ousmane, I commissioned an embroidered bedspread for a friend's wedding costing 100,000 CFA (£100). This represented approximately six weeks' work, during which time I sat by his side every morning and learned some basic stitches. It was agreed that I would embroider a circular design on a small piece of cloth, a component "patch," which is then sewn on to strips of cloth that are sewn together to make the bedspread or some of the other embroidered products. The component patches come in a variety of different designs, ranging from the simple to the very complex and can also be embroidered in one of two colours: cream or gold. I was to attempt the simplest patch with cream coloured thread.

On the first day I learned the first and most basic stitch, named *dioré* (Brunet-Jailly, 1999: 99), although I was never taught the names of the stitches by Ousmane. He sat me down on a mat next to his and on a wooden board placed the bit of white cotton material on which he drew the pattern with pencil tracing around small and large Nescafe tops. Ousmane owns a collection of designs drawn in pencil on paper and kept in a waterproof file. He can refer to these when discussing designs with apprentices or clients, as well as refer to the photos in *Djenné d'Hier à Demain*, a copy of which he keeps by his side. Creating a catalogue of the products for sale in the shop was a priority for both Ousmane and Alpha, and I helped them do so by photographing the products and saving the images digitally for them. They could then retrieve, send, or print the images at a later date.

Ousmane showed me how to stitch and hold the material for the patch properly. It is important to hold the material in one hand with the fingers splayed to stretch the fabric as if a canvas. This is harder than it looks and takes some weeks of practice to do with ease. The stitch was shown to me a few times, and then the material was handed over for me to continue. After a few of my own stitches, Ousmane inspected my work and allowed me to continue. From the outset, I was made to understand that the small piece of material, the cotton I would use to embroider, and the needle were all valuable and would be costly to replace. There was no assumption that being new to embroidery, I would need several attempts and scrap pieces of material. In fact, when I made a mistake with a stitch a few days later (they were too far apart), Ousmane showed me how to unpick the stitches with a razor blade and start again. Over the weeks, I learned further stitches, each a little harder to do than the previous one. The stitches are used to "colour in" the different parts of the patch, creating different patterns and textures. One stitch involved making a small hole in the cloth with a sharpened feather and sewing around the outside to create a focus for the pattern.

Figure 6.2 Cream thread on white bazin cloth, part of a *grand boubou*

Ousmane was unfailingly patient in his teaching; he is used to having apprentices and regularly outsources pieces of work to the apprentices who have "graduated" from his tuition or to other embroiderers in the town—for example, he may commission a pocket for a *grand boubou*, or *tilbi* (see Gardi et al., 1995). He sketches the designs and tacks the material together, and then it is delivered to the person, sometimes in an outlying village, who has a couple of weeks to complete it and return it to the *atelier*.

Figure 6.3 Sketch design of embroidery patterns on paper

Ousmane was always coming up with new ideas for products to sell to tourists. As well as the traditional *grands boubous* for sale, there were bedspreads, cushion covers, small handbags, and his newest innovation, a lampshade. The frame of the lampshade was made of wood and metal, and the embroidered material was stretched over it and held in place with a cream-coloured zipper. Unlike the bedspread, the lampshade was not made of material with component patches; instead, the embroidery was stitched directly on to the material. This had the effect of creating a projected design when the lamp was turned on. One of his lamps was permanently on in the shop, and some others had been given to local hotels to place in rooms as advertisements for his work.

The handbags were best sellers with tourists, because they were economically accessible, costing between 5,000 CFA (£5) and 8,000 CFA (£8), depending on how many were bought and the negotiating skills of the tourists or their guide. The bags are made of cotton strips sewn together with only one embroidered "patch" on the front. The embroidery is the labour-intensive part of making the bag, so, by just including one patch, bags could be made fairly rapidly. The handle of the bag was a piece of rope sewn into place, and the closing was a handmade "button." The cotton strips were sometimes dyed blue, so the bags could also be produced in a variety of styles and colours. The cushion covers also sold well and retailed at around 15,000 CFA (£15). They either had embroidery sewn straight onto the material, like the lamps, or they were made of plain cotton with patches.

Ousmane's newest idea was to make belts for the tourist market. One morning I took in some photos taken from an old copy of *Marie Claire* magazine to show him some of the fastenings I had been trying to describe in conversation. Although he was open to trying different things, he contemplated using only traditional materials—for example, the little sewn buttons and not metal fastenings—when thinking about a design for the belt. It seems that the reason was a combination of tradition and practicality. If he could not make the fastenings himself, then he would have to buy them or outsource them, and it could very rapidly become too expensive. He also explained that a metal fastening would not be authentic and not in keeping with the Djenné embroidery style. This came as a surprise to me, since he not only was contemplating making belts but had also conceived of new designs for ties, two products that are not traditionally found in Djenné. Therefore, authenticity did not reside in the product itself but instead in its means of production and the choice of materials used. Embroidery was a technique that could be applied to any number of products to make them *Djennenké*.

As I worked in the *atelier* every morning, I came to get to know the stream of daily visitors, mostly elderly men who came to give their encouragement and greetings. Many of them inspected my work, and some of them sat for a long time on the bench just inside the shop and discussed the day's events with Ousmane and Alpha. Tourists coming to the *atelier* were also very interested to talk to me about my apprenticeship, and I sometimes helped to translate from English into French for them.

Ousmane has been an embroiderer since he was seven years old and has never entertained the idea of a different life. He learned his work from his father and has passed on his knowledge to his sons. Unlike most people in Djenné, Ousmane has travelled extensively. Together with some of the Djenné masons and other artisans, he was invited to the Folklife Festival in Washington in 1995. He had also travelled to Brussels to a trade fair and was preparing another such trip during my time of being an apprentice as well as participating in the twin town exchange between Djenné and the town of Vitré in France. On the floor by his side, Ousmane keeps an album in which he collects photographs from his travels, as well as photographs of him with tourists and visitors whom he has befriended in Djenné. His skill as an embroiderer has allowed him to travel and make business contacts throughout the world. This, in some ways seemed to have changed his view of Djenné. For example, he was very struck that in Europe and America animals were far more controlled than in Djenné (where they are often left to wander freely in the streets), and this observation had led him to fence in his own animals. He was also struck by the high-rise building in the United States and the large scale on which food was available during his stay. His visits abroad had not, however, fundamentally altered his way of living in Djenné or his appreciation of his hometown. Like other people who had travelled abroad and returned, his view was that, compared to Djenné, many places are cold, big, anonymous, and overwhelming.

Despite his international business contacts and fairly regular income from commissioned work as well as passing trade, Ousmane, like most people in Djenné, was often short of money. For example, when he wanted to send his son to Ségou to take part in the *Biennale* (described shortly) he asked me for an advance of 20,000 CFA (£20) to fund the trip. This came as somewhat of a surprise, because I knew that he had recently received an order from a French woman for a *grand boubou* at the cost of 500,000 CFA (£500). It seems, therefore, that for even the most successful artisans in Djenné, cash flow is a problem. A possible explanation is that being responsible for a large family he may have had many demands on his income. As I found out, money in Djenné is in constant movement, and it is only yours for as long as you can keep hold of it. Once a social relationship is established between two people, the borrowing and lending of money is a very regular occurrence. This is true within professional groups, such as the guides (described in the next chapter), but most particularly within families.

Many people in Djenné described the difficulty of accumulating wealth as capital for future projects. For example, young men often had to sacrifice their small savings to help an older male relative to do the *Hadj* (travel to Mecca). The only way to save money is to somehow take it out of circulation (Mauss, 1990), but this is difficult to achieve, since even people travelling to the nearby town of Mopti to use a bank were rarely able to confer an "out of bounds" status on their money, with the exception of money earmarked for specific projects. Like money, material goods also seemed to be in constant circulation unless explicitly placed out of bounds, as I found out when my room became the sometime depository for electronic goods, personal belongings, and occasionally, money.

6 • ARTISANS, EMBODIED KNOWLEDGE, AND AUTHENTICITY

Many people in Djenné can fit their worldly belongings into a bag. Owning material goods is a source of security owing to the lack of an adequate savings mechanism (the first bank came to Djenné in 2007) and the temperamental nature of rain and harvests. Ousmane explained to me how a person's wealth used to be invested in the clothes they wore (an embroidered *boubou* can cost up to 500,000 CFA, [£500]). Today, expensive embroidered clothes are ordered only by a few of the richest people in the town, and most of Ousmane's orders come from rich Malians living outside Djenné and from tourists. Similarly, the traditional heavy jewellery that used to be passed down through families is increasingly disappearing. A jeweller in Djenné told me the story of a woman who owned a 300 gram, 23.5 carat gold bracelet. She used to wear it for big events and festivals. She ended up selling nearly all of it over a period of 20 years: "I was the one who started to cut it," he told me.

The woman managed to successfully bring up her family through sacrificing part of her family's material heritage. She came to him for the first time when she needed 50,000 CFA (£50), so they cut 8 grams off. Over the years, little by little, she sold off nearly the whole bracelet. When she first came to him, she had just lost her husband and had small children to care for. She managed to pay for their upbringing on her own, and I was told that one of her children now works in Bamako and another in Mopti, signalling their success. She now has only two small earrings left from the original bracelet.

This story was related to me without value judgement. The original function of the bracelet, to be a portable form of wealth, had served its purpose and allowed her family to survive. The jeweller did not mention the loss of the object itself. Similarly, another jeweller in Djenné told me how he regularly bought old jewellery from women in the countryside. He saw himself as providing a valuable service to these women by freeing up the capital the jewellery represented. Once he had taken a photograph of the jewellery he would either sell it to Western collectors or melt it down and make more modern adaptations using some of the original designs. He spoke about his work in terms of improving the old designs to fit with women's new aspirations for lighter jewellery in a more modern style.

At first glance, therefore, it appears that people in Djenné have a pragmatic attitude toward their cultural heritage and will adapt and dispose of it to suit their needs and ambitions. The reality, however, is more complex. The task of identifying what is and what is not considered important cultural heritage in Djenné is not straightforward. For example, local attitudes toward the surrounding archaeological sites, discussed in Chapter 2, show how Islamic attitudes toward pre-Islamic material culture are determining the success of Western antilooting sensitisation projects. In many cases, cultural heritage is something that is identified as a potential resource and therefore appropriated and offered up for tourist consumption. The importance this heritage has for the individual appropriating it beyond its financial significance needs further scrutiny.

Artisan Associations

The artisans in Djenné have organised themselves into an association since 1995. Each subgroup of artisans (tailors, carpenters, jewellers, leatherworkers, and so on) pay 15,000 CFA (£15) a year to be a part of the association. Each subgroup also has its own "industry" associations. Alpha told me about the Jewellers' Association, set up in 1998 with the aim of developing the work of jewellers in Djenné. The long-term aim of the association is to forge links with other jewellers' associations in Mali, and they are currently exploring the idea of involving a nongovernmental organisation to help them to identify a source of funding for the purchase of a machine that mechanically produces metal sheets and wire (the cost of the machine is approximately 8 million CFA [£800]). In Mopti, the jewellers have acquired two such machines and own them communally, paying a small fee every time they use them (5 CFA [£0.005] for each gram of metal). In 2006, however, there was only one way of making jewellery in Djenné and that was with a hammer and an anvil.

The limitations of the technology in Djenné mean that the jewellers must limit their designs to those that are viable using traditional methods. One such design is the ubiquitous "Peul earring" that is found in all the jewellers' shops in Djenné and that is a regular export product for Alpha. The size and weight of the earrings can vary from approximately 5 to 20 grams. The Peul earring is very hard to make, because the metal must be hammered into a conical shape, and consequently some apprentices never master the technique. Despite this, Alpha was happy to show me the steps necessary for its production, as he explained: "It's not a secret, just a job."

The work of being a jeweller in Djenné, like that of embroidery, is learned through a system of apprenticeship, usually drawn from the family circle. There are five main families of jewellers in Djenné; two of them are separate branches of the same family. Despite spending the majority of his time in the *atelier* shared with Ousmane, Alpha has his own workshop adjacent to his house in which he employs a dozen or so young men, mostly relatives. Over time, the young men learn the skills necessary to judge the quality of metal (using a special acid and a control stone), melt it down, and fashion it into the component shapes necessary for jewellery making.

At first their jobs are quite basic, such as stoking the fire and learning to use the bellows, made of animal skin. Most apprenticeships start around the age of seven, although the children usually have been exposed to jewellery making all their lives. It is important when children first become apprentices for them to learn the dangers of the job, and so they

Figure 6.4 Alpha Sidiki Touré, jeweller in Djenné, in his shop

are warned off harshly if they attempt to tamper with the fires. Next, they are taught the skill of hammering metal into sheets. This is taught with bronze or copper, because silver is too valuable to waste on the potential mistakes made by the apprentices. Gradually, and depending on their individual competence, the apprentices will learn all the skills they need to make jewellery, usually making their first ring or small Peul nose ring around the age of ten (these rings are often made of bronze and sold to local women for as little as 100 CFA [£0.10]).

Figure 6.5 Handmade jewellery in Djenné

Once an apprentice has mastered the necessary skills to become a jeweller he works in the workshop fulfilling orders. Jewellers are not paid a salary but instead paid per piece of jewellery produced. For example, if a pair of earrings is sold at 5,000 CFA (£5), the artisan will be paid 1,000 CFA (£1), since it will cost 2,500 CFA (£2.50) to buy the silver and another couple of hundred for cleaning products, charcoals for the burners, and other equipment. At times when there are no orders, the jewellers are free to use the workshop in a self-employed manner and innovate to create new designs. If these new products appeal to Alpha, he will buy them and sell them in his shop. If the new design is popular, more orders will follow.

As a result, there is constant innovation in the jewellery found in Djenné, with the limiting factors of the technology available and the difficulty in finding certain materials. Precious and semiprecious stones and materials available in other parts of Mali (for example, rubies, ivory) are rarely found in Djenné, so the jewellery makers limit themselves to gold, silver, and amber. In 2005, 24-carat gold cost 8,000 CFA (£8) per gram of unworked metal and 10,000 CFA (£10) per gram of worked gold (already in some jewellery form). Eighteen-carat gold was less expensive at 7,500 CFA (£7.50) per gram. As well as the design and difficulty in making a piece of jewellery, its weight is therefore integral to its final

6 • ARTISANS, EMBODIED KNOWLEDGE, AND AUTHENTICITY   141

value. In fact, when bargaining over the price of a piece of jewellery, Alpha would often resort to putting it on the little weighing scales in front of the customer to assure him or her of its value. A ring usually weighs 4 or 5 grams and is consequently a very costly item when made out of gold. Silver, in contrast, is a much cheaper raw material, costing 1,750 CFA (£1.75) per gram (approximately four times cheaper than gold). Alpha regularly goes to Bamako to buy silver and comes back with large quantities at a time. Sometimes, semiprecious stone and amber can be sourced from old women who come into Djenné to sell their jewellery. Gold can occasionally be bought in Djenné or from *ateliers* in Bamako who buy it directly from the source (Mali is a gold mining country).[1]

Negotiating Authenticity

Alpha describes inspiration for his work as coming from personal experience, which can include seeing women on television or in the street, when certain patterns or designs lodge themselves in his memory. When the time comes for making new jewellery, the inspiration will be recalled first as a drawing on paper and then through translating it into a prototype:

> Alpha was working on a leaf design necklace. He makes the templates out of old phone cards. He showed me his equipment—a locally made hammer that he puts in water before he uses it so that the wood swells and the metal head doesn't fly off. He also uses a locally made anvil (piece of metal wedged into a piece of wood). The little scales he uses he bought for 50,000 CFA from Bamako second hand. They are a very expensive but indispensable piece of equipment.[2]

If the prototype can be sold successfully, then more will be made. In his experience, very few new designs fail. When asked about keeping the tradition of jewellery alive in Djenné, Alpha does not see a contradiction between innovation and tradition. However, some of the jewellers in Djenné locate traditions in the technology and reject newer technologies such as welding, preferring only the old techniques of hammering and twisting.

Although the raw materials used to make jewellery are important for determining their final financial value, their provenance is not important to confer authenticity on the object. For example, a key component used by Alpha in his jewellery is old French 10-franc pieces from the 1960s (costing 7,500 CFA [£7.50] each) that are melted down and mixed with pure silver (which is very soft) to make bracelets. This recycling is not referenced in the final product. Similarly, old (some would say antique) amber beads or silver bracelets are melted down or recycled to make new products.

Authenticity in the materiality of the objects therefore does not seem to be a concern for jewellers in Djenné, because the provenance of the raw material is of little interest or note. Jewellery is *Djennenké* through being made in Djenné by jewellers who usually belong to one of the five big jeweller families in the town. A debate sometimes arises about the technology that should or not be employed, but it does not seem that the jewellers are capitalising financially with tourists on the uniqueness of their products or the techniques used to make them. This being the case, their production is not tied to a particular technology, and they are free to seek funding to buy labour saving machines.

Both Alpha and Ousmane calculate the financial value of the products they sell through a combination of the cost of raw materials and the amount of labour and the different degrees of specialist skill they represent. However, unlike jewellery, the "technology" of embroidery (*broderie à la main*) is central to the value of Ousmane's work and distinguishes it from machine-produced products that can be bought much more cheaply. These methods of calculating value are only two of a number of ways found in Djenné; other artisans, such as leatherworkers (described in Chapter 4), calculate the value of their *gris-gris* based on their potency.

Embodied Knowledge

Understanding the mechanism by which embodied knowledge is transferred from one artisan to the next is a priority for such bodies as UNESCO, who are currently developing their work with intangible cultural heritage. Marchand (2003) discusses this mechanism in reference to his work in the Yemen. He explains how after the inclusion of the city of Sana'a in Yemen on UNESCO's World Heritage List, several Western-trained architects promoted the idea of establishing officially regulated trade schools to protect the town's architecture, thus replacing the competitive families of traditional builders in the city. This was meant not to only to secure the survival of the Sana'ani style of architecture but also to impose a form of "quality control." However, Marchand argued that:

> Trade schools, which would aim to revive or sustain traditional craft production and building techniques, might successfully train corps of craftspeople to reproduce accurately the material products in question, *but the traditional building trade, defined by its distinctive set of human relations and methods for transferring knowledge, cannot easily be replicated.* (Marchand et al., 2003: 35, original emphasis)

He concludes that a different focus should be adopted when one is thinking about cultural continuity: "Ultimately, 'tradition' lies in the

6 • ARTISANS, EMBODIED KNOWLEDGE, AND AUTHENTICITY

process and qualitative aspect of the human relations, not in the materiality of the object" (2003: 35).

Consequently, in common with the work of other artisans in Djenné, the work of the Djenné's masons, the *barey-ton*, can be seen to be both an embodied and a social practice. Additionally, it would be hard to disembed and capture the masons' knowledge to ensure its transmission (through for example, a trade school or archival records).

Marchand concludes that, to ensure the survival of Djenné's architecture, the social cohesion of *barey-ton* is paramount:

> I will ultimately assert that the maintenance of an apprenticeship system that endows young men with not only technical skills but a sense of social identity and professional responsibility is the most effective way to guarantee a sustainable reproduction of a distinct architecture and an urban landscape imbued with changing and dynamic meaning for the Djennenké population. (Marchand, 2006: 51)

He therefore puts the masons at the centre of any future plan to protect Djenné's architecture. This position echoes the work UNESCO is now undertaking with intangible cultural heritage, where transmission, identity and continuity are taking precedence over "outstanding universal value." However, it is hard to see how in practice an accommodation could be reached between the dominant "archival" knowledge of the town and a more dynamic embodied one.

To some extent, the Dutch Housing Restoration project did achieve such an accommodation through positioning Djenné's masons at the heart of the project. However, the "authenticity debate" surrounding the project (choice of houses to restore, documentation and historical analyses) took place to a large extent outside Djenné and involved "experts" from Dutch universities. As has been stated in Chapter 1, the locus of authenticity in Djenné is seen as residing in the façades of the houses, and these were considered authentic because they closely resembled early photographs of Djenné.

UNESCO states that no material changes can be made to Djenné as a "monument" without endangering its World Heritage status. The archival approach to Djenné is therefore resistant to change and unwilling to give up its power to local negotiations of authenticity. A knowledge monopoly is in force, whereby local voices find themselves drowned out by archival imaginings:

> In short, it would seem that the practice of prioritizing the material by (largely) Western trained specialists is vested with (potentially neoimperialist) ambitions to monopolize what has been constructed as a tangible resource. Cultures are effectively reduced to, and constrained by, a positivist discourse that reconfigures cultural resources as classifiable and quantifiable objects. (Marchand, 2001: 138)

Unlike other artisans in Djenné, the masons find themselves part of an ongoing debate about authenticity and cultural continuity. Whereas the jewellers are free to change their design and "improve" their products for new markets, UNESCO condemns the use of tiles by the masons.

A Western focus on the town's architecture has no doubt increased the status of the town's masons and their income. However, more important, the masons are bound by their responsibility to Djenné's residents. They cannot solely bear the burden of negotiating between the desire of the residents and the restrictions of the officials in the town (such as the Cultural Mission); a debate about authenticity and architecture in Djenné should include the whole of the town. In the same way that early writings and photography about Djenné should not be considered a unique source of knowledge about the town, the embodied practice of its masons should not be so considered. Instead, houses in Djenné should first and foremost be thought of as people's homes, places of shelter, comfort, and pride for their inhabitants.

Voices of Authenticity in Djenné

There does not seem to be any "authenticity anxiety" among the artisans in Djenné. Instead, it seems that authenticity in terms of cultural production resides within the embodied knowledge achieved through kinship and apprenticeship. However, as is discussed in Chapter 8 in relation to the Artisan Hall during the *Festival du Djennéry*, some organisations in Djenné, such as *Djenné Patrimoine* and the Cultural Mission, are becoming increasingly concerned that Djenné is losing its unique cultural appeal.

In 1999 *Djenné Patrimoine* drew up an inventory of typical *artisanat* made in Djenné. The association's position is that being unique to Djenné, these objects should be protected through sensitising artisans to the needs of the tourists (who, it is assumed, are seeking authentic *Djennenké* objects). These objects—which include locally produced *bogolan*, leather goods such as boots, jewellery, beadwork, and embroidery—are contrasted with the masks, Dogon statues, Tuareg jewellery, and imported cloth also for sale in Djenné. During the *Festival du Djennéry*, the issue of authenticity took on particular importance, because many of the objects on sale in the artisan's hall were not made in Djenné.

Additionally, some artisans in Djenné are involved in the production of *faux* terracotta statues, primarily on sale in the shops operated by the guides. Most of these objects are clearly recent reproductions, or "fakes," and tourists purchasing them would not be under the illusion that they were buying an ancient object. However, other *antiquaires* in the town blur the line between a reproduction terracotta object and one acquired from the archaeological sites surrounding the town. Despite very strong

6 • ARTISANS, EMBODIED KNOWLEDGE, AND AUTHENTICITY   145

sensitisation programmes warning against the purchase of archaeological objects, tourists may buy a fake in the hope that they are getting an authentic archaeological object. In relation to archaeological objects, therefore, people in Djenné are aware that there is a desire for authenticity, and some *antiquaires* will go as far as artificially ageing objects to give them the patina desired by tourists.

Biennale de Ségou

The event now known as *Biennale Artistique et Culturelle* was first started by Mobido Keita after Independence in 1960. During Keita's era, they were annual events called *Les Semaines de la Jeunesse* (1963–1968). Their antecedents had been the *1er Festival Africain de la Jeunesse* in 1958 and the *1er Festival Nationale de la Jeunesse* in 1962 (Arnoldi, 2006). Speaking of *Les Semaines de la Jeunesse*, Arnoldi states that: "Many local performance genres were ethnically or regionally based, and their insertion into a national cultural pantheon was intended to allow citizens at large, regardless of their specific affiliations, to identify with and embrace these arts as wholly Malian" (Arnoldi, 2006: 58).

After having being suspended for a period of 12 years between 1989 and 2003 (although in 2001 there was a *Semaine Nationale des Arts et de la Culture*), *Biennales* were re-launched in 2003 by President Amadou Toumani Touré. During the opening ceremony the former Minister of Culture,[3] Cheick Oumar Sissoko said:

> The *Biennale* will never be again as it was before. It will now rest on four considerations around which the Ministry of Culture is actively working and mobilizing its resources. 1 - Culture as a factor in economic development; 2 - culture as a factor in the stability of the country; 3 - culture as a factor in the preservation of cultural expressions; 4 - and culture as factor in developing fertile partnerships.[4] (my translation)

In 2005 the Cultural Mission, along with some artisans and masons from Djenné, formed a delegation that took part in the *Biennale de Ségou*. Ségou was chosen as suitable location by the government in order to support its policy of decentralisation. The Djenné delegation was the representative for the *Région de Mopti*, and it chose architecture as the theme for its exhibit. Each *région* had exhibit space in which to showcase their cultural heritage. The exhibits tended to refer to the production of *artisanat*, and so Djenné's entry with its emphasis on architecture was unique. It also benefited from having a multimedia dimension to it (in the form of a projected slide show) and a number of model houses and exhibits donated by the Dutch. A committee of experts judged the exhibits, and a prize of 1 million CFA (£1,000) was awarded to the best entry.

Despite the financial awards available, the Mopti delegation did have some difficulty in motivating people from Djenné to attend the *Biennale,* because there was no assured financial reward. In fact, to their disappointment, the *Région de Mopti* delegation's exhibit came in second in 2005 to the *Région de Gao.* As it turned out, the artisans in Djenné had also been well advised to think about attending the *Biennale,* because the sale of *artisanat* to tourists was very disappointing. Ousmane's son, despite spending three days in the space set aside for artisans, made only a handful of sales owing to a lack of tourists participating in the event. However, his presence at the *Biennale* was an important part of his apprenticeship and an important way of gaining more experience and responsibility.

Conclusion

A discussion of the work of artisans in Djenné demonstrates that authenticity, while being of utmost importance both externally, to organisations such as UNESCO, and internally, to the Cultural Mission and *Djenné Patrimoine,* is in fact of little immediate concern for the artisans themselves. This is because the artisans are the locus of their own authenticity, and they pass on their cultural knowledge through embodied practice in the form of apprenticeships. Architecture, embroidery, and the production of jewellery in Djenné is *Djennenké,* because it is made by local people trained in a local tradition. In this context, change is part of the adaptation of the tradition to new economic, political, religious, and social realities. Through its work protecting intangible heritage, UNESCO has recognised the dynamic nature of cultural transmission through embodied knowledge. In Djenné itself, UNESCO and the Cultural Mission recognise the irreplaceable role of the masons for the ongoing preservation of Djenné's architecture. However, at the same time, a reevaluation of UNESCO's original vision of Djenné as a monument (World Heritage) needs to occur to allow space for the cultural life of Djenné to continue evolving. This evolution need not be conceptualised as posing a threat to Djenné's architecture but instead should be seen as breathing a vital life force into the town.

CHAPTER 7

Guides and the Regulation of History in Djenné

The Malian Government is increasingly regulating tourism in an attempt to standardise the industry. The introduction of tests for guides across Mali has marked a move toward attempting to establish stable historical narrative of the country, since the knowledge of the guides is assessed against a national norm. In a discussion of the complex lives of the guides, the complicated place they inhabit within Djenné is revealed: they are at once socially marginalised and a very important part of the town's economy. Most guides in Djenné have not attended school for many years and will therefore have bypassed the historical education that is part of Mali's national curriculum. Their knowledge is therefore a pastiche of oral history, information from guidebooks (for those who are literate), and information from tourists. Although the guides are now being judged against the new criteria set out by the guide test, interviews with tourists reveal that what they seek from guides during their time in Djenné are often personal insights that make them feel they have a degree of emotional complicity with their hosts.

Figure 7.1 Hama Lamine Traoré, called "Phillipe le Magnifique," guide in Djenné

If we are to understand many of the new challenges facing the guides of Djenné, we need to put their profession into its larger political and economic context. Unbeknown to many of the guides, the tourist industry is one of Mali's greatest economic hopes, and consequently the government is taking an increasing interest in its promotion and regulation. The United Nations World Tourism Organisation (UNWTO) for Africa reported that tourism to the continent grew at a greater pace than tourism to the rest of the world (6.6% between 1995 and 2000, as opposed to 4.9% for the rest of the world[1]). The UNWTO is optimistic about Africa's future, owing to its proximity to Europe (both Africa's and the world's main source of visitors) and a new agreement aiming to liberalise air traffic within Africa, the Yamoussoukro Declaration (UNESCO, 1999). However, a few countries attract the bulk of tourism to Africa (Tunisia, Morocco, and South Africa) and Sub-Saharan Africa still accounts for only 1.5% of world tourism receipts.[2] In 2004 Mali recorded 148 million U.S. dollars in tourist receipts, compared to France, which recorded 40 billion U.S. dollars, and Morocco, which recorded 4.5 billion dollars. The tourist industry in Mali is reliant on a few key locations in the country to attract tourists, three of which are World Heritage sites: "It is said that the Mopti-Dogon-Bandiagara-Djenné-Timbuktu area has a potential of attracting about 20,000 tourists a year. This could under global estimates generate annual revenues of 10 million US$ in foreign exchange" (UNESCO/PNUD, 1997: 13).[3]

However, the tourist situation in Mali is unpredictable, given the worrying developments in the north of the country. Because of the recent activities of AQIM (Al-Qaeda in the Islamic Maghreb, discussed in Chapter 4), as of the end of 2010 all of UNESCO's World Heritage sites in Mali (Djenné, Timbuktu, Dogon Country, and the Tomb of the Askias) are now officially in the British and Commonwealth Office's red zone, meaning that travel to the area is not advised. The French travel advisory has placed Djenné and Dogon Country in an "orange" category (no unnecessary travel to the region) and Timbuktu firmly in a prohibited red zone. Despite these warnings, some travel companies and independent tourists persist with their travel plans, often foregoing any form of travel insurance. However, it seems that the dominant trend among tour operators is modification or cancellation of trips to the area. Although Ségou (a town that hosts a successful music festival every February, discussed in Chapter 8) is not affected by the travel advisory, the appeal of the music festival for many tourists is that it is a highlight of an organised tour around the country and not a sole destination.

The Status of the Guides

The guides in Djenné occupy a complex space linking the town to the outside world through tourism. They are an exclusively male group,[4] and their profession is considered to be of low status. The negative reputation of guides is known in Djenné and is also documented in travel guides (Hudgens & Trillo, 1999: 337). Local people do not like the guides' flashy ways or the way they run after tourists. Parents and teachers are worried that young boys, seduced by the easy money to be made from tourism, will increasingly abandon their studies and the promise of traditional jobs. The guides are also associated with non-Islamic behaviour through their contacts with tourists, because they are regularly exposed to alcohol consumption and other negative behavioural traits attributed to tourists, including inappropriate dress and public displays of affection. The guides are the catalysts for broader changes in the town, since they have taken up "modern" or "westernised" dress, have a perceived lack of respect for older generations, and engage in conspicuous consumption of new technology, such as mobile phones and the Internet.

Dramane's Story

I first heard about the guide, Dramane, from other guides. He was considered by the other guides as one of the success stories of the profession. I tried to catch up with him on various different occasions, but he was often travelling away from Djenné. When we finally did meet, six months into my fieldwork, I found him to be a very charming and well-informed man, unusually self-deprecating for a guide.

Dramane is now in his early thirties. He was born in Abidjan, where his father had a job working at the port. His parents were both originally from Djenné and had gone to the Ivory Coast as migrant workers. His earliest memories are of the people who came to his home in Abidjan from Djenné, seeking work and shelter. At one time, his father was employing up to forty people from Djenné at the port of Abidjan. He told me that from this early exposure to a constant stream of people from Djenné he learned about the town's culture, the way of speaking, preparing food, and social greetings.

Having been named after his grandmother's father, Dramane had a very special relationship with his grandmother, who called him "father" all her life. This bond meant that after five years in Abidjan, his grandmother in Djenné called for him, and he moved there to be by her side, leaving behind his father, his father's three wives, and his eighteen siblings. In Djenné, he was sent to the local Qur'anic and French schools and lived with his grandmother on the little money his father sent them. After his father's retirement, the money ran out, and the savings that had been assumed to have been invested in cows in Djenné had also gone. This was due to a combination of the death of many cows in the droughts of the 1980s and the fact that cows entrusted to others from a great distance are often stolen, sold, or taken by other members of the family without permission. As Dramane told me: "You have to follow your cows closely if you don't want to lose them."

The next stage of his young life was very hard; he and his grandmother had no money and had to rely on the generosity of their neighbours for food and clothing. Finally, in desperation, his grandmother left for Abidjan to plead directly with his father and left Dramane in the care of her neighbour, a teacher at the local school. This arrangement was arrived at through a protracted process of establishing a kinship link between the two families, which, however tenuous, ensured that Dramane could be accepted by the neighbour as a family member. On the return of his grandmother, he got "lost" between her home and the home of his adoptive mother; this allowed him to say he was in one place when in fact he was in the street or hanging around in the market with other children. He started to avoid going to school.

Dramane's first encounter with tourists was in the market when he was ten years old. An elderly Italian woman was trying to buy a fan from a Bamama trader and was failing to be understood. Dramane interpreted in French for her and was rewarded by spending the rest of the day helping the Italian woman with her shopping. At the end of the day, she gave him 500 CFA (£0.50), a considerable sum of money at the time. He rushed

7 · GUIDES AND THE REGULATION OF HISTORY IN DJENNÉ   151

home to give it to his grandmother, who did not believe he had earned it honestly and so frog-marched him back to the hotel where the Italian woman was staying. After the Italian woman reassured the grandmother that the money had in fact been earned honestly, they spent the money by celebrating with a big meal, and it was at this moment that Dramane says he definitively abandoned school for a childhood spent following tourists, despite the best efforts of teachers and fellow pupils sent out to try to catch him.

Tourism at the time in Djenné was organised through a government-run association named the *Société Malienne d'Exploitation de Resources Touristiques* (SMERT). At the entrance of every tourist town in Mali, a SMERT office stood alongside a police control barrier, ensuring that tourists had to go through a local guide to visit the town. There was no training in place for the guides, and many of them did not speak French, so their job was more one of accompaniment than cultural interpreter. The SMERT guides were obviously very hostile to the *petits guides*, the children like Dramane who hung around in front of the Mosque hoping to show tourists around. Dramane was regularly beaten by the SMERT guides, had his earnings stolen from him, and was dragged to the police station, where they threatened him with a re-education camp in Bamako. One loophole the SMERT office could do nothing about was the diplomatic cars, which were not required to stop at the barriers. These diplomats were free to walk around Djenné as they pleased, and conse-quently Dramane and children like him could befriend them. One such lucky encounter enabled Dramane to befriend a man from the French Embassy, who, having heard his tale of hardship went with Dramane to the police station and asked them to leave him alone. In the end the SMERT guides gave in and let him have the job of making tea at their office. There he found that the guides were mostly illiterate; consequently he relied on the elderly Great Mosque guard to tell the tourists the history of Djenné. Dramane spent time with this man, learning his oral history by heart. He also came across a guidebook to Djenné, *Le Guide du Routard*, and set about teaching himself Djenné's history.

His first trip to tourist destinations outside Djenné came through an international travel company. Some tourists he befriended asked if he could accompany them on the rest of their trip around Mali to help with their bags and interpretation. His grandmother gave her permission, and they set off to Timbuktu and Gao. The trip enabled him to befriend other guides and begin to learn some of the history of these other towns. On his return he was paid 20,000 CFA (£20) in tips, with which he repaired his grandmother's house, which had fallen into a state of ruin. This is the point at which he saw his status within the town changing as he moved on from his status as a *petit guide*. *Petits guides* still bring deep shame on their families. Dramane told me: "A well-educated child would never become a guide."

Through being one of the first guides in Djenné to work all over Mali, and through his contacts with big travel agencies, Dramane soon started making a very good living out of tourism. He spoke a bit of English picked up from tourists along the way, but Anglophone travel agencies were increasingly asking him to learn English formally. This he did through the help of an American friend who worked at the *Banque Africaine du Développement* in Abidjan. The man paid for him to attend the American Business School in Abidjan for six months and acted as his host. He would go and see his parents on weekends, and when he left and started to work again, he sent his father money from Djenné. His father was surprised that for the first time money was leaving Djenné to go to Abidjan; for years it had been the other way around. Dramane's new-found English skills allowed him to work not only in tourism but also for Anglophone television production companies. He worked on the BBC's Michael Palin documentary as well as with other journalists and photographers. Most recently, he helped a German production company make a documentary about illegal immigration to Europe through northern Mali and Algeria.

Dramane is now a wealthy man in Djenné. He has opened his own bar/nightclub in the previously derelict *Maison des Jeunes* that he rents out for weddings and special occasions. He also took the lead in setting up the new Guides' Office in Djenné in 2005, SMERT having closed in 1988 and the profession being essentially unregulated since then, until recent measures taken by the Malian Government.

Dramane's story is illuminating on a number of levels. Despite coming from a Peul family, he does not mention cattle herding as a viable option for him. As mentioned, his father had to leave Djenné to find work, and the cattle that were intended as a form of wealth for the family were lost through drought or bad management. For a child, the tourists in Djenné are a symbol of wealth and fascination. It is not unusual for parents to encourage their children to ask white visitors for sweets or money. For many children who do not speak French, the phrases *toubabou cadeaux* and *toubabou bonbons* are learned by heart at an early age. There does not seem to be shame associated with such behaviour. However, giving up school or employment to become a guide does bring shame on the family. To a certain extent, this is due to religious conservatism and a distrust of non-Islamic behaviour. The fact that children abandon school to become guides is also considered ill advised, because education (both Qur'anic and French) is considered important. However, the reality is that many guides earn a better living than the majority of the population of Djenné. Their jobs are, however, seasonal, precarious, and dependent on an unpredictable flow of tourists.

The guides' presence in Djenné is very conspicuous. They are conspicuous not only through their consumption of Western style clothes, music, and technology but also through their youth and fearless attitude toward the outside world. Tourists and locals feel their physical presence, since the places they choose to spend time in are public, such as the main square and the entrance to the town. The guides are always watching what is going on in Djenné, because they are forever on the lookout for new business. They are also suspicious of any threats to the monopoly they have over the tourists. When visitors sought me out in Djenné, I had to make it very clear that they were in the town to see me. In fact, I had to make sure one of the guides was informed of their visit so that the message not to harass my friends was passed on to all the guides. On two occasions, I was indirectly accused of being a guide myself when a series of visitors came to visit me in the space of a few weeks. Similarly, one of the Peace Corps volunteers in the town was accused of being a guide when some of the other volunteers from Mali paid her a visit.

The accusations were interesting on several levels. First, they were part of a wider speculation about the true reason for my presence in the town. Second, they demonstrated that despite the guides' contact with tourists and a Western way of life, it was credible to some of them that I would be secretly operating as a guide, earning 5,000 CFA (£5) in an afternoon. This suspicion seemed to contradict the assumption that white people are rich and potentially an endless source of financial support (such as the three expatriates who have built houses in the town). Whatever the reason for their suspicions, it seemed to indicate that the guides believe their position is precarious, and that they are alert to any threat that may undermine their role as the cultural brokers between Djenné and visitors from the outside.[5]

Like Dramane, many of the guides have travelled to other tourist destinations in Mali and beyond. To successfully operate in the tourist economy, the guides have acquired a wide range of communication, business, and practical skills and are often imaginative and highly adaptive in the face of new opportunities. For example, one of the guides was very keen to borrow a book I owned entitled *Birds of West Africa*. He was aware that tourists are interested in the wildlife around the town and wanted to be in a position to exploit this market (specialist ornithological tours have begun to come to Djenné and the surrounding area). Another guide used some capital he had been sent from a friend in France to open a tourist art shop. The shop had the advantage of being situated on the main square, so it attracted through-business as well as tourists brought to the shop by the guides. Other attempted business ventures included selling T-shirts with prints of the Mosque on the front (the result of the collaboration between a guide and a Japanese tourist). Some of the guides are also employed in other roles, such as language teaching and traditional subsistence activities.

The Tourist Season

As is true for the rest of Mali, the tourist season[6] in Djenné is short, and the income generated during these few months must sustain those working in tourism for the rest of the year. Additionally, tourism in Djenné tends to be restricted to Sunday nights and Mondays, with very little tourism for the rest of the week. The number of tourists visiting Djenné has been increasing gradually over the years. In 1996 the *Mairie* declared receiving tourist tax from approximately 5,000 tourists. In 2004 the figure had risen to approximately 8,000[7] (although in an interview in 2007 the Director of the Cultural Mission reported a figure of 15,000 tourist visits to Djenné[8]). However, the competition for tourists' income is still high and leads to aggressive and underhanded business techniques.

The tourists arriving in Djenné have to cross the river outside the town before travelling the last few kilometres into Djenné. This crossing is the first point of contact between incoming tourists and local guides. There is a clear hierarchy of guides and a "code of honour" that dictates that once a guide has made an agreement with a tourist, another guide may not come along and *gache son marché* ("spoil his deal"), however underhanded the manner in which the original agreement was made. Techniques to entice tourists include telling them that they have been sent to meet them, pretending to know their guide from the tourists' previous destination, and declaring that they are the official guide from the tourist's intended hotel.

The river crossing is a perfect place for guides to hunt for business. Guides use the analogy of hunting especially when a large group of tourists arrive at once. Tourists who arrive in large groups are labelled by the derogatory term *chumpas,* and the tourist season is referred to as *la chasse aux chumpas* ("*chumpas* hunt"). As a vehicle approaches the river crossing, the dust and noise announcing its arrival triggers calls of *chumpas chumpas* among the waiting guides, who swarm on the vehicles as they cross the river. Many tour groups are brought by guides from outside Djenné who are well practiced in the art of deflecting the attention of the guides and tend to have long-standing relationships with one particular guide in Djenné. Once this is found out, the other guides will lose interest and move on to the next group of tourists. Unaccompanied tourists will usually be hounded until they give in to one guide, and any attempts at "going it alone" in Djenné usually fails owing to the guides' sheer perseverance.

Figure 7.2 Impromptu Djembe dance session in Djenné

The creation in 2005 of the *Bureau des Guides* in Djenné was meant to impose a turn-taking structure on the guides and therefore start to diffuse the aggressive competition. One merchant reported that he was outraged after talking to a tourist in his shop who had originally intended to spend three days in Djenné but had decided to leave after only one day owing to the constant pestering of the guides. The Tourist Office, *Mairie*, and the Cultural Mission are all concerned with this problem and are trying to regulate the guides' behaviour through a series of bureaucratic measures.

The guides themselves do, however, have a high level of agency in the negotiations with the Tourist Office, the Cultural Mission, the hotels, and the restaurants. Through being the main point of contact between the locals and the tourists, the guides influence the tourists' choice of hotels, restaurant, and shops. All the artisan shops in Djenné pay the guides a commission on any sale made by the tourists they accompany, as do hotels and restaurants. I was perplexed as to why hotels and restaurants allowed the guides to sit around menacingly in close proximity to the tourists until I realised the full extent of this symbiotic relationship. I witnessed an example of the lengths that hotel managers will go to in order not to offend guides when a tourist bought a *bogolan* cover with the help of a hotel manager as a translator. The manager was very uncomfortable with the request but nevertheless obliged, and the merchant delivered the purchase later on his bicycle. The tourist was surprised that he was not able to carry his purchase back to the hotel himself, but the manager explained to me afterward that if a guide had seen him in the company of a tourist who had bought something with his help they would automatically assume he had taken the commission, something that in their minds was rightfully theirs.

Guides also have access to tourists through means of contact through the Internet and mobile phones and are regarded as having good links with the outside world. Personal relationships between guides and tourists do occur and are often a way to have access (often temporarily, very occasionally permanently) to the resources of the Western world. Although these relationships sometimes reflect reciprocal affection, relationships between young guides and older Western women are the subject of discussion and amusement among the guides.

Some of the older and more established guides have a regular supply of tourists, recommended by their past clients, guidebooks, or travel

Figure 7.3 Hotel Djenné-Djeno on the outskirts of the town; tourists come in search of a particular vision of Djenné

agencies. These guides are usually closely affiliated to a hotel and rarely hang around touting for business. Most of the guides in Djenné are also closely linked to the wider tourist circuit in Mali, sometimes through travel agencies and often through business contacts in other main tourist destinations. In the final analysis, however, the guides are entirely reliant on tourists visiting the town. During the visit of Mali's President, Amadou Toumani Touré, to Djenné in February 2005, one of the guides said to me: "*ATT [Amadou Toumani Touré], je n'en n'ai pas besoin. Mon ATT c'est les touristes*" ("I don't need ATT, my ATT is the tourists").

The guides therefore live in a strange space somewhere in between the tourists and the town, a space that sometimes circumvents local officials and national control. They have a very sophisticated understanding of the tourists and know which nationalities are most likely to be generous (German, English, Chinese) or not (French). The guides have a large insight into the lives and attitudes of the tourists through spending so much time with them, often eating and travelling with them for several days or weeks. Unlike the findings of van Beek (2003) in Dogon Country discussed later, the majority of guides I spoke to wanted to leave Djenné, sometimes to go and live in another West African country but most often to go and live in the West. Life in Djenné did not compare favourably in their minds to life elsewhere.

One of the main difficulties facing guides seems to be their inability to hold on to the wealth they acquire during the tourist season. Bumping into a guide I knew well one day, I listened to him explain that he was in bad financial trouble, because he had not managed to make the money he had anticipated during the tourist season. Consequently, he had had to sell his motorbike (which he originally bought on credit and was still paying off at 30,000 CFA [£30] per month) and also has a monthly debt to a tailor for some clothes he had bought for his wife. He also had to sell his DVD player for money to pay for healthcare. It is perhaps hard to feel sorry for a guide in Djenné who has to relinquish material luxuries such as a motorbike or a DVD player when the majority of the population is extremely poor, but it is symptomatic of a wider phenomenon in Djenné that something is yours for only as long as other demands are not made on it. In the minds of the guides, this situation contrasts sharply with the seeming ease with which tourists acquire and hold on to their material wealth.

OMATHO

The *Office Malienne du Tourisme et de l'Hôtellerie* (OMATHO) office in Djenné first opened its doors to guides and tourists in 2004. The office is situated on a main street and consists of a desk, a few promotional posters of Malian tourism on the walls, and a framed map of Mali leaning against the wall. The man in charge at the time of the office's opening was at first met with some hostility from certain quarters as part of a wider feeling that levels of bureaucracy are brought to Djenné without solving the immediate problems faced by many householders.

The creation of an OMATHO office in Djenné is part of the process of decentralisation. A decision was made that OMATHO should have a permanent presence in the main tourist towns in the country. One of OMATHO's most important everyday roles is looking after tourism locally through being an arbitrator for problems between tourists and guides or hotels. OMATHO is the first port of call for any disputes and has the power to refer them to the authorities for arbitration. Hotels and restaurants need to be registered with OMATHO, and those who fail to do so are issued with warnings until they comply or are shut down. The hotel and restaurant inspections are intended to check basic things such as fire exits and hygiene standards. The attempt to crack down on guides who let people sleep in their homes comes under this same umbrella of measures, since the authorities are worried about food poisoning or accidents that may lead to them being sued. Tourists are seen as powerful, because they have resourceful embassies to back them up.

For this reason, travel companies operating in Mali need to pay 2 million CFA (£2,000) into a trust fund when they first set up business. This fund is then used to pay off any tourist or legal fees arising from disputes. If a company closes, the money is returned. As well as the main tourist tax, tourists pays a second tourist tax for each night spent in Djenné (500 CFA [£0.50] per room per night). This goes to central government to pay for the work of OMATHO.

As part of its drive to standardise the tourist's experience in Djenné, OMATHO is listing all its accredited guides on a website and hopes to set fixed prices for visits, thus allowing tourists to prepare their holiday and have greater control over their time in Mali. A big aim for OMATHO is to be able to negotiate complete tourist access to Djenné's Great Mosque during non-prayer time for people who are appropriately dressed. The suggestion has been made to the mayor in terms of potential income and is still under discussion. (As mentioned earlier, the issue of allowing tourists access to the Mosque was one of the flashpoints in setting off the riot in September 2006. Consequently, any decision to allow tourists to enter the Mosque would be very unpopular with many *Djennenkés* unless they could see visible and immediate economic benefits.)

The OMATHO office also had to collaborate with the Cultural Mission. In some ways, their remits overlap, albeit with different foci. Whereas the Cultural Mission is restricted to undertaking the work of the protection of cultural heritage and sensitisation of local populations, OMATHO is tasked with the promotion of cultural heritage for the purpose of developing the tourist industry. OMATHO's success can be measured in economic terms, whereas the Cultural Mission measures its success in terms of visibility and protection. It was interesting to note than one of the first ideas of OMATHO was to establish a museum in Djenné, an ambition that stepped on the toes of the Cultural Mission, which had been drawing up plans for a museum for years. OMATHO had concrete plans (and budgets) to bring hotels, restaurants, and guides in Djenné in line with its vision. It was also helped by the fact that because its aims were overtly economic OMATHO immediately had the ear of the people it sought to influence.

The Cultural Mission, however, brings money to Djenné in a far more opaque and indirect way and consequently suffers from mistrust of the population. Juxtaposing the stated aims and functions of OMATHO and the Cultural Mission brings to light one of the central problems with UNESCO's World Heritage Project in Djenné. For *Djennenkés* to respond to UNESCO's pleas for restraint vis-à-vis the architecture and archaeology of the town, UNESCO must develop a direct relationship with the population and explicitly show how its vision for the town will benefit the local population. If the Cultural Mission is not tasked with developing tourism, it needs to define itself as a useful contributor to Djenné's economy in some other way. In Djenné, heritage and tourism are inextricably linked. In a chapter entitled "Heritage for People" Howard argues: "Tourism, is to an extent, peripheral to heritage. It is a very important periphery, particularly as regards money, but heritage is conserved first and foremost by people for themselves . . . tourists then come along and want to see it, but no one supposed that if people stopped visiting the Tower of London we would destroy it" (2003: 50).

This argument may ring true for the Great Mosque in Djenné; however, the entire "town as monument" model advocated by UNESCO makes sense only if tourism can provide vital remuneration. In Djenné, tourism is not peripheral to heritage but central to its survival.

The regulation of tourism in Djenné can therefore be broken down into a number of areas. First, it is part of a broader attempt to regulate behaviour and ensure that tourists have a safe and pleasant experience. Second, it is an attempt to regulate what is said by the guides: historical accuracy and standardisation are the two main objectives. Third, it is an exercise in making visible the tourist industry through the issuing of guide badges, the creation of websites, and documentation.

Becoming a Guide in Djenné

In 2003 the Malian Government decided through a vote at the National Assembly to impose a structure on the guide's profession by introducing national exams and a regulatory body. The exams, widely advertised through the media and administered by OMATHO in 2005, were a compulsory requirement for all people in Mali wanting to operate as a tourist guide. For the first time a formal structure was being established that required would-be guides to prove their Malian nationality and identity. The exams, which were held in regional capitals across the country, allowed people to apply to be either regional or national guides. Successful candidates were issued with a guide badge bearing their photographic identification. OMATHO set up a website listing all the official guides. A complaints procedure has been put in place so that a guide will lose his licence if he has three upheld complaints made against him.

The exam was intended to test the guides' knowledge in three areas: health and safety, historical knowledge, and courtesy and behaviour. It was by all reports very straightforward and was arrived at after a series of compromises. The initial intention was for all Malian guides to have a high level of education. At first, the OMATHO wanted guides to have reached a level of *Baccalauréat* + four years of higher education; then this was adjusted down to *Baccalauréat* level; then it was suggested that a *Diplôme d'Études Fondamentales* would suffice (achieved after nine years of education), but this requirement would still have excluded many of the people already operating as guides, such as Dramane. Finally, the national test was devised, and training courses offered, to dispense of any formal educational requirements. However, a few of the Djenné guides still failed the exam, adding to the others in Djenné who either did not turn up on the day of the exam (owing to scepticism about the whole process) or were excluded for not having Malian nationality.

This minority of unlicensed guides became an on-going problem for OMATHO in Djenné in attempting to impose the new legislation. The problem was exacerbated by the fact that the guides closed ranks around those who had failed the test and colluded in helping them to obtain work. The Director of OMATHO in Djenné, himself a former guide in Bamako and generally on good terms with the guides in Djenné, was given clear instructions to report any guide operating without permission to the police. The guides were also required to register their clients at the OMATHO office to allow the Ministry of Tourism to have a clearer idea of the number and provenance of tourists to Djenné. These restrictions led to a number of clashes, arrests, and even short spells in jail for some of the unlicensed guides. As a result, the Director of OMATHO was subjected to physically aggressive behaviour and threats of witchcraft.

The national guide tests encroached on a system of power and self-regulation that was already present in the town. The attempt to exclude the guides who failed the test from the profession was undermined by the guides' solidarity in the face of outside intervention. Despite the often aggressive competition among the guides, the exams were not seen as an opportunity for the majority who passed to exclude the minority who did not. Instead, the guides allowed their former colleagues to work illegally either by turning a blind eye or by working with them and halving the money, to bypass the legislation. (There is a keen awareness in Djenné that taking away a man's livelihood often commits his family to destitution.) Additionally, like other all male groups in Djenné, like the age-groups or *grins*, the guides have a strong sense of identity, reinforced by the use of nicknames (all the guides have a nickname, such as John Travolta, Chirac . . . drawn from an aspect of their appearance, biography, or personality). Before the exams were established, being a guide in Djenné apparently was simply a matter of being recognised as such by the other guides. The guides see a strong distinction between themselves and the young boys and teenagers known as the *petits guides*. However, most of the guides were at some stage *petits guides* themselves. Some of the *petits guides* do attach themselves to older guides in a version of an apprenticeship, or they are the older guides' younger siblings and are therefore tolerated. Before the test, however, there was no official mechanism to prevent tourists using children to guide them around the town, despite posters put up to discourage them from doing so.

A few months after the exams, the guides seemed to be responding proactively to the new interest being shown in their activities. With Dramane as the main instigator, they set up an office—the *Bureau des Guides de Djenné* at the entrance of the town—and they established a turn-taking system to ensure that all the guides worked regularly. The new system also had the effect of reducing some of the aggressive behaviour among the guides competing for tourists. Most of the guides who had failed the exams intended to sit them in the next round, so despite bypassing the new rules temporarily, the new system seemed to have been accepted in principle. By early 2008, however, the *Bureau des Guides* had ceased to operate, and guides were once again fending for themselves.

Papa's Story

Papa is one of the guides in Djenné who did not attend the national test. He was consequently left in a difficult position in which he runs the risk of being fined and imprisoned if he carries on working with his regular clients. In part, he did not make the effort to attend the test because he did not think that he needed to—most of his clients come to Djenné with his name. At the time of the test, he was in Timbuktu with photographers. On his return he went to the testing centre with his documents, but he was too late. Papa feels angry that many of the guides who passed the test are not in his view very good at their jobs. He believes that they do not possess the "art of speaking" in front of clients. He thinks that the history of Djenné is very important and that the test was not hard enough and consequently did not distinguish between good and bad guides. Despite these misgivings, he says he will attend the next national test (although the tests were intended to take place only every five years).

Having not passed the guide test, Papa has to rely on his colleagues to give him a share of the income they make from the tourists he passes on to them. He is finding the situation particularly difficult, because his father has recently died, and he is left with the financial responsibility for the family. Several times Papa was caught illegally accompanying tourists in the town, and once hosting them in his home. After several warnings, he ended up spending a day in jail as punishment. His long-term ambition is to open a hotel, but, like many people in Djenné, he guards his ambitions fiercely, afraid that someone will make trouble for him if he speaks of them publicly.

Papa feels that many people call themselves guides, but to truly be a guide is something deeper. He says that if you put ten guides in Djenné next to one another and ask them the history of the town, not even two of them will tell you the same thing. He says that most of them make up dates, that many of them are illiterate and pick up the bits of information they can from what they hear on the street.

Papa is aware of UNESCO and thinks that it is protecting Djenné's architecture from the outside world. To him, the threat comes from people who have left Djenné for work and who may come back with higher ambitions for their homes. (However, this is contradicted by interviews undertaken with those who have left and returned to Djenné and who tend to be very conservative.) He says that if Djenné's architecture changes, the tourists will stop coming, because they would not come to Djenné to see what they can see at home. Despite feeling positively about the Dutch Housing Restoration project and the new sanitation project, Papa is uncomfortable with the town getting used to outside help; in his words: "If every time we need something we cross our arms and wait, that's not an attractive thing."

Djenné and Multiple Histories

According to Adame Ba Konaré, Malian history is inextricably linked to the country's colonial experience:

> Malian historiography, indeed African historiography, cannot be understood outside the colonial domination from which it came and in relation to which it is defined. French colonialism, in approaching the history of African people, had as its principle objective to transform the barbarous and bloody past of Africans to the current benevolence. (2000: 17)

Konaré goes on to explain that after Independence in 1960, the government launched a programme of pedagogical reform to rehabilitate the heroes of the precolonial state. History therefore became a nationalistic project—"a narrative without objectivity" (Konaré, 2000: 17). A romanticisation of the precolonial period saw past leaders, such as Sunjata and Askia Mohammed, recast as heroes. Konaré judges this as problematic:

> The perpetual agitation of the past and its heroes does not permit us to move forward: rather it leads us to the hardening of positions around values that are undoubtedly shared but which belong to another era. Too much remembering can become an obstacle. (2000: 22)

The guides in Djenné tend to talk about the history of the town through a discussion of its architecture. However, as has been shown by Bourgeois (1987) in relation to the construction of Djenné's three mosques, establishing an accurate history of events is far from straightforward. In fact, as he reveals, the "accepted" history in Djenné hides a series of controversial events, such as the suppression of smaller neighbourhood mosques and the destruction of Djenné's second mosque (built between 1834 and 1836) by deliberate neglect and the blocking of the drains. Negotiating history in Djenné is therefore always a means of imposing a narrative on past events to best suit contemporary purposes.

For Papa, it is important for the credibility of the guides for them to be conversant in the "correct" history of Djenné. However, as will be discussed shortly, the history of Djenné is only one element of tourists' interest in the town. Furthermore, it is hard to establish, from a largely oral tradition, a precise chronology of events. Before the guide tests, many guides did indeed get the facts and dates "wrong"—when checked against travel guides (for French speakers, *Le Guide du Routard Mali, Petit Futé Mali*; for English speakers, *The Rough Guide to West Africa, Lonely Planet Guide to West Africa, The Bradt Travel Guide to Mali*) that become the repositories of "true" knowledge. The guidebooks also had the effect of fixing prices for guided tours of the town, causing some concern to guides who want to have the freedom to negotiate prices themselves.

It is as yet unclear whether or not the guide test has imposed a new uniformity on the guides' discourses. What seemed to be the case at the time the guide test was being implemented is that with reference to historical "facts," tourists trusted their books more than their guides, although the books were written by people who to some extent relied on local guides for their content. From interviews (discussed shortly), it seems that tourists are comfortable with a multivocal approach to the history of Djenné, incorporating oral history, folklore, and their guidebooks. In fact, the guides can go beyond the official narrative of the guidebook to provide an insight into local culture. The imposition of regulated history

Figure 7.4 Blocked storm drain in Djenné

through tests came at same time as other regulations affecting the tourist industry in Djenné, implemented through OMATHO.

Access to Income from Cultural Heritage

The negotiations about the nature of historical knowledge in Djenné and the qualifications needed by guides to talk authoritatively about the past become visible in relation to tourist access to archaeological sites. Currently, guides are unable to take tourists to the protected site of *Djenné-Djeno* without being accompanied by an official guide from the Cultural Mission. This restriction serves two purposes: first, to regulate

7 • GUIDES AND THE REGULATION OF HISTORY IN DJENNÉ   165

access to the site and ensure no further looting and, second, to ensure that the person showing tourists around the site has received adequate training in archaeology and is able to answer the tourists' questions.

This division between the town guides and the guides from the Cultural Mission (who are in fact Cultural Mission employees who derive additional income from their guiding activities) inevitably causes tensions. It serves to further alienate Djenné's population from its archaeological heritage, because the Cultural Mission staff are all from outside Djenné and are therefore not always well assimilated into Djenné's population. A possible solution would be giving interested Djenné guides adequate training, which would allow them to disseminate knowledge about the sites to both tourists and the wider *Djennenké* population. The current division between the guides serves to reinforce existing power structures in the town by placing the professional knowledge of the Cultural Mission in opposition to the lay knowledge of *Djennenkés*.

Although the guides are the most visible part of Djenné's population to benefit from tourism, many other people earn a living from the industry. With the help of the director of OMATHO, we devised a diagram to show the impact of tourism on Djenné (Appendix 4). As well as local people working in the restaurants and hotels in Djenné (cleaning, cooking, serving), some home-grown produce is sold to the hotels by local women.[9] Artisans and local shops benefit as well, as do people working in transport. In fact, although much could be done to improve the distribution of income from tourism, a lot of people in Djenné are already in some way reliant on the industry.

One such person is a drummer named Djakité. He was born and brought up in Djenné and taught himself how to play the drums on a big *Nido* (powdered milk) tin. When he was a teenager, a professional drummer moved to Djenné and took him on as an apprentice. His skill as a performer has allowed him to travel to Vitré in France (a town twinned with Djenné) during a cultural exchange. Although his day job is milling flour, he earns good money from drumming both for *Djennenkés* (10,000 CFA [£10]) for a *Jembe* session and during the tourist season, when he performs at the hotel Chez Baba a couple of times a week.

The Tourist

An exploration of the motivations of tourists who visit Djenné allows a conceptual link to be made between UNESCO's preoccupation with the preservation of the town and the demands of the tourist industry (Joy, 2010). It is assumed that tourists come to Djenné to see its unique architecture and archaeology. Although this may be the case for some, many combine this interest with a search for an emotional authentic experience, a search that is often unsettled by the reality of the town.

Using Urry's definition of the three important dichotomies defining tourist sites, one can characterise Djenné as historical, romantic, and authentic (Urry, 2002: 94). Urry's analysis centres on a Foucauldian concept of an organised and systematised "tourist gaze." Despite the limitations of the concept (addressed by Urry, 2002: 145), its application to Djenné is particularly illuminating. Although Djenné can be seen as the object of a collective (and international) gaze, a tourist travelling to Djenné tends to be seeking the romantic, or individual, experience. In fact, for many tourists, the presence of a large number of other tourists, especially at the Monday market, detracts from their enjoyment of the town. This discomfort with the presence of other tourists can be analysed in different ways.

As well as the many organised tours that stop off in Djenné for a day, many tourists travel in small groups with a guide, and a high number of independent travellers also come to the town. For some independent travellers, such as two young students from Belgium cycling across Mali, the presence of other tourists detracted from their feeling that their travels were an adventure. They described Djenné as "touristy," a negative attribute that encompassed their feeling that there was nothing new to discover. To get around this and have a satisfying "adventurous" experience, they sought out small villages and stayed there overnight, sleeping on floors and eating with families. For them, the liminal phase of their tourist *Rite de Passage* (Cohen, 1988) has to include a physical separation from all forms of familiarity, including language. Their compass throughout their travels was a *Petit Futé* guidebook; however, they rejected the idea of employing a guide in person. Instead, they trusted that through serendipity they would meet people who would welcome them and give them an original or different insight into Malian culture. This required a level of trust that they were aware was risky, for instance, in entrusting their bicycles to strangers or drinking water from unknown sources. The element of "danger" or unscripted adventure was, however, central to their idea of travelling, a fact that became clear in their recounting of their travels in other parts of the world. They conceptualised their time in Djenné as a short interlude on their journey during which they enjoyed meeting other tourists, visiting the town, and drinking beer in the hotels.

The Belgian cyclists' quest for the authentic can be defined by the urge to get off the beaten tourist track and interact with people who are not sensitised to the needs of tourists. Lindholm (2008: 39) describes this behaviour as being motivated by a modern desire for self-realisation and an attempt to gain a heightened sense of who you really are by testing your physical and psychological limits. Lindholm rejects the idea that most tourists are satisfied with a staged or "fake" experience (an idea he says has come from Jean Baudrillard's [1994] *Simulacra and Simulations*) and states that, instead, the concept of authenticity in travel has remarkable resilience.

Another quest for authenticity can be seen through tourists such as Betty, who tend to linger where others move on, thus gaining access to behind-the-scenes experiences. Betty, a woman in her sixties, has travelled alone all over the world. She is of mixed Chinese and French background and stood out owing to her small stature and apparent vulnerability. Unlike many tourists who spend one or two nights in Djenné, Betty spent a few weeks in the town and came to know my host family well. Adopting many strategies of fieldwork, she ensured that she ate with the family and accompanied them in their daily activities. Travelling on a small budget, she also quickly managed to negotiate cheaper accommodation by moving from the tourist quarters to the family's rooms, therefore making a move from the usual "outside" space occupied by tourists to the "inside" intimacy of family living. She insisted that the family refer to her as "grandmother," establishing a symbolic kinship tie and ensuring that she was looked after and included by the family. Betty's presence coincided with Djenné's 2005 *Festival du Djennéry,* and Betty asked me on several occasions whether she should attend the evening performances, phrasing her question in terms of whether what she would see was "authentic."

It seems that in Betty's mind, as in the minds of many other tourists, there are two types of culture: "unmediated culture" (authentic) as opposed to "mediated culture" (monument). Her strategy was to access unmediated culture through literally walking into people's lives and to a certain extent circumventing the tourist structures put in place to guide her trajectory around the county. Unlike the Belgian cyclists, she was not on a quest for an adventure in terms of physical danger and unpredictability but instead sought a meaningful encounter with people from a different culture. This approach was reinforced by the fact that after her departure she kept in touch regularly with the family through postcards, each time signing the card with "grandmother." Like the cyclists, Betty made reference to the *Petit Futé* by carrying with her photocopied pages of the book, which she constantly annotated and edited. The pages provided a reference point and structure around which to understand her experiences and plan her travels. They were her point of entry into the culture, although by photocopying them and annotating them with comments and suggestions made by the people around her, she managed to personalise them and to a certain extent visually distance herself from the many tourists who conspicuously carried their guidebooks with them. Her quest for authenticity was not based around a desire for historical or cultural accuracy in the Festival performances she witnessed but instead lay in the desire for an emotional authenticity that seemed to be at the heart of her impulse to constantly travel around the world. As noted by Selwyn commenting on MacCannell's seminal work *The Tourist*: "If we agree with MacCannell and others that tourists seek the authentic, we need to add that such authenticity has two aspects, one of which has to do with feeling, the other with knowledge" (Selwyn, 1996: 7). And as MacCannell remarks: "The touristic critique of tourism is based on a desire to go beyond the other 'mere' tourists to a more profound appreciation of society and culture. . . . All tourists desire this deeper involvement with society and culture to some degree; it is a basic component of their motivation to travel" (MacCannell, 1973: 10).

As the guides' understanding of tourists' expectations has become more sophisticated, the number of tourist locations in Djenné has increased from the traditional route (the tomb of *Tapama Djennépo* [the sacrificed virgin], the Holy Well *Nana Wangara*, the house of the *Chef du Village*) to take in more unexpected sights, often brought about by tourists' questions and interests. These include local schools, people's homes, agricultural practices, visiting the fishermen by the river, and taking part in local sporting activities. Consequently, "knowledge" about Djenné is, for many tourists, much less about facts and figures but more about a certain intimacy, taken to extremes by Betty.

Tourists therefore have the power to enfranchise certain parts of Djenné's population, who have found themselves excluded by an elitist and archival reading of their heritage. Such enfranchisement has been the case for some of the women artisans in Djenné, who have organised a cooperative space to sell their work, and for women working in the gardens, who benefit materially from showing tourists around. However, these "excursions into the ordinary" are possible only because of the wider framing of Djenné as a World Heritage site and one of the top three tourist destinations in the country.

The Mali Circuit

Almost all the tourists I spoke to in Djenné were undertaking in some form the traditional Mali tourist circuit of Bamako, Ségou, Djenné, Mopti, Dogon Country and Timbuktu. These places are widely acknowledged by the tour companies and travel guides as the places to visit in order to successfully "do" Mali. The completion of the circuit is especially important as many tourists will only make one visit to the country in their lifetimes. Other tourist destination such as the Northern town of Gao (home to the World Heritage site of the *Tomb of the Askias*) are starting to change some tourist circuits but only peripherally as the North of Mali remains both physically inaccessible due to the road running out and considered by some foreign governments as dangerous owing to the perceived threat from AQIM.

Unlike the cyclists or Betty, for whom the guides are the ugly face of tourism that emphasises the self-consciousness and staged experience of being a tourist, most tourists visit Mali through the mediation of a guide. However, many of Betty's attitudes can be perceived in diluted forms in tourists' discourse and expectations. For example, tour companies often employ a national guide who will accompany the tourists throughout their journey around the country (usually ten days to two weeks) as well as local guides on an ad hoc basis in towns such as Djenné. The additional use of local guides reassures the tourists that they are gaining access to "authentic" or inside knowledge about a place. Local guides can also ensure that tourists gain access, if only temporarily, to inside spaces such as houses and rooftops. The guides in Djenné tend to include a degree of personal narrative in their descriptions of the town, and the tourists are reassured by the lively way in which they or their guide are received in the different spaces they move through around the town. The indigenous guide can also share information about a place in a conspiratorial way with the tourists and become the embodiment of the annotated comments about a destination.

The majority of the tourists visiting Mali come from a Western rationalist tradition that is often at odds with many of the synchretic and superstitious beliefs found among their hosts. The tourists therefore tend to adopt a different persona for the duration of their time in the country. Examining the element of role play present in many tourist encounters, Urry (2002: 98) describes how tourists taking part in organised package tours "play" at being a child by letting all the arrangements relating to their daily needs be taken over by the tour company. Similarly, tourists in Mali have to some extent to entrust their daily needs to the guides, especially in the Dogon Country, where the guides provide an interesting contrast with the guides in Djenné.

Van Beek's (2003) description of tourism in Dogon Country is contrasted with tourism in Northern Cameroon. His argument is that whereas in Dogon Country the encounter between tourists and local people is largely positive and reinforces Dogon feelings of cultural pride, among the Kapsiki of Northern Cameroon the tourist encounter engenders negative feelings among local people about their own self-worth and reinforces their desire to leave. He accounts for this by saying that it is the prime interest of the tourist that has consequences for how the host culture defines itself within the tourist encounter. In Dogon Country, tourists primarily come to experience Dogon village life (dances, architecture, animistic beliefs), thus reinforcing Dogon pride. In Northern Cameroon, by contrast, tourists come to see the stunning scenery and to a certain extent avoid too much contact with the villages by keeping to certain defined tourist areas. This marginalisation of the local population reinforces feelings of inferiority in contrast to the tourists' perceived wealth and prestige.

Van Beek states that each tourist encounter creates its own subculture. In Dogon country, the tourists (many of whom have come from or are shortly about to go to Djenné via Mopti) enter an extraordinary

Figure 7.5 Dogon Country

world of villages perched on cliff tops, stunning views, and stories of the mythical ancestors who used to inhabit the escarpment, the Tellem, who are believed to have had magical powers, such as the ability to fly. Van Beek describes the attitudes of the Dogon guides toward tourists:

> The setting of the cliff villages is for them a backdrop to what is valued most, the cultural performances. The physical and cultural attraction of their country is not a source of wonder but a self-evident fact. Dogon view the relation with their visitors as more or less permanent, and on the whole are prudent not to rupture it: they should give value for money. (Van Beek, 2003: 269)

For the tourist, the experience of visiting Dogon Country is largely escapist, as one is lulled by rhythm of walking through ever-changing scenery punctuated by stops in villages and taking photographs from vantage points. During my two visits to Dogon Country in 2004/2005, the guides described their services not only as pathfinders but also in terms of cultural mediation, nearer to the role of "mentor" described by McGrath in her analysis of guides working in Peru (McGrath, 2005). They recounted warning tales of foolhardy tourists who had tried to explore the area alone only to run into difficulty. In particular, the guides explained that a tourist would not have the necessary cultural knowledge to know which parts of villages to avoid, and so they would inevitably cause offence.

A story I heard several times told of a Scandinavian family who unwittingly strayed into a sacred part of a village and had to pay reparations to the village *Hogon* (priest) in the form of a black cow and a black chicken. The guides in Dogon Country therefore know themselves to be indispensable on two levels: first, as physical guides, showing a path through the vast countryside, finding food, water, and accommodation every night; second, as cultural guides, negotiating access to villages and masked dance performances and steering tourists away from tabooed areas. The stories told by the guides of the flying Tellem ancestors blend in with the radical feeling of *dépaysement* experienced by the tourists who spend their nights climbing up Dogon ladders to sleep under the stars and awake to the sight of stereotypical African villages punctuated by Baobab trees and surrounded by spectacular scenery.

By contrast, in Djenné the guides have a harder job of selling their services. Many tourists feel that they can explore the town alone, as they would a European city, armed with their guidebook and rudimentary map. In the end, unaccompanied tourists tend to accept a guide to avoid constant pestering more than through a desire for a cultural commentary. The precariousness of the guides' position in some part explains their aggressive behaviour. In Djenné, a guide sells his services very much on the basis of accessing inside knowledge, not in terms of regulating behaviour or physical safety. Tourists who have come to Djenné from Dogon Country will often be exhausted and want to use their time in Djenné as a relaxing interlude before starting their journey to Timbuktu, or back to Bamako via Ségou. Like Dogon guides, Djenné guides are very aware of providing value for money (usually assessed in terms of hours spent with the tourists) and will be disappointed if a tourist does not want to take them up on their offer of visiting an outlying village or *Djenné-Djeno*, the archaeological site.

In Djenné, more so than in Dogon Country, there is an issue with the accuracy of the guides' historical knowledge—tourists may have a keen interest in vernacular architecture or the archaeological sites. The skills required from guides in Djenné therefore differ somewhat from guides in Dogon Country. The guide test, however, licensed guides based on the regions of Mali, and so a Djenné guide will have a *Region de Mopti* license and be allowed to be a guide in Djenné, Dogon Country, and Mopti. A minority of guides in Djenné passed the test to become a *Guide National*, thus allowing them to accompany tourists anywhere in the country.

The role-playing stance adopted by tourists visiting Djenné allows them to overlook the historical and factual discrepancies in the guides' discourses. Many of the tourists who visit Djenné are highly educated and will have researched the active interests they may have in Djenné's history, archaeology, or architecture. What they are looking for from the guides is therefore often not the "hard" facts that they can look up in their guidebooks or on the Internet but the "soft" facts, or the "art of speaking" described by Papa. A good guide in Djenné can reveal exciting trajectories through the town and introduce people to different experiences, such as the women's gardens on the outskirts of the town or a jeweller's workshop.

In Djenné the collective gaze and the individual gaze are somewhat at odds as people seek a personal authentic experience while being confronted by the presence of numerous other tourists. As discussed, some tourists find strategies to navigate this tension, while others are content with a tour-guide approach to their visit. Although OMATHO Director in Bamako is keen to promote "cultural tourism" in Mali, an examination of some of the discourses of tourists coming to Djenné reveals a number of motivations, more or less catered to by the present tourism industry. OMATHO sees its role as one of regulation, promotion, and standardisation. The desire to draw up a predictable "tourist calendar," in which key cultural events such as the remudding of Djenné's Mosque and the annual transhumance of the cattle are highlighted, would for some remove the joy of serendipitous discoveries. Similarly, banning guides from allowing tourists to stay in people's homes in

Djenné (*chez l'habitant*), although enacted for legitimate health and safety reasons, can also be a disappointment for tourists seeking an "authentic" experience. This authentic experience is for many rooted in an image of Mali as a preindustrial society, where symbols of modernity are an intrusion and should be as much as possible airbrushed out. Within this context, regulation of guides' discourses and the tourist experience is not necessarily a desirable thing.

Cultural tourism in Mali is being transformed by the international rise in the popularity of Malian photography and music. Amadou and Mariam's internationally acclaimed album *Un Dimanche à Bamako* is one of many symbols of a new Malian modernity, embraced by international travellers and expatriates alike. Music festivals in Mali, described in the next chapter, can house a broad Malian identity, at once being rooted in authenticity and tradition (for example, Salif Keita is a modern day *griot*) while at the same time dealing with present conflicts (for instance, the Festival in the Desert and the Tuareg Rebellion). The "culture" sought by tourists can therefore be highly personal and may even change throughout their time visiting the country.

It is hard to say whether the architecture of Djenné and the consequent lifestyle of its residents denote for tourists a "performative primitive" (MacCannell, 1992: 26). From interviews with tourists, it seems that their understanding of Djenné is much more sophisticated than simple acceptance of the UNESCO or guidebook rhetoric. People repeatedly reported an uneasiness or anxiety about what was being asked of the town: to remain materially the same in order to retain World Heritage Status. When asked explicitly about the viability of such a project, the majority of tourists interviewed said that it was untenable, and at some point in the future UNESCO would have to rethink its World Heritage project in Djenné. Many found the idea of imposing architectural restrictions on people patronising and wrong, while appreciating that it was in large part the architecture that drew them to Djenné. All the tourists I spoke to seemed keen to take part in what could be described as the "UNESCO debate" in Djenné.

UNESCO and Tourism

The symbiosis between tourism and UNESCO is not as straightforward as it may appear. Although tourists do tend to visit Mali's three main World Heritage sites, and they are the focus of the government's OMATHO efforts, tourists do not do so solely because UNESCO has brought them to their attention. For example, the *Tomb of the Askias* in Gao has not yet been included in many of the tourist circuits. Beck (2006) has found that although World Heritage can act as an international top brand or "collectible set" for tourists, it is unclear without further research how aware people are that the places they visit are World Heritage sites. Furthermore, she states that the reliability with which travel guides identify a destination as a World Heritage site is very variable depending on the publisher. I would argue that tourists' awareness of Djenné's World Heritage status is quite high owing to the discourse around the protection of the architecture. However, if UNESCO had ignored Djenné, its Great Mosque, being the biggest mud-brick structure in the world, may well still have attracted similar numbers of tourists to the town over the years.

Particularly for a relatively unfamiliar tourist destination such as Mali, there is a strong correlation between "must see" places and World Heritage sites. However, Timbuktu, Djenné, and Dogon Country were well known to tourists before their listings, and their identities cannot be reduced to their World Heritage status. For example, people would continue to go to Timbuktu (if present security problems allowed) owing to the renown of its name, with or without the endorsement of UNESCO. Perhaps a study of visitor numbers to the recently declared Tomb of the Askias and the Intangible Masterpiece of the *Yaaral* and *Degal* (declared in 2006) would allow a more accurate assessment of the effect on tourist numbers.

Tourism in Mali is heavily reliant on infrastructure and repetition, especially before 2005, when most guides did not possess mobile phones. A regular tourist circuit allowed tour companies and guides to negotiate preferential and predictable food and accommodation arrangements and meet up with friends and family at prearranged times and places. Speaking with the male Director of a tour company in Bamako, I was told that Djenné was included in nearly all his circuits, because its non-inclusion would arouse suspicion among tourists. In his view, Djenné is *une belle femme sale* ("a beautiful dirty woman"). He would prefer not to take his tourists there but is worried about its omission. He compromises by going to Djenné on Monday mornings and then leaving to stay overnight in Mopti or nearby Sevaré, where the hotels are more suited to European tastes. In some ways, he is dealing with a paradox central to the tourist gaze—the fact that what people gaze upon are often idealised versions of the reality, before and after the event:

> What people "gaze upon" are ideal representations of the view in question that they internalize from postcards and guidebooks (and TV programmes and the internet). And even when the object fails to live up to its representation it is the latter which will stay in people's minds, as what they have really "seen." (Urry, 2002: 78)

By spending only a day in Djenné tourists can capture their experiences, often through photography, while mentally (and literally) airbrushing out the lack of sanitation, the poverty, and the begging children. Some tourists explicitly come to Djenné for its photogenic potential. One tourist whose hobby is photography told me that it was very difficult to take photographs in Djenné without elements such as electric wires spoiling the view. The only time he felt that the wires did not detract from his photographs was during the Monday market when there is such a mix of colours, shapes, and movement that the wires blend in. The man, who is a French expatriate living in Benin and was travelling through Mali with his wife and two young children, was at once bemoaning the fact that Djenné has been spoiled by electrification while being very aware of the poor living conditions of people around him.

Similarly, UNESCO can be accused of suffering from a highly romanticised "gaze" in relation to Djenné. In an interview with the head of the African Division of the World Heritage Centre in 2005, I brought up the subject of loosening some of the restrictions imposed on Djenné to allow for limited development. I was told that this was unthinkable. Reaching for a postcard that showed an aerial view of Djenné clearly surrounded by water, he told me that it was the "architectural integrity" of Djenné that made it a World Heritage site. No part of that architecture could be changed without threatening the whole. It is attitudes such as this that have led dissenting voices within the town to ask for UNESCO representatives to come to Djenné and listen to their concerns. In November 2010 a UNESCO delegation did indeed hold a three-day meeting in Djenné, covering issues raised in the management plan and future projects such as the restoration of the *Maison des Jeunes*.

Conclusion

Tourist visits to Djenné are motivated by many different factors. In some ways, World Heritage status has had the effect of reducing Mali for tourists to a few "must see" locations on a circuit around the country. The Malian government's recent attempt to regulate the tourism industry further focuses the tourist gaze away from the general toward more uniform discourse and forms of hosting. However, tourists go beyond this analysis of what is and is not of interest and seek to go farther than the material heritage on display by finding strategies to access intangible or "emotional" heritage. This may be corporeal, for example, tourists playing football with children on the outskirts of town, or linguistic, through unstructured dialogue with people who take them beyond the usual tourist narrative. In part these strategies are strategies of distinction and accruing cultural capital (Bourdieu, 1984), but they are also about the emotional need of the tourist to gain complicity with their hosts.
Moreover, this desire for complicity is not one sided, since many people

in Djenné look on tourists as potential links to the outside world and are therefore very keen to cultivate friendships with them.

Unfortunately, the long-term relationship between tourists and *Djennenkés* is often one of broken promises—tourists forget to send the promised photographs, letters, and gifts once they have re-entered their real worlds. Some do send gifts and aid to people in the town, with mixed results. For example, the T-shirt making business venture between the Japanese tourist and the guide floundered owing to a lack of communication and trust. The guide wanted start-up money, and the Japanese tourist wanted a business plan (which the guide was unable to produce) before committing any funds.

Accurate historical knowledge in Djenné is being demanded of the guides for the benefit of an outside audience, the tourists. Regulating history in Djenné is part of a wider government programme to improve the country's tourism industry and to make it come into line with other such industries found throughout the world. It is assumed that tourists have certain standards and expectations that must be met and that the best way to do so is to as much as possible reflect back to them the image of a place they already have in their minds. An accurate historical discourse is seen as important in lending credibility to their experiences. However, as has been discussed, the credibility sought by tourists may have more to do with emotional authenticity than facts or figures.

In some ways the historical knowledge demanded of the guides can be juxtaposed with their lay knowledge of the town. Discussing the work of guides in Cusco, McGrath (2005) identifies three types of guides who act as bridges between the tourist, the local people, and the site: the official guides who have degrees in tourism or archaeology, the college-level guides who put more emphasis on the social aspect of visitor management and communication, and the indigenous guides who have had no formal training but are sometimes employed by tour companies to give local insights to tourist visits. In Djenné the guides are a mix of all these things. The Cultural Mission guides who accompany the tourists to the archaeological sites are also asked to accompany important visitors and dignitaries around Djenné in favour of the city guides. This is because they are more closely associated with McGrath's first category: the official guide. However, knowledge in Djenné is not just a matter of education or historical accuracy. An indigenous guide may be able to provide tourists with more insights about life in Djenné than his Cultural Mission counterpart and in doing so, impart the kind of emotional knowledge sought by the tourist. The boundaries of what constitutes an understanding of cultural heritage in Djenné need to be widened to include an understanding of the lives, past and present, of the people who give the town its life.

7 • GUIDES AND THE REGULATION OF HISTORY IN DJENNÉ

The *Festival du Djennéry*, discussed in the next chapter, is a case study of how the heritage elite in Djenné came together to plan and run a cultural festival. It brought to light not only the tensions between the various factions in the town but also their assumptions about the expectations of tourists. First and foremost the *Festival du Djennéry* was devised as an opportunity to raise money from outside funding bodies for the promotion of cultural heritage to paying tourists.

CHAPTER 8

Festival du Djennéry

The *Festival du Djennéry* held in February 2005 presented itself as an opportunity to work with a small group of people on the preparation and execution of a cultural festival in Djenné. I had previously come across many of the organisers in relation to other parts of my research, many of whom I had identified as belonging to the "heritage elite." They joined others whom I had not previously met, who worked for the *Mairie* and were consequently part of the political elite of Djenné. I was particularly interested in becoming involved, because this festival was to be the first one to be held in Djenné (apart from a small-scale event organised by *Djenné Patrimoine* in 2002 to celebrate the new year[1]). It gave me an opportunity to see how the festival was being conceptualised and executed from beginning to end. It also allowed me to measure the impact on the local community, note participation, and examine networks of communication about cultural heritage. And it was most interesting that the festival brought together all the different factions within Djenné's heritage landscape, described in the previous chapters. Additionally, the festival provided me with a case study of the kind of intangible heritage of increasing interest to UNESCO ("festivals" is one of the subcategories within the *Masterpieces of Oral and Intangible Heritage*).

When I first heard, through Ousmane the embroiderer, that there was going to be a festival, I intended to find out as much as I could about it through interviews with organisers and festivalgoers. However, after attending a few open meetings, I was asked to join the festival committee as part of the communication team, which allowed me to gain access to all the negotiations and compromises first hand. Gradually, I became more involved as more tasks were delegated to me. The difficulty with joining the festival committee was trying to keep some distance from events. At times, I had to give my (what they saw as Western) point of view, and I was forced to take sides on certain debates (for example, the entry price) while shying away from getting involved in others (filming permits, discussed later). The experience ended up being a constant negotiation between my personal involvement in the festival and a desire for it to succeed, while maintaining friendships with those who saw themselves as excluded or aggrieved by its preparation.

Becoming a festival committee member did cause certain problems, because I was inevitably identified with the committee's work. Asking me to join the committee was not a big departure from protocol, since the precedence of Peace Corps volunteers getting involved in projects was established long ago in Djenné. In fact, a Peace Corps volunteer was also part of the 2005 committee, because he was at the time working on the town's sanitation project. In the end, I decided that because the festival was of such direct relevance to my research I should participate. People also knew that I was interested in the subject for my research, so my presence was expected. However, with hindsight, one of the major drawbacks of participation was the fact that the festival turned out to be surrounded by accusations of corruption.

The organisation of the *Festival du Djennéry* began in December 2004, when a few people got together with the intention of holding the event the following February. Although it was at first put forward as a nonpolitical activity, it soon became apparent that the newly elected members of the *Mairie* were behind the project. A number of people connected to the previous administration refused to have anything to do with the festival, and some even tried to put a stop to it. It is interesting to note that in 2005 the *Mairie's* role in the festival was played down, and even hidden. In 2006, by contrast, the *Mairie* was happy to identify itself as the organiser of the festival. As was the case for the sanitation project, the political dimension of the festival became clear to me only with the passage of time.

Although behind the scenes the festival was being conceptualised by the organisers as primarily an economic activity, it was presented to the general public as a not-for-profit venture, a trial run for what was intended to be Djenné's big celebration, the 2006 *Festival du Djennéry,* which would mark the 100th anniversary of the building of the Great Mosque. Looking back on events, it is easy to see that people became involved with the festival to make money, not least because most negotiations in the meetings revolved around money. However, as discussed shortly, the negotiations, although clearly about money in the final analysis, were also about how the money would facilitate the presentation of cultural heritage through clothes, hairstyles, performance, and craftsmanship. There was genuine enthusiasm and excitement on behalf of the participants, because as well as presenting performances for live audiences, the festival was going to be broadcast on national television (see Schultz, 2007, for a discussion of the success of cultural heritage programmes on Malian television). It is therefore difficult to untangle economic motivation from other forms of motivation. The exchange of money in some guise had become so much a part of every activity I undertook in Djenné that it had almost become invisible to me.

The committee members undoubtedly worked hard, and at times, especially as the deadline approached, people pulled together and worked well beyond their specific duties. However, at the end of the festival, we found out that a significant proportion of the money raised was unaccounted for. This left some of the performers and employees unpaid and was a great source of shame for those of us on the committee who had loaned the festival credibility through our involvement. The deception came to light gradually, and it was only when a festival was proposed for 2006, nine months after the first event, that explicit reference was made in public meetings to the unacceptable behaviour surrounding the 2005 festival. My close involvement with the 2005 festival presented me with first-hand experience of the kind of corruption allegations I had heard associated with most of the other heritage projects coming to Djenné. It led me to conclude that the reason that accusations of corruption were of such significance to me was that they symbolised a different kind of "hidden" knowledge operating at the heart of all negotiations about cultural heritage in Djenné.

This hidden (some would say pragmatic) knowledge is, on the one hand, about being able to make claims on behalf of a community one identifies strongly with while, on the other hand, keeping the reality of one's life, and the financial demands made on one, at the forefront of one's mind. What confused me was the apparent sincerity and pride with which people turned the idea of a festival into reality, while it seemed that some were deriving illicit economic gain from it. In this context, cultural heritage, like any other project in the town seeking funds from the outside, is a temporary resource. Although the money raised came in the name of all the residents in Djenné, it apparently did not always find its way into the hands of those it was intended for.

Festivals in Mali

On its website, the *Ministère de la Culture du Mali* lists sixty-nine festivals and cultural celebrations supported by the Ministry in 2004. They vary in size from small-scale local events to international festivals such as *Essakane*. *Essakane* is widely known internationally as the Festival in the Desert. Officially starting in 2001, a largely Tuareg annual musical gathering has become a world renowned meeting point for world music fans. Its popularity is helped by the fact that it is difficult to get to. (It was held in the town of Essakane, about 65 kilometres northwest of Timbuktu, until 2010, when it started to be held just outside Timbuktu, owing to security concerns.) Therefore, it retains some of the credentials of "authenticity" (Lindholm, 2008: 48) much prized by those attending. However, perhaps paradoxically, the festival has become famous through commercialisation owing to the presence of international singers such as Ry Cooder and Robert Plant. This commercialisation has greatly raised the profile of Tuareg bands such as *Tinariwen*, which has achieved international cult status and now regularly plays alongside Western mainstream bands at concerts throughout the world. According to their website:

> The Tinariwen story is already well marinated in startling myths; fierce nomadic desert tribesmen toting guns and guitars, Ghadaffi's poet-soldiers spreading their gospel of freedom throughout the world, turbaned rock'n'roll troubadours, Stratocaster on one shoulder, Kalashnikov on the other, 17 bullet wounds and rawest desert blues on earth.[2]

Unlike other festivals in Mali, The Festival in the Desert gets wide media coverage in the international press (for example, *Vanity Fair*, July 2007 issue), because it combines music-star glamour, romantic images of turbaned men riding through the desert, and the slightly dangerous edge, and current affairs credentials, of the aftermath of the 1996 violent conflicts involving the Tuareg and the Malian Government. UNESCO has taken an interest in *Essakane* and in 2006 gave their support to the event through the Artists in Development programme funded by the Norwegian Ministry of Foreign Affairs. The intention is to professionalise the organisers of the festival through a twinning programme with European specialists. The long-term aim of the programme is the development of sustainable tourism as the basis for economic growth in Mali. However, as described in the introduction to this book, this sustainable development is threatened by increasing security concerns and stark travel advisories issued by Western governments, which have led the organisation committee to secure the presence of the Malian President at the 2011 Festival to help to dispel fears.

A second festival in Mali, which is increasingly gaining international attention, is the *Festival sur le Niger* held in Ségou. In 2003 Lebanese, German, French, and Malian hotel and restaurant owners formed an association named *L'Association des Hôteliers et Restaurateurs pour le Tourisme à Ségou* (AHRTS). They used their expertise and international contacts to launch a very successful music and cultural festival, attracting big name performers such as the singer Salif Keita. In 2005 they had also found the funds to build a dedicated walled-off festival area on the banks of the river (in traditional Ségouvian mud-brick architectural style) and a large floating stage. The organisers were successful in attracting a high number of Malian ministers, whose presence lent an element of gravitas to the proceedings (owing to their official vehicles and armed guards).

In contrast to the *Festival du Djennéry*, the *Festival sur le Niger* in 2005 had taken a year of careful planning. Despite involving local people, the festival team was dominated by European and Lebanese hotel owners, all experts in local tourism. They had also successfully recruited unpaid students from France to help to run the festival. The success of the Ségou Festival has assured its organisers a regular economic return, and since 2005 every hotel in Ségou has been fully booked for the duration of the festival (in fact, tour companies block book the hotels up to a year in advance). Additionally, the *Festival sur le Niger* ensures its profit by successfully charging Western prices for entry, 100 Euros per non-Malian visitor for a three-day pass.[3]

The widespread media coverage in Mali of festivals such as *Essakane* and the *Festival sur le Niger* undoubtedly had a catalysing effect on the people organising the *Festival du Djennéry*. Before the decision to hold a festival in 2005, the idea of a festival was increasingly seen by groups such as the Cultural Mission, *Djenné Patrimoine*, and the *Mairie* as desirable. During the festival preparations, a few disgruntled people from the previous mayor's administration tried to put a stop to it with the justification that it had originally been their idea. This was, however, dismissed by everyone on the committee who did not consider the idea of a festival as something a person (or administration) could own. Because there was no precedent for such an event (apart from the event organised by *Djenné Patrimoine*), the shape and content of the *Festival du Djénnery* emerged gradually, until in its final form it became a hybrid of local performance, the sale of *artisanat,* and the annual celebration of the *crépissage* of the Mosque as the central event.

Whose Festival?

The first festival meeting was called in December 2004. Some preliminary negotiations must have taken place behind the scenes, since there was no debate as to who the president would be, and he immediately took his place at the desk at the front of the meeting room, whereas everyone else sat in the audience. The president not only worked for the *Mairie* but is also a member of a powerful *Grande Famille* in Djenné. The meetings were held in the *Maison du Peuple* and at first were open to all. Later, they moved to a smaller office, and the people present were there as members of the festival committee or by invitation. The proceedings opened with a proposal to hold the festival February 19–25, 2005. Many people in the audience were sceptical that everything needed for a festival could be achieved in such a small amount of time. It also emerged that there was very little money already in place (2 million CFA [£2,000]) and that the first priority of the committee would be to raise funds (an estimated 12 million CFA [£12,000], was quoted as a budget).

After some negotiation, it was agreed that the president and his assistant would go to Bamako to hand out "letters of support" (*lettres de soutient*) soliciting money. A further meeting would be needed to identify the people who were going to be targeted by the letters. Next, the different committees were named. Committees were established for: sanitation, *artisanat*, exhibit and events, communication, accommodation, security, and transport. Each committee was then free to appoint additional members and delegate tasks.

During all the subsequent festival meetings, although issues surrounding budgets were always contentious, a consensus over the content of the festival was very quickly achieved. Without any discussion, the title of the *Festival du Djennéry* was adopted, which refers to the town of Djenné and its surrounding villages. Each night a different ethnic group would perform: Bambara, Bozo, and Peul. There was also to be a Hunter Night and a *Djennenké* Night, when a few women from each women's association in Djenné were chosen to perform. With the exception of the *Djennenké* and Hunter Nights, the performers were invited from surrounding villages.

The villages that surround Djenné tend to be mono-ethnic and in fact are referred to in such terms to tourists: *Sénoussa, le village Peul* (Sénoussa, the Peul village); *Sirimou, le village Bozo* (Sirimou, the Bozo village). I was struck by the fact that the festival was conceptualised as a *Djennéry* affair and not a Djenné Festival. All the ethnic groups chosen to perform are adequately represented in Djenné, but the performers were invited from the outlying villages. Moreover, the villages seemed to be regarded by the committee as interchangeable, so when Sirimou was uncooperative financially, they were simply replaced by performers from another Bozo village, Djéra. I was never given an explicit explanation as to why the festival was a *Djennéry* affair, although, as discussed before, the concept of *Djennéry* has deep historical roots. Additionally, the *troupes de danses* (dancers) from different villages are famous in Djenné. Djenné in a UNESCO-bounded sense therefore perhaps does not exist in *Djennenkés'* minds.

From the outset, the festival both reflected and challenged my perceptions of what constituted cultural heritage in Djenné. It was intended for an outside audience (tourists) as well as for *Djennenkés*. The parameters of the festival were taken from similar ones found throughout Mali: an evening event and some daytime activity, revolving mostly around the work of artisans and an exhibition. The festival was also going to have an opening ceremony, in which dignitaries would be invited to participate, and a closing ceremony that would include a prize giving. In the initial stages, the organisers hoped to include a conference during the festival with the title *Djenné: Ville classée Patrimoine Mondial, quel avenir?* ("Djenné: A World Heritage Site, What Future?"). The conference was going to be organised by *Djenné Patrimoine*, who wanted to invite Malian scholars to put forward their views on the Djenné's cultural heritage. There was, however, neither the time nor the budget to realise it.

During the festival meetings, it became clear that the initiators of the festival thought that the festival, as well as providing long-term economic gain, could be used as an opportunity to carry out work in Djenné that most people believed should be paid for by the *Mairie* (through the money raised by the tourist tax). Three examples of this work were (1) restoring the *Tribune* in Djenné, to be used during the opening ceremony; (2) a cleaning project covering the whole of Djenné, employing local women's associations; and (3) restoring the Djenné Archway, lying derelict at the entrance of the town. This banco archway had fallen down sometime in the second half of 2004. It had been built by the masons of Djenné and was intended to welcome people coming into the town, a symbol of the town's great architecture.[4] It was erected near the Cultural Mission and was the pride of the masons who built it, the guides who pointed it out to tourists, and many *Djennenkés*. However, when it came down to a negotiation of who would pay for its repair, people were quick to disassociate themselves from it. The festival committee believed that the archway should be back in place by the time the festival began. However, first the *Mairie*, then the Cultural Mission, followed by the masons all declared that they did not have a budget to pay for it. The committee took a decision that any profit from the festival could be put toward this good cause. However, there was no money left over, and the archway was simply reabsorbed into its surroundings.

Negotiations Concerning the *crépissage* of the Great Mosque

The festival committee understood that to attract funding the festival had to refer to the importance of Djenné's cultural heritage and the pride that the festival would instil in the town. A particular event that in many ways embodies such pride is the annual *crépissage* (remudding) of the Great Mosque. Consequently, it was decided that the festival would have to coincide with the *crépissage*. This turned out to be the single most contentious issue between the population and the committee during the festival.

According to the *Chef du Village*, traditionally the *crépissage* of the Mosque took place over a period of a month, at times decided on by *quartiers* elders in conjunction with local authorities. More recently, the Mosque has been divided up into sections, with each *quartier* responsible for one section, and this approach has allowed the whole process of *crépissage* to take only a matter of days. Each *quartier* now elects one young man and woman to lead their peers. The young woman is responsible for coordinating the collection of water for the mud and organising the food and the music. The young man is responsible for organising the preparation of the mud and the actual work on the Mosque. Before 2005 the *crépissage* usually happened after the tourist season, in late March or April, depending on the river level. During the festival, however, the *crépissage* needed to take place on the February 25 to fit with the festival calendar.

The *crépissage* was undoubtedly the major attraction for tourists at the festival (previously a date had never been set for the event so far in

Figure 8.1 *Chef de Quartier* meeting held to decide on the date for the *crépissage* of the Mosque

advance, and so tourists would have seen it only through serendipity). However, negotiations about the exact date of the *crépissage* brought to light tensions about who or what ultimately decides when it should take place: the Imam, the *Chef du Village*, the Cultural Mission, the mayor, the *quartiers* elders, or climatic conditions. Behind the scenes, difficult discussions took place between the Cultural Mission, the Imam, the *Chef du Village*, and the *quartiers* elders, and money changed hands to convince the *quartiers* elders to cooperate. In part, their cooperation was due to the fact that since 2002, 1 million CFA (£1,000) has been given each year toward the *crépissage* by the Cultural Mission. Before 2002 money had been given informally to different *quartiers* elders. However, now the 1 million CFA was being given directly to the *Chef du Village*, and he distributes it as he sees fit.

Despite the initial tensions, the date, Friday February 25, was finally agreed on. A *quartier* meeting on the eve of the *crépissage* was filmed as part of the documentary of the festival made by an ORTM (*Office de Radiodiffusion Télévision du Mali*) television crew. The meeting consisted of about thirty elderly men sitting on mats outside some houses, each making a declaration of support accompanied by a small (now perhaps mostly symbolic) donation. One man wrote each donation down into a notebook. After each man spoke, a younger man dressed in dark blue would repeat it loudly. After a while young men gathered around, and I was told that the old men were giving formal notice to the young men, whose responsibility it was to make sure the *crépissage* was a success.

Owing to the water level at the time of the *crépissage* in 2005, holes were dug near the river's edge to speed up the process of fermenting the mud. On the eve of the *crépissage* young boys began to make the journey from the river to the front of the Mosque to deposit the mud. Old men traditionally gather in the Mosque on the morning of the *crépissage* to ensure the success of the event. These old wise men (known as *Albada*) have a special ritual role to play by helping the young men to assemble the ladders they use to climb the Mosque. They use secret knowledge to ensure that the ladders don't fall down and that no harm comes to the masons working on the Mosque.

The actual event of the *crépissage* starts at daybreak, and it is a matter of only hours. Young men from the different *quartiers* approach the Mosque with music and flags to ensure their presence is noticed. Once they have erected their ladders, the men work together, with younger boys passing up the mud to older, experienced masons.[5] The smaller boys are kept busy mixing the mud with their feet and working on the lowest parts of the Mosque. Each *crépissage* is also an opportunity to renew the sand inside the Mosque.

Figure 8.2 Young boy bringing mud for the *crépissage*

Setting the date for the *crépissage* of the Mosque was part of a wider attempt to bring Djenné's biggest cultural asset into line with the needs of tourism. As discussed previously, OMATHO has for a long time been trying to negotiate tourist entrance to the Mosque, which has been officially *Interdit aux non-Musulmans* (forbidden to non-Muslims) since an incident involving disrespectful behaviour of white people inside the Mosque in the 1980s. In this case, "non-Muslim" is most often understood as being synonymous with white people.[6]

At the time of the negotiations around setting the date for the *crépissage* of the Mosque, it struck me that I had never been inside the building despite walking past it repeatedly every day. My view of the Mosque remains therefore completely external; I can only imagine the inside from the photographs and descriptions I have seen. In fact, I had long since ceased imagining the inside, because to me, in common with many tourists visiting Djenné, the Mosque is only a façade. Yet the feelings and conceptions of *Djennenkés* toward their Mosque as they walk past are radically different. They can recreate the inside while being on the outside. It does not strike *Djennenkés* as contradictory that a monument that has been declared part of the World Heritage of humanity can be apprehended by a big part of that humanity only superficially. The tension between World Heritage and local heritage is therefore constantly present in Djenné, whether in reference to its houses, access to its archaeological sites, or even the hospitality of its monuments.

Organising the Festival

Attracting media interest in the festival was seen as a priority. Two televisions crew were invited to the festival, the first from the Malian national television channel (ORTM) and the second from the *Centre de Services de Production Audiovisuelle* (CESPA). The ORTM team that was sent had won an award for a documentary about the *Essakane* festival near Timbuktu the previous year. CESPA is a UNDP-funded initiative to train people in Mali in the use of audiovisual equipment and to help to support development through education. Despite the need to raise the profile of the festival through television and radio advertising across the country, in 2005 the total advertising and media budget in place was only 115,000 CFA (£115), although to be able to do its job adequately the communication committee believed it needed 2 million CFA (£2,000).

The choice of people and organisations approached to solicit money through "letters of support" was an insight into the way money is seen to flow into the town. The list was arrived at after a brainstorming session involving the whole festival committee. It was made up of a number of international donors already present in Djenné, as well as businesses and local and national organisations concerned with cultural heritage.

In the first few weeks a few responses arrived. The department of *Patrimoine Culturel National* wrote back saying that they had no money with which to help, as did the Dutch government, who expressed support for the idea of the festival but stated they had already given money through the Cultural Mission. The European Union wrote back saying it was too late in their budgetary calendar for them to be able to contribute. Negative responses also came from UNESCO and the Canadian government. *Ikatel* (the mobile telephone company) and *Nestle* were approached as potential sponsors, and *Ikatel* responded positively. OMATHO released 500,000 CFA (£500) to show their support, and the *Association des Ressortissants de Djenné* (a network of *Djennenkés* living away from the town) gave 725,000 CFA (£725). The *Conseil de Cercle* gave 50,000 CFA (£50), the *Mairie* gave 250,000 CFA (£250), and the president's office 500,000 CFA (£500).

However, after initial regular communication about the success of the fundraising effort in the first few weeks of the festival organisation, there was suddenly a lack of communication from the festival treasurer. This was timed with increasing hostility among some of the committee members toward what they saw as excessive expenses during the two fundraising trips to Bamako (735,000 CFA [£735] was claimed for two people for two five-day trips to Bamako).

Despite repeated attempts on behalf of the committee to get the treasurer to provide receipts for expenses or donations, she simply refused to attend meetings. On the one occasion when she did, she claimed to feel victimised by the vicious rumours she had heard and left after only a few minutes. It was therefore impossible to gain an accurate picture of the financial success of the fundraising, since no receipts were available for the majority of the donations. In the end, after a few people on the committee got in touch with some of the donors directly (and calculated the difference between the declared amounts and amounts the donors claimed they had given), it was estimated that approximately a third to half of the money raised was unaccounted for. The festival consequently officially made a loss,[7] and many people were left unpaid, including the *troupes de danse* from the villages, the women who had been employed as hostesses throughout the festival, the women responsible for cleaning, the ticket sellers, those responsible for lighting, and the advertising by *Radio Jamana*. No formal complaint was made against anyone on the committee, and therefore no clear conclusions can be drawn about exactly what went on during the fundraising process. Many accusations were made off the record, but no one was prepared to directly confront people with questions. It was only when the next festival meeting was held that it seemed widely accepted that corruption had taken place and should be put behind everyone in order to move forward with the 2006 festival.

Through their international networks, the guides were identified as key to mobilising tourists. However, from the outset there was tension between Dramane, who was acting as the guides' representative on the committee, and a few other committee members. Dramane believed that he had a good understanding of the expectation of tourists, and he wanted the festival to be more focussed on their needs. But some of the committee organisers saw the tourists primarily as sources of income and wanted to extract the maximum amount of profit from them in the short window of opportunity represented by the festival. One particularly contentious issue was the setting of the entry price for tickets. The Cultural Mission, who explicitly claimed to be "heritage professionals," wanted to charge a flat fee of 15,000 CFA (£15, to be collected as tourists entered Djenné) for a four-day pass regardless of how long a tourist was in Djenné. The pass would allow a tourist entry into all the evening activities. Dramane and a few other people on the committee argued that it would be more appropriate to have two prices: the four-day pass price and 3,000 CFA (£3) for a ticket to a single evening event (sold at the box office).

In the end, the Cultural Mission was convinced to change its mind, because most people on the committee realised that tourists coming to Djenné rarely spend more than a day in the town. In the end, less than twenty 15,000 CFA passes were sold; the majority of the seventy or so tourists paying to attend[8] the festival chose to buy individual tickets for events. Additionally, the tourists present for the *crépissage* did not necessarily also attend the festival activities. A similar discussion took place when it came to setting the *Djennenké* entry price: the Cultural Mission pushed for the tickets to cost 500 CFA (£0.50) each but were finally convinced that *Djennenkés* could not be expected to pay more than 200 CFA (£0.20). The decision meant that the evening activities were well attended by *Djennenkés.*

On the third day of the festival, a disagreement arose between the guides and the Cultural Mission that led to a few guides boycotting the festival performances with their tourists for the rest of the week. The argument arose from the issue of filming permits. During the evening performance (Bozo night) a few tourists who were filming the event were told by one of the employees' from the Cultural Mission that they were not allowed to film unless they bought a permit. Incensed and embarrassed by this, the accompanying guide had a very heated discussion with the Cultural Mission employee, nearly ending in a physical fight. Finally, the then-Director of the Cultural Mission stopped proceedings to take the microphone at the front of the stage and announce that while photography was permitted, filming was not allowed without a permit.

On the following day, an extraordinary meeting of the festival committee was called to discuss filming permits. To avoid the expected confrontations during the meeting, I chose not to attend. Despite many people on the committee arguing against permits (since tourists would have already paid once to attend the events), the Cultural Mission got their way, and filming permits were printed at 13,000 CFA (£13) each. Not a single permit was sold.

These events were of interest to me, because they were further evidence of a cultural heritage hierarchy at work within Djenné. First, the ex-Director of the Cultural Mission had legitimacy through being an agent of the state but also from being a powerful man politically in his own right. He also presented himself as an expert on the value of cultural heritage and its commodification. The guides, however, while actually having quite a sophisticated understanding of the tourists coming to Djenné do not have the power or the legitimacy to influence the Cultural Mission. The director of OMATHO and the director of the local radio station *Radio Jamana,* while both opposing the filming permits and being committee members themselves, did not intervene in the Cultural Mission's decision. Like the former director of the Cultural Mission, they were both agents of the state and came from outside Djenné; however, they lacked personal political power to gain any influence over decisions.

The majority of the difficulties encountered by the committee in the preparation of the festival were solved through the promise of future money, with a small amount paid in advance. Infrastructural problems, such as transport (for example, getting the dancers from *Kwakourou,* which is 45 kilometres away with no road and very few cars in Djenné) and sanitation (at the time the sanitation project had only just begun) were dealt with as well as possible given the resources available. Financial negotiations with performers always ended in a compromise. For example, the women's association representative (head of the CAFO in Djenné, *Coordination des Associations et ONG Féminines du Mali*) wanted the committee to provide the money for the clothing and hairdressing of ninety women for the Djenné night. They were convinced to cut the number down to twenty-seven, three per *quartier* in Djenné (although there was a lot of discussion about whether Djenné really has nine or eleven *quartiers,* depending on how they are counted—in the end it was decided that there were ten). However, there are twenty-eight women's associations in Djenné, and all needed to be represented. Finally, the decision of whom to choose was given to the head of CAFO, who was also a committee member. Similarly, the leader of the hunters in Djenné accepted to cut their costs from 500,000 CFA (£500) to 100,000 CFA (£100). The performers were therefore all making an effort in the understanding that the committee was operating with a very small budget. They were, however, assured that they would share in any eventual profit made by the festival.

Despite having been a committee member myself and having had first-hand access to many of the conversations, both formal and informal, during the festival's preparations, I was left feeling that I hadn't really fully grasped what had gone on behind the scenes, and the experience made me aware of the very great limitations of my local knowledge—perhaps because internally in Djenné people have a very sophisticated understanding of political, economic, and cultural hierarchies and can adapt this understanding to fit a range of situations. Although the *Festival du Djennéry* was an original event, people had been rehearsing their relative positions toward one another in every encounter they had had over the preceding years. Changes that occur in the political landscape in Djenné—such as the arrival of the Cultural Mission, decentralisation, the rise of wealth of *marabouts* or *guides,* and the new status of the masons through their international fame—all serve to recalibrate the existing relationships. They do not, however, seem to fundamentally alter the power base of the *Grandes Familles,* who manage to be very well represented politically (for example, *Chef du Village,* Imam) and now seek to benefit economically from cultural heritage projects coming to the town. Festivals such as *Essakane* and the *Festival sur le Niger* served to highlight the economic potential of festivals to Djenné's heritage elite.

Those people on the outside who did not have control over significant budgets (such as the director of OMATHO and the head of *Radio Jamana*) appeared to be powerless during the festival committee discussions. Power in Djenné is therefore twofold: old power derived from family membership facilitating access to positions of influence, and new power, which can be financial or political but is generated through national political links or access to significant international budgets. The direction the population's anger took during the 2006 riot toward old established positions of power as well as new brokers of wealth in the town (such as the Cultural Mission) therefore comes as no surprise.

The Opening Ceremony

The opening ceremony was a mix of politics and the celebration of Djenné's cultural heritage. Chairs were set out on the raised platform in the main square (*tribune*), and a large tarpaulin provided shade for the invited dignitaries. A banner had been made declaring the opening of the *Festival du Djennéry 2005*. Drumming was followed by the parading of a group of ten women, each representative of one of the *quartiers* in Djenné. The women were elaborately dressed in white *bazin* (wax cloth), with hairstyles and jewellery revealing their ethnic affiliation (see Schulz, 2007, for a discussion of the negotiation between traditional dress and women's identities in Mali).

After the women's parade, the audience stood up for the arrival of the *Chef du Village*. In fact, many of the invited dignitaries similarly made entrances throughout the opening ceremony. Speeches were made on behalf of the Cultural Mission, by the *Préfet*, the Imam, the *sous-Préfets*, the mayor, and the festival president. Representatives from the Ministry of Culture and the Ministry of Artisanat and Tourism were present, although no ministers actually came to Djenné until the day of the *crépissage,* when the then-Minister of Culture made an appearance, going as far as applying some mud to the Mosque.

In his speech, the festival president told the story of *Tapama Djennépo,* and, at the mention of her name, everyone in the crowd cheered. He concluded his speech with the words: "We wish everyone a good stay in Djenné the religious, Djenné the mysterious, cradle of ancient human civilization and the pride of humanity. Long live the Djenné Festival, a prosperous Mali, and a united Africa.'"

Later, the ten women were once again presented to the crowd in a form of beauty pageant with a little explanation given as to their dress and ethnicity. When it was the turn of Fatimata Djennépo, who is regarded in Djenné as a descendent of *Tapama*, the *Chef du Village* rose from his seat and joined her centre stage. He raised her arm in the air to great cheers from the crowd and stood by her side clapping as she danced.

At the end of the ceremony a brand new police car was formally presented to the mayor by a government representative from Bamako. The car was a symbolic gift to Djenné from the President of Mali. It seems that the car had been promised long ago and that the occasion of the festival was chosen as a fitting event at which to formally hand it over.

Soirées Culturelles

The *Soirées Culturelles* were held in the *Maison des Jeunes* (a venue traditionally used for plays, musical events, and talent shows in Djenné). A small budget of 50,000 CFA (£50) was found to clean and paint the stage. The first night was the *Nuit des Marionettes* ("puppet theatre night"), representing the Bambara culture. The performers came from a village named *Diabolo* and were paid 100,000 CFA (£100) in expenses. Owing to the secrecy of the preparations for their performance, they asked for a high walled area near the stage in which to prepare, so a makeshift corridor was hastily assembled to protect their privacy. Despite efforts at getting the evening started on time and the successful preparation of the venue (chairs, lighting, hostesses), there were major technical difficulties every night with the sound system owing to problems with the electricity supply.

A few themes emerged from the evenings that were of particular note. First, *Djennenkés* tended to favour the performances in which their own ethnic group was represented, so the Peul night was mostly frequented by Peuls, the Bozo night by Bozos, and so on. The Djenné night, on which representatives from all the women's associations took part, was a unifying event and was the best attended by *Djennenkés*. It also seemed to be the most interactive, with women from the audience spontaneously joining in on stage. Many of the women had their youngest children with them on stage and simply handed them to one of their neighbours when they felt it was their turn to dance. During the Djenné night, the stage acted less as a barrier between the performers and the audience than it seemed to on other nights.

The most "professional" night was said by all (tourists and *Djennenkés* alike) to be the Bambara night (see Arnoldi, 1988, for a discussion of the organisation and meaning of Bamana puppet theatre). This was in part due to the strength of their performance but also to their attitude toward the event. After the night's performances they went out *en brousse* ("into the countryside") to spend the night going over the parts of their performance they believed still needed improving. The Hunter Night was poorly attended by both *Djennenkés* and tourists. This could have been because of the technical difficulties, which meant it started very late, but was also because of the very loud noises (repeated gunshots) during the performance that many *Djennenkés* disliked. UNESCO has turned its attention to hunters' music and in 2004 launched a programme entitled "Support for safeguarding traditional music of hunters in Mali" with the aim of publishing an audio CD as well as getting involved in local activities of identification, safeguarding, and promotion. However, nobody I spoke to in Djenné was aware of UNESCO's activities in relation to traditional music.

As Arnoldi points out in reference to the youth festivals held in Mali, all the performances during the *Festival du Djennéry* were limited and standardised by the time constraints that were imposed by the festival program and by the stage setting (Arnoldi, 2006: 58). It was very clear to tourists attending the events that the performances were not adapted specifically for the stage and in fact would have probably have been more enjoyable to them (and felt more "authentic") had they been experienced in their original village settings.

The Exhibition Hall

The festival committee spent 500,000 CFA (£500) on turning the old OPAM (*Office des Produits Agricoles du Mali*) building in Djenné temporarily into *la Salle des Expositions* (the exhibition hall). After much negotiation, each artisan was charged 2,500 CFA (£2.50) for a space in the hall for the duration of the festival.

The *Salle des Expositions* was declared open at the end of the opening ceremony, and immediately a big crush of people attempted to get through the entrance gates. The hall was divided into the front section for the artisans and the outside space at the back, which housed the Cultural Mission exhibition. The artisans came not only from Djenné but also from all over Mali and as far as Burkina Faso and the Ivory Coast. This situation led *Djenné Patrimoine* to complain that a *Festival du Djennéry* should be showcasing the talent of Djenné artisans and to bemoan the fact that ubiquitous Malian tourist art was for sale. However, the artisans were financially successful owing to the high number of tourists present and the fact that they were all grouped together in one place (without having to pay the guides a commission). *Djennenkés* also visited the artisans enthusiastically but tended to buy little, because they would be able to source the products (for example, jewellery) more cheaply from local kinship networks.

The Cultural Mission exhibition made up of photos, explanation panels, and replica models of houses on loan from the Cultural Mission museum was a great success, especially with *Djennenkés*. The photographs, showing local masons at work, were appealing, because they immediately provided people with familiar discussion points. The Cultural Mission is aware of the appeal of their collections; they mounted a photographic exhibition between December 1996 and March 1997 that was seen by an estimated 4,000 *Djennenkés*. The exhibition hall therefore made a very strong case for the permanent presence in Djenné of an artisan's hall and a museum in Djenné with photographic exhibitions for all *Djennenkés* to enjoy.

Conclusion

The suspicions of corruption during the 2005 festival were of particular interest to me. First, they shed light on the reasons why cultural heritage in Djenné has become so contentious. Second, corruption in the domain of cultural heritage is complicated analytically by the discourses of pride and identity that accompany it. In the final analysis, the *Festival du Djennéry* was primarily an economic resource (like *Essakane* or the Ségou Festival); however, it was put forward as a not-for-profit venture. Whereas *Essakane* is an international music festival, the *Festival du Djennéry* was an intimately local affair, put together on a local budget using people's personal contacts and limited resources.

Figure 8.3 Exhibition put on by the Cultural Mission at the Djenné Festival in 2005

While somewhat expecting corruption to accompany international projects coming to Djenné with large budgets and little local knowledge, I assumed that a locally organised festival would have its own internal checks and balances (and perhaps it did). Compared to abstract funding from abroad, a significant proportion of the money raised for the festival was from personal sources (for example *L'Association des Ressortissants de Djenné, Djenné Patrimoine*, Jean-Louis Bourgeois).

Working as a member of the festival committee therefore further revealed to me the sources of official and unofficial power in Djenné. It also strengthened my feeling that the promotion of cultural heritage in Djenné often reinforces divisions between those people in society who can legitimately mobilise money for its promotion and those for whom the money is intended (directly and indirectly) and who remain disenfranchised from the whole process.

Throughout the festival, issues of authenticity were raised only by tourists and *Djenné Patrimoine*. Tourists repeatedly asked me (as an anthropologist) whether what they were seeing was authentic. The answer is perhaps that the festival was an authentic representation of how cultural heritage is performed and negotiated in Djenné today. While elements of the festival, such as the *soirées culturelles,* took place with very little input from the festival committee, they were performed on stage in front of tourists and filmed for a national television audience. Cultural activities during the festival were altered and influenced by financial intervention (such as setting the date for the *crépissage*); however, this situation in fact represents a form of continuity, although the balance of power has shifted from the *quartiers elders* to the Cultural Mission and the *Chef du Village*.

The *Festival du Djennéry* took place within the wider framing of Djenné's identity as a World Heritage site. The letters soliciting money for the festival all made mention of the importance of Djenné's cultural heritage and the future *crépissage* of the Great Mosque in 2006, which would mark its one hundredth anniversary. However, owing to the controversy accompanying the 2005 festival, the 2006 festival was a scaled-down and largely insignificant event, since many of the people who had previously been committee members refused to participate. Therefore, at certain times, there seems to be a tipping point when the power imbalances within Djenné are no longer tolerated. Although the 2006 riot is officially played down as being the result of the activities of a few troublemakers (unsurprisingly, the guides, who occupy a difficult space between the town and the outside), I would suggest that it represented a time in Djenné when local political struggles had reached another tipping point, and the violence that erupted was a message from those disenfranchised from the wealth coming to Djenné in the name of its cultural heritage to those repeatedly profiting from it.

CHAPTER 9

Conclusion

On its website, UNESCO showcases a short film about Djenné entitled *Enchanting Town of Mud*. As the camera winds down narrow streets, the narrator talks about Djenné's architecture and declares that "a unique way of life still exists in Djenné today."[1] Whereas previously UNESCO did not think of its work in Africa as development work, a change of mood has taken place within the organisation, as was witnessed through the institution's 2010 resolution on Culture and Development calling for sustainable development through the promotion of cultural capital.

However, the term *sustainable* in Djenné has multiple meanings. For many *Djennenkés*, trying to achieve sustainability through the practice of rendering the outside of their houses with fired clay tiles, their focus is on maintaining the originally intended purpose of the house as shelter. For organisations such as *Djenné Patrimoine*, who are concerned with authenticity and preserving the knowledge of the masons, sustainability would be achieved through a flourishing *barey-ton* and the revival of old techniques, such as the use of *Djenné-Ferey* bricks. Until recently, UNESCO would consider their project in Djenné as sustainable if they could enforce the rule that no material changes are to be made to the town's buildings.

Intangible heritage—for example, the work of the artisans—is sustainable if it continues to find a client audience, thus ensuring its relevance to subsequent generations of artisans.

In terms of cultural transmission, the recent creation of UNESCO's programme of Living Human Treasures,[2] which has seen the declaration and protection of people considered to be in possession of a high degree of cultural knowledge, is an additional step away from the material toward the human actors that give the tangible/intangible heritage its meaning. Within UNESCO, a new focus on intangible heritage and "heritage landscapes" has allowed the organisation to go beyond Eurocentric conceptions of the primacy of tangible (built) heritage. A discussion of this position can be found in the Getty Conservation Institute's edited volume entitled *Historical and Philosophical Issues in the Conservation of Cultural Heritage* (Price et al., 1996). The volume brings together historical writings from some of the most influential Western thinkers on the value of cultural heritage—for example, John Ruskin (1849: 42):

> When we build, let us think that we build forever. Let it not be for present delight, nor for present use alone; let it be such work as our descendents will thank us for, and let us think, as we lay stone on stone, that a time is to come when those stones will be held sacred because our hands have touched them . . . it is their lasting witness against men, in their quiet contrast with the transitional character of all things.

For Ruskin, therefore, great buildings, like the stones from which they are made, are the only tangible "witnesses of history." Alois Riegl (1903), in his famous essay "The Modern Cult of Monuments," sets out an analytical framework with which to measure age value, historical value, commemorative value, and use value of monuments or works of art.

The age value can be perceived through outward signs of decay and incompleteness and contrasts strongly with newly completed pristine works. The work of art or monument is considered organic and suffers the same fate of disintegration as nature imposes on everything else. Age value is therefore radically undermined by outside interference to halt the decay or sudden violent destruction. Age value is considered by Riegl to be universal and to be comprehensible to everyone, whatever their background or level of education.

A second value, historical value, is the value the monument has as a representative of human creation at a particular time (for example, Djenné, a medieval town). It therefore loses historical value through decay, since it is in its completeness that it can best be understood. To preserve historical value, the most accurate documentation possible must be made of the monument for future generations. Although somewhat in opposition, age value and historical value are never truly separable, since it is through the categorisation of historical value (Renaissance, Baroque, and so on) that we perceive age value. Commemorative value links both age value and historical value with the demands of the present. UNESCO's World Heritage project can be thought of as being in this category: "Deliberate commemorative value simply makes claims for immortality, an eternal present, an unceasing state of becoming. The disintegrating forces of nature, which work against the fulfillment of this claim, must therefore be fought ardently, their effects paralyzed again and again" (Riegl, 1903: 78). UNESCO's World Heritage in Danger list and the World Monuments Fund's *Watch List of 100 Most Endangered Sites* are both examples of this constant battle for immortality.

Finally, the use value of a monument refers to the fact that a monument must be kept in a suitable condition to accommodate those within it and not endanger their lives or their health. Use value is indifferent to the other types of value as long as the monument's existence is not threatened (for example, the use of fired clay tiles in Djenné to ensure the houses do not fall down during the rainy season). Riegl therefore provides an analytical framework with which to think about the competing claims made on the buildings in Djenné. From the *Djennenkés'* perspective, the use value of their homes is primary. From UNESCO's perspective the commemorative value (outstanding universal value) of Djenné's architecture and archaeology is of utmost importance. This is not to say that each position is mutually exclusive, simply that different motivating factors are at work.

UNESCO's World Heritage project in Djenné is faced with two great challenges. First, there has been a failure in communication. While UNESCO officials maintain that they work only indirectly with World Heritage sites, through the mediation of the state parties (in this case, the Malian government), people in Djenné want a direct relationship with the organisation; whether this is possible in practice remains to be seen. For many of the reasons discussed throughout this book, there is mistrust between *Djennenkés* and the Cultural Mission, and it is unclear to many *Djennenkés* whether the Cultural Mission is there as a representative of the State or of UNESCO. For *Djennenkés* to connect with the town's World Heritage identity, they need to have far more positive experiences with cultural heritage projects. Second, UNESCO is reviewing its position toward the management of historical urban landscapes (see the *Mémorandum de Vienne*, adopted by UNESCO in 2005[3]). A new focus on the amelioration of people's quality of life through cultural heritage projects is changing UNESCO's discussions with state parties and the design and implementation of management plans of World Heritage Sites.

UNESCO's recent focus on intangible heritage is conceptually useful, since perhaps Djenné's architectural heritage could be constructively conceived of as intangible cultural heritage—because it is the regular process of *crépissage* that maintains the buildings as viable structures. During an informal interview in 2005, the Director of the Intangible Heritage section at UNESCO spoke about the protection and transmission of cultural heritage through "enabling spaces,"[4] meaning the promotion of the structures that surround the cultural heritage. In this instance, it is not possible to preserve "the thing in itself" without supporting the social and economic structures that make it possible. The recent focus of heritage projects in Djenné (such as the Dutch Housing Restoration project) on the *barey-ton* and the transmission of their embodied knowledge is a step in the right direction. As a discussion of the artisans' practice in Djenné has shown, cultural knowledge is a dynamic force, invested with potency and innovation through transmission. However, this focus is still limited by the fact that it leaves out the inhabitants of the houses. When they do make choices—for example, choosing to cover their houses in clay tiles—they are considered ill informed, and their actions are seen as a threat to the integrity of Djenné's cultural heritage.

The use value of the houses in Djenné must be considered separately from their historic value. A consideration of use value alone would reveal a problem with sanitation, space, ventilation, and light. New practical measures must be developed to help those householders failing to meet the regular demands of upkeep on their homes. A vision of Djenné as intangible cultural heritage could also perhaps help break down the divide between the heritage elite and the rest of Djenné's population. If the use value of the buildings becomes the primary focus, then an understanding of the lives of the people within the buildings becomes a priority.

The Lessons from Intangible Heritage

UNESCO's approach to the protection of intangible cultural heritage still operates broadly within a eurocentric conceptualisation of archivisation and transmission. However, by coming to an understanding that it is impossible to protect "the thing in itself" without a thorough appreciation of the "enabling context," officials at UNESCO are taking a big step toward heritage policy that better encompasses the needs of those for whom cultural heritage is also their daily economic responsibility. The case of Djenné is unique not only because of the conditions of extreme poverty encountered in the town but also because it poses a deeper moral question: what standards of living are universally acceptable? If, as many architects assert (Malian and non-Malian alike), living in mud-brick houses in Djenné is the best possible adaptation for people given their current circumstances, how can one accommodate the dissenting voices in the town? Should one dismiss the views of those *Djennenkés* who would

9 • CONCLUSION

like to "improve" their homes by using new materials and changing their layout and appearance?

In his discussion of the controversy over the preservation of the historic town of Rethemnos in Crete, Herzfeld (1991) documents how many of the residents in the old town resent the state's intervention in decisions over the upkeep of their homes. Too poor to be able to move to the new town, they must abide by the state's vision of historical Rethemnos. Many of the richer residents are able to procure a spacious home in the new town while keeping their links with the old town through the ownership of houses let to tourists. Herzfeld therefore demonstrates how "monumental time" in Rethemnos is prescribed by the state and how those living within the old town are often powerless to assert their rights to modernity (1991: 6–7):

> Soon, people are talking about history in monumental terms, and the awareness of social time—a time defined by both formal relationships and daily interactions—appears to slip away. . . . Monumental time is calibrated in well-defined periods. The bureaucratic measure of history, it is no less *managed* than social time, and its proprieties are no less contingent on access to sources of power; but it has the power to conceal the props of its management and to insist on the rightness of its results.

In Djenné, there is not yet a new town for disgruntled residents to move to (although despite restrictions some homes are being built on the outskirts of Djenné). There is a view expressed by some masons that a "third" Djenné will eventually emerge, and, just as in the move from Djenné-Djeno to present-day Djenné, many residents will decide to move to the more spacious and unregulated land outside the town. This view has to be heavily counterbalanced by the fact that homes on the outskirts of Djenné are often occupied by newcomers and consequently have a lower status than those homes found in the historic parts of the town. Although some older *Djennenkés* may envisage building a home on the outskirts of Djenné for their sons, none of them seemed able to envisage such a move for themselves.

UNESCO's work with intangible cultural heritage is again useful at this point, because it is through the recognition that intangible cultural heritage is something dynamic, efficacious, and transmitted from one generation to the next that questions can be asked about the appropriateness of trying to conceptually remove tangible cultural heritage from its social context for protection purposes. Throughout my fieldwork, it became clear that people's homes were primarily talked about by their inhabitants as "places": specific locations within a distinct *quartier* in the town, bounded by other familiar families, landmarks, and predictable events (such as the daily return of the cattle, call to prayer, noises from the women's market). Asked to describe their favourite location in the town, the overwhelming majority of residents answered that it was their *quartier* (although some older respondents chose the Mosque). Individual houses in Djenné are therefore part of the rich fabric of the town and have acquired their meaning through their individual biographies; they cannot usefully be considered as "monuments" in a reifying sense for *Djennenkés*.

Democratising Heritage

The "voices of heritage" that are heard coming out of Djenné are those of the heritage elite, and to a large extent they reflect Western heritage organisations' preconceived views of what is and isn't important in the town. These elite voices have international credibility through being conversant in the "Authorised Heritage Discourse" (Smith, 2006). In her study of Stonehenge, Bender (1998) reveals that labelling anything as *heritage* is a deeply political act. Similarly, Western heritage organisations are acting politically when they work in Africa and can inadvertently reinforce existing power imbalances within societies. There needs to be a democratisation of cultural heritage within Djenné and a validation of everyone's knowledge, whether it be that of a mason, a mother living through her first rainy season with a newborn baby, or a man struggling to pay for the upkeep on the home he has inherited from his father. As Rowlands and Butler have commented in reference to the current situation in Liberia: "Instead of privileging a dominant heritage, we need a mosaic approach that considers each identity as having an equal knowledge of the other and a tolerance for its place. A pious hope perhaps, since such heritage pluralism assumes that resources available to each are similar in content and form" (2007: 2).

All the different forms of "knowledge" about Djenné's cultural heritage are inextricably linked. However, the case study of the *Festival du Djennéry* shows that although its realisation was dependent on many people's participation, the presentation of Djenné's cultural heritage to the outside world is channelled through existing power structures within the town. Outside intervention does in some cases alter the balance of power (for example, money from the Cultural Mission for the *crépissage* of the Great Mosque); however, long-standing political and economic structures in Djenné are resilient to change.

Djenné's Future

As in most other parts of the world, older *Djennenkés* remember a "golden age" when the town was richer and water more plentiful. The increasing

9 • CONCLUSION

tourism in the town together with the arrival of satellite television, mobile phones, DVD players, the Internet, motorbikes, and all the other accoutrements of modernity have certainly radically changed Djenné over the last twenty years. This shift has left many older *Djennenkés* concerned with the behaviour of the younger *Djennenkés* (such as the guides). It is clear that certain events, such as the building of the water tower, have had an immediate transformative effect on the town (through at once freeing women from their daily chore of getting water from the river while at the same time causing an acute problem with the accumulation of waste water). However, it is very hard to accurately assess UNESCO's effect on the town since 1988. I would suggest that the inclusion of Djenné on UNESCO's World Heritage List in 1988 has had a gradual cumulative effect, and only now, in the particular political, economic, and climatic conditions the town is finding itself in, are many of the underlying tensions resulting from its classification finding a voice. Conversely, these tensions seem to be caused as much by wealth as by poverty, more particularly by the emergence of a widening gap between rich and poor in the town. Conspicuous signs of wealth (for example, the Imam has three cars, the Cultural Mission staff have use of a car and a driver) cause resentment and distrust among the wider population. It is interesting to note that the guides, who are also often conspicuous consumers of status symbols such as mobile phones and motorbikes, do not seem to attract the same degree of hostility from other *Djennenkés*. Instead, as discussed, they are often looked down on owing to their involvement in non-Islamic behaviour and their lack of education.

Of most use to further contextualise events in Djenné such as the 2006 riot would be an historical analysis of how the status of political factions in Djenné (*Chef du Village*, *Grandes Familles*, Imam) has changed over the years. Then, the influence of newer factions, or factions that have changed in status owing to decentralisation—such as the *Préfet*, mayor, and the Cultural Mission—could be better understood. As the situation currently stands, Djenné's World Heritage Status is apparently seen positively by all the "heritage elite" in Djenné, with perhaps the exception of the Imam and his followers, who would put more emphasis on Djenné's Islamic rather than architectural identity. It is hard to come to a definitive conclusion about the feeling of the majority of *Djennenkés* toward their World Heritage status, because many of them have very limited information on the subject and are therefore not in a position to judge the long-term economic benefits of the classification. What does seem to be the case is that very practical economic factors are at the heart of any judgement about UNESCO classification. "Softer" benefits such as prestige are secondary considerations, owing to the severe economic and climatic conditions found in the town.

Djenné seems to be in need of a more democratic discourse about its cultural heritage. As UNESCO states in "Our Creative Diversity": "Finally, freedom is central to culture, and in particular the freedom to decide what we have reason to value, and what lives we have reason to seek. One of the most basic needs is to be left free to define our own basic needs" (World Commission on Culture and Development 1996: 4).

Owing to its World Heritage Status, one of *Djennenkés'* most basic needs, the need for shelter, is being defined by officials outside the town. The question therefore needs to be asked: on what scale is freedom being talked about? Is it the freedom of the individual? A majority voice within the town? The National Government? An international organisation such as UNESCO claiming to act for the good of the heritage of 'humanity'? Would declassifying Djenné allow *Djennenkés* a greater degree of freedom?

Although declassifying Djenné does not seem likely in the near future, especially in light of UNESCO's recent investment in a new management plan for the town, Djenné could still potentially lose its World Heritage status if more and more houses are covered in tiles, drastically changing the town's appearance. I suggest that a more constructive approach would be to open up a dialogue between UNESCO, the National Government, and *Djennenkés*, wherein the original classification criteria could be rethought in light of the new economic and social conditions faced by people today.

At the same time, an essential part of the democratisation of cultural heritage could be established by finding mechanisms through which to redirect the income from heritage tourism into the local economy. An obvious starting point would be the ring-fencing of the tourist tax to pay for local initiatives such as planting, fishing, and herding cooperatives. Despite alleged local corruption, heritage organisation could make greater transparency a condition of working in the town.

In terms of education, the archaeological objects found at Djenné-Djeno, some of which are now on display in the National Museum, could become part of a travelling exhibition to Djenné (physically or through the medium of photographs). Guides in Djenné should positively be encouraged to find out more about Djenné-Djeno so that they might pass on their knowledge to others in the town. UNESCO's concept of World Heritage could be communicated to people in Djenné through an exhibition of photographs of other World Heritage sites found throughout the world. This measure would at least give *Djennenkés* the impression that UNESCO was willing to enter into a conversation with them about the wider meaning of the town's identity and create a sense of solidarity with other World Heritage sites.

In a focus group with *Djennenkés* on the subject of Djenné's World Heritage status, one man expressed his impotent rage at what he saw as

9 • CONCLUSION   207

the unacceptable living conditions in Djenné: *On est là dans nos nids de rats.*[5] ("We are here in our rats' nests."), while he perceived that other towns such as Mopti, free of restrictions, were evolving and changing in the right direction. For *Djennenkés* to believe in the future of their town as a World Heritage site, they need to see their cultural heritage working for them in an efficacious way, contributing to a better collective future.

UNESCO's World Heritage project in Africa has successfully moved attention away from a discourse that defines Africa as a continent beset by poverty and corruption. It is a way of celebrating Africa's rich history and cultural heritage and a successful means of promoting tourism. The success of Africa 2009 has seen the launch of a new programme, Africa 2017, continuing the work of training heritage professionals and protecting built heritage. Yet poverty and corruption still exist, and people's lives still need improving. In addition to these problems, the new destabilising effect of international terrorism in the north of the country threatens to undermine the potential economic benefits represented by tourism. At the end of 2010 Djenné is on the red part of the international community's map of places that can be safely visited by tourists. If this remains the case, even for a limited period, a completely different question needs to be asked about the future of Djenné's World Heritage status: without an outside tourist audience, what value remains in Djenné's architectural and archaeological cultural heritage? As UNESCO's mission is to build peace in the minds of people, will the inaccessibility of once frequented sites such as Djenné and Timbuktu become a rallying cry around which the international community will mobilise to fight terrorism? If tourism in Djenné declines over the years, what will have been the risks of moving toward a model of economic development reliant principally on tourism? While the heritage elite may well see a continuation of money flowing into Djenné in solidarity with the aims of preserving its cultural heritage, the guides and other residents in Djenné are unlikely to find the adjustment to a life without tourism income straightforward. Already, young guides in Djenné are looking toward the Malian State to solve the problem of the dwindling number of tourists visiting their town and are considering actions such as demonstrations in the capital, Bamako, to make the state aware of their plight.

In their approach to the protection of tangible and intangible cultural heritage, UNESCO seem to place the human actors involved on a scale, from detached to absolute embodiment, from a World Heritage site to a Living Human Treasure. In the final analysis, however, any discussion of the importance of cultural heritage in Djenné must begin with an understanding of the conditions in which people live their lives. This cannot be merely academic, reduced to facts and figures about life expectancy and educational outcomes. Cultural heritage in Djenné should not be burdensome but redemptive.

Sometimes a choice between building in banco or in concrete in Djenné comes down to matters of practicality and health and safety. When a school was built on the site of Djenné's second mosque, the Cultural Mission fought hard to have the building constructed entirely in banco. However, both teachers and parents firmly believed that the school should be built in concrete, because the authorities could not be counted on to pay for the annual upkeep that such a large banco building would require. Some parents had had the experience of part of the previous school collapsing around their children, endangering their lives. In this instance, the teachers and parents won, and the school was built in concrete covered with fired clay tiles. Like the administrative buildings near the entrance of Djenné, on the outskirts of the town to the west, the hospital and radio stations are both concrete structures, for similar pragmatic reasons.

According to its staff, the Cultural Mission was praised by the director of the UNESCO World Heritage Centre in Paris, who came to visit Djenné in 2005. Because he comes to Africa very infrequently, Djenné was lucky to welcome him. He is reported to have said that Djenné is the only "original" town in the world, the only one that stays the same while living in the modern world. This may be the case for now, but at what price to its residents? Is it only a Western sensibility of nostalgic remembrance of the past that would consider as desirable a town forever staying materially the same?

The Cultural Mission argues that the only reason any money comes to Djenné in the first place is its World Heritage Status (although money does comes from Saudi Arabia and other Muslim countries because of the importance of Djenné as an Islamic centre). It is therefore crucial to protect Djenné's cultural heritage to ensure the future economic success of the town. When asked if people will still be living in banco houses in one hundred years' time, staff at the Cultural Mission feel confident that the answer is yes. One of them expressed his certainty by stating that:

> If a Djenné man makes money and he wants to show his wealth he will build a beautiful house with a *façade Toucouleur*, he will express himself in banco. He will be proud each year to re-mud his house. The maintenance of the front of the house is a symbol of wealth, people walking past can see if the house owner is rich or poor.[6]

At the moment, a house owner may be expected to gain money through the monumental status of his home and the outside income and interest it will generate. However, a longer term view of the situation may begin by validating the traditional livelihood strategies in the town—supporting fishing, farming, herding, trading, and artisanat and promoting this "enabling context" in its broadest possible sense.

Heritage Ethnographies

Throughout this book, I hoped to illuminate certain "heritage logics" present in Djenné. For example, the embodied practice of artisans (constantly evolving. improving, and developing new designs) is a useful counterbalance to an approach to cultural heritage that hopes to "freeze" architecture in time and space. Another example is how the historic discourse used by guides ("the art of speaking") is a long way from the historical accuracy demanded by the national guide tests.

What seems to have developed in Djenné is therefore a very strategic attitude toward cultural heritage and the imaginative use of cultural heritage as a resource to improve the economic lives of *Djennenkés*. Where cultural heritage becomes burdensome (such as the cost of the upkeep of houses), new strategies are devised to try to circumvent problems. These new strategies (such as tiling houses) cannot be dismissed as uneducated and short-termist reactions. Instead, they fit within wider strategies to ensure that a family has access to a more reliable form of shelter and can afford to eat. If it is to be successful, an international organisation such as UNESCO, even acting through a state party, cannot remove itself from the different "heritage logics" found throughout the world.

Two broad conclusions therefore emerge from the research. First, it is not appropriate to divorce attempts to protect cultural heritage from considerations of development and poverty alleviation. In cases such as Djenné, the potential income from tourism must be balanced against the economic burden presented by the protection of a particular vernacular architectural tradition, especially if this potential income is subject to revocation through terrorist threats. In a situation where it is often difficult to ensure that people have enough to eat or have access to healthcare, what is at stake are people's lives.

Second, the successful protection of cultural heritage requires a much deeper dialogue between heritage professionals and local constituents, one that starts with an understanding of people's everyday lives and concerns. Building on the work of Smith (2006), I have argued that heritage professionals, such as those employed by UNESCO, operate within a very specific institutional culture that can be studied historically. Only through the theorisation of this institutional culture as one of many "heritage logics" (albeit an extremely powerful one) can room be made for an engaged debate about the importance of cultural heritage in people's lives. As this theorisation evolves, and organisations such as UNESCO continue to rethink their approach to their mandate, a democratisation of different visions of cultural heritage would ensure that the work of heritage professionals becomes increasingly relevant and dynamic.

Butler (2007: 272) states that Euro–North-American museum and heritage culture has for a long time failed to come to terms with different worldviews:

> My point has been that museum and heritage culture, like Narcissus looking into his pool (as a "world in itself"), still fails to engage in alternative conceptualisations of itself within a wider global context. . . . Moreover, Euro-North American core values continue to function as museology's resource for its own legitimation, and, crucially, for its professionalism and expert culture. I have demonstrated that as a consequence there has been a failure, in particular, to imagine "non-Western" landscapes/cultural influences other than as stereotypes and thus to give a reality to their history and humanity.

Through detailed case studies and life histories, heritage ethnographies can further problematise the dominant heritage discourse. The theoretical objections to a dominant Western approach to cultural heritage are already present in the literature (Konaré, 2000; Olaniyan, 2003; Turtinen, 2000); however, detailed ethnographic accounts can increasingly provide vital clues to what an alternative (and plural) heritage landscape may look like. Fieldwork in Djenné has shown that many concepts such as "authenticity" and "cultural transmission" are not stable entities. For example, authenticity among the jewellers in Djenné is not about the reproduction of a stable prototype but about the materials and skills used to produce the object. Additionally, cultural transmission occurs as much through "improving" an object for modern-day use as it does through ensuring that old designs are not lost.

In fact, as Herzfeld (1991) has revealed, this re-theorisation of the role of cultural heritage in people's lives not only is applicable to non-Western heritage landscapes but also serves to reveal a subaltern, alternative, or more democratic appreciation of what people find meaningful in their lives. In Herzfeld's ethnography, as in the case of Djenné, it is people's homes that become the domain of contestation between heritage professionals and local people. And, as in the case of Djenné, Herzfeld argues that people express themselves through their homes in a great number of complex ways that are intimately linked to ideas of hospitality, prestige, modernity, and economic rationality.

Instead of reinforcing an opposition between a Western heritage discourse and a local level reality, ethnographic fieldwork can reveal the history of different heritage discourses—where they meet, the consequences of these encounters, and the way in which lessons from the encounters can be used to improve the practice of heritage professionals. This revelation will be achieved primarily through striving for a more inclusive and iterative method of heritage management, one that is low in initial assumptions and high in understanding future aspirations.

Appendices

Appendix 1
Imams of the Great Mosque in Djenné

List compiled by the Mosque Committee established in Djenné in 2007.

1907–1918	Baber Tawati
1918–1922	Sofia Gomeda
1922–1932	Amadou Tinanka
1932–1942	Alphamoye Djeïté
1932–1945	Amadou Nafogou
1945–1958	Alphamoye Tenentao
1958–1992	Samoye Korobara (father of current Imam)
1992–1993	Bakamia Djeïté (died suddenly)
1993–1994	Mamadou Traoré (died suddenly)
1994–	Alman Korobara

Appendix 2

Chefs du Village

List compiled by the Mosque Committee established in Djenné in 2007 (no dates available to show when the *Chefs du Village* held their posts).

1. Aimame Siaka Traoré (1st *Chef du Village*, daughter married a Maiga)
2. Bassoumaïla Maiga
3. Bahasseye Maiga
4. Sékou Hassan Maiga
5. Aba Sonmayla Maiga
6. Bahasseye Alhadi Maiga
7. Aba Sékou Maiga (Aba Sékou had a dispute with the *Commandant de Cercle*. The *Chef du Village* position was passed on to another family).
   —Salmoye Baber Traoré (died before he took office)
8. Sory Demba Cissé (relative of Maiga)
9. Nyemy Maiga
10. Bahasseye Sékou Maiga (current *Chef du Village*)

Appendix 3

Ministry of Culture **Organigram**

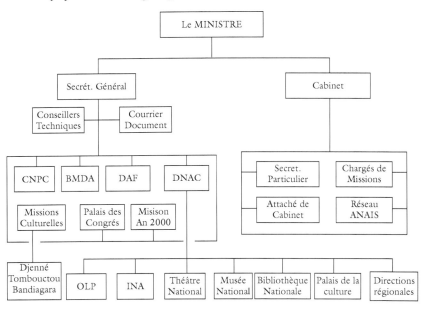

Appendix 4

Impact of Tourism Diagram

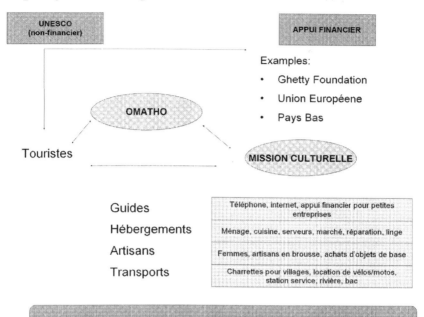

Notes

Introduction

1. Research diary entry, 10th September 2005.
2. See *http://portal.unesco.org/culture* for a comprehensive coverage of their "Slave Route" initiative, coinciding with the 200-year anniversary of the abolition of the slave trade. Many other heritage organisations and museums throughout the world also participated in the celebration of the abolition anniversary.
3. See *www.akdn.org* for more information.
4. *www.africa2009.net*
5. UNESCO (2005), Document WHC-05/15.GA/INF.7
6. UNESCO (2010), Document A/C.2/65/L.50
7. *http://instat.gov.ml*
8. See Plan de Conservation et de Gestion des «villes anciennes de Djenné» Préparé par la Direction National du Patrimoine Culturel du Mali et la Mission Culturelle de Djenne avec le soutien du Fonds du Patrimoine Mondial et Le Bureau multi-pays UNESCO à Bamako, *http://whc. unesco.org/en/list/116/documents/* (accessed January 20, 2011).
9. Of the representative national sample of households recruited for the survey, ethnic identity broke down as Bambara (29.1%), Malinke (8.1%), Peulh (14.5%), Sarakole/Soninke/Marka (12.6%), Sonrai (9%), Dogon (5.8%), Tamachek (4.1%), Senoufo/Minianka (8.9%), Bobo (2%), Other West African (1.7%), Other (3.8%).
10. This census revealed that of a population of 6,809, Djenné was dominated by Marka (1,462) and Bozo (1,389), with smaller numbers of Somono (510), Songhai (662), Arma—who are said to be descended

216 NOTES

from the Moroccan invasion of the 16th century—(668), Fulani (807), Rimaibe (467), and Diawanbe (618).

11. The Dutch government financed all the original equipment for the Cultural Mission: the architect's office, the computers, printers, photo equipment (as well as a 1995 photo exhibition), a 1999 exhibition held in a Qur'anic school, and a 2004 exhibition held to mark the end of the first phase of the housing restoration project.

12. Projets de Conservation du Patrimoine Culturel du Mali: (deuxième phase), Ministère de la Culture Bamako (Mali). Rijksmuseum voor Volkenkunde Leiden (Pays-Bas).

13. ADEMA is the political party that held power in Djenné until 2004.

14. The latest person to build a house in Djenné is the Dutch architect Pierre Maas. The house is currently under construction for use by visiting students and researchers to the town.

15. See *http://jeuneafrique.com* for recent articles relating to the problem of assuring security in the north of Mali and the impact on tourism.

16. See, for example, the Jamestown Monitor for further information: *www.jamestown.org*.

17. Personal communication with UCL researchers, October 2010.

18. Second Press Release, Eleventh Edition of the Festival in the Desert; *www.festival-au-desert.org* (accessed December 2010).

Chapter 1

1. See *www.craterre.org*.

2. Le Livre d'Or de l'Exposition Coloniale Internationale de Paris, 1931. Paris: Exposition Coloniale Internationale.

3. «Les visiteurs . . . se trouvent transportés au cœur de l'Afrique Noire à travers les ruelles étroites de Djenné, fidèlement reproduites, avec leurs maisons a terrasses et a étages, aux grossiers murs de pisé rouge, telles qu'on les rencontrent sur les bords du Bani. . . . Dans une construction toute proche, reproduisant a une échelle forcément réduite, la célèbre mosquée de Djenné, est installé un cinéma permanent où le public voit défiler les film récemment tournée en Afrique Occidentale Française. » (Le Livre d'or de l'Exposition Coloniale Internationale de Paris, 1931. Paris: Exposition Coloniale Internationale: 85).

4. Personal communication with Director of Aga Khan project in Djenné, January 2010.

5. "Ma joie put s'épandre en moi. J'étais bien face à ce dont j'avais rêvé dans l'année de préparation au vieux lycée de la montagne Sainte-Geneviève, dans les années d'école et sous les arbres du Luxembourg, dans le temps d'armée, face à ce que j'avais tant espéré et tant attendu.»

Chapter 2

1. Cities and urbanisation seminar series, Prof. Kevin Macdonald (2003), Institute of Archaeology, University College London.
2. Personal communication with Prof. Rogier Bedaux, May 2008.
3. For a full breakdown of costs including labour costs, see *Djenné Patrimoine Informations*, No. 21, Automne 2006.
4. This is disputed by the Cultural Mission, *Djenné Patrimoine,* and most other "heritage experts," who claim that tiles last only for a few years and cannot be considered a long-term solution.
5. Personal communication, February 2005.
6. «C'est pour ça que les touristes viennent. Voir des maisons, faites il y a un ou deux siècles, en banco, qui ne sont pas tombées. Bon, cela fascine, cela attire. C'est ce qui fait notre valeur.»
7. Personal Communication, January 2006.
8. Personal Communication, December 2005.
9. The transcription of the debate can be found at www.djenne-patrimoine.asso.fr/racine/dp8.htm.
10. The terms of the 1964 Venice Charter can be found at www.icomos.org/venice_charter.html.
11. According to K. Epskamp, 2002: "World heritage: Bilateral cooperation between the Netherlands and Mali," *Boekmancahier* 14(54): 433–45, the collaborative relations between the Netherlands and Mali (1996–2003), which focused on supporting Mali's World Heritage, was in accordance with Dutch development policy. The policy identified the cultural sector as a future sustainable source of income. Heritage is seen as a way of creating jobs through tourism, thus leading to development. However, the work was judged in terms of capacity building and heritage site should be given the opportunity of becoming sustainable in terms of maintenance and management, security, and site management. Efforts were therefore made to train people both locally and nationally.
12. To contextualise the giving of aid money through cultural heritage projects in 1997/1998, PNUD Mali Report stated that 74% of aid came from six sources: the World Bank, France, EU, UN, United States, and Japan. Other donors were the IMF (5%), *Fonds Africain de Développement* (4%), and the Dutch government (4%) (*Aide, Endettement et Pauvreté, Rapport 2000 sur le Développement Humain au Mali,* PNUD/MSPAS /Banque Mondiale).
13. Fear over the loss of houses was prompted by a Dutch study that showed that of 134 monumental houses documented in 1984, 40 were gone completely and another 34 replaced by the time a new census was carried out in 1995 (Personal Communication, Prof. Rogier Bedaux, May 13, 2008.)

14. The choice of houses to restore was made by the Dutch project team and the Cultural Mission, approved by the project's *Comité de Pilotage* (made up of local leaders, representatives of masons, local associations, and development committees) and the *Comité Scientifique* (made up of the Malian ministries involved, the Cultural Mission, UNESCO, the National Museum in Bamako, the *Institut des Sciences Humaines* in Bamako, architects, the Dutch embassy, and the National Museum of Ethnology, presided over by the Dutch Minister of Culture) (personal Communication, Prof. Rogier Bedaux, May 13, 2008).

15. In May 2008 the Cultural Mission finally confirmed that it had received the ongoing funds (personal communication, Prof. Rogier Bedaux, May 13, 2008).

16. In Dogon Country, where the Dutch are also undertaking architectural restoration work, their project included immediately effective measures to help local populations such as digging wells and building new roads to allow access to abandoned villages, thus protecting the architecture.

17. This was due to the fact that architectural criteria were used for selection. Representative houses owned by poorer *Djennenkés* were also included, as were a certain number of restored monumental buildings owned by poorer residents (personal communication, Prof. Rogier Bedaux, May 13, 2008).

18. Although *Djenné-Ferey* bricks were used in exceptional circumstances, such as the restoration of the house of the *Chef du Village*.

19. Bigger cities in Mali have their water and energy run by EDM (state monopoly). Cities with population of 5,000–15,000 inhabitants have nonprofit Water Users Boards. Two local representatives are elected for every public fountain and one for every twenty homes with water. These elected delegates go to the *Assemblée Générale* to approve the by-laws relating to water distribution. In Djenné these delegates number almost 200 people; they work alongside permanent employees who manage the accounts and the technical aspects of water supply. Djenné is at the limit of what can be managed under a Water Users Board system, since Water Users Associations are meant to operate in places where it is not economically viable for National Agency (EDM) to operate. The Board is supposed to be audited twice a year by an organisation linked to the National Hydraulic Agency, which also gives them technical advice and ensures there is no misuse of funds. The Board in place until 2005 was a continuation of the ad hoc administration in place since 1988, before the system formalised in the mid-1990s. This ad hoc Board comprised many ADEMA supporters and had left itself open by not renewing its mandate when it was time to do so. Following a change in administration after local elections (a coalition of parties excluding ADEMA came into power),

NOTES 219

a struggle began to replace the old Water Users Board. An interim Board was appointed, and new elections were held—in effect completely replacing the old Board (that had a large amount of expertise) with a new Board made up of people more politically aligned to the new administration in September 2005.

20. Forsythe, Lacour, & Roignant (2007) *Mesures d'urgence pour l'évacuation des eaux usées de la ville de Djenné, Mali: Rapport de Mission.* ENGREF/Groupe d'Assistance Française de Développement.

21. Personal communication with one of the project leaders, December 2006.

Chapter 3

1. "Since wars begin in the minds of men, it is in the mind of men that the defences of peace must be constructed" Imber (1989: 98).
2. *www.un.org/millenniumgoals*
3. Document 34C presented at the General Conference, 34th Session in Paris, 2007.
4. Personal communication, June 2004.
5. Personal communication, member of the British Delegation at UNESCO in Paris, June 2004.
6. His son, Laurent Lévi-Strauss, is currently the Chief of Sector for Tangible Heritage and Deputy Director for the Division of Cultural Heritage at UNESCO.
7. For full text see *http://whc.unesco.org/en/conventiontext/*.
8. For full text see *www.unesco.org/culture/ich/index*.
9. *http://whc.unesco.org/en/list*
10. From the ICOMOS website www.international.icomos.org.
11. From the ICOMOS website www.international.icomos.org.
12. For a full discussion of the events see K. Warikoo (ed.), 2002. *Bamiyan: Challenge to World Heritage*, New Dehli: Bhavana Books & Prints.
13. *www.unesco.org/culture/intangible-heritage*
14. See *http://unesco.org* for more information.

Chapter 4

1. See, for example, Human Rights Watch, *www.hrw.org*.
2. Mali ratified the United Nations Convention on the Rights of the Child in 1990. As part of the agreement, the Malian Government submits a report every five years detailing its progress in promoting the rights of children, protecting them from exploitation and ensuring they have access to healthcare, education, and leisure. Despite this, there is still much progress to be made.

3. The Mosque in its current form, however, may well have been changed radically if it had not been for the intervention of Alpha Oumar Konaré as early as 1975, opposing a plan to rebuild it using concrete and blue tiles (personal communication, Prof. Rogier Bedaux, March 13, 2008).
4. See *www.timbuktufoundation.org*.

Chapter 5

1. Research diary entry, December 27, 2004.
2. The Malian government distributed rice to families in Djenné in 2005 to help with the consequences of a poor harvest brought about by drought.
3. The UN Human Development Report can be found at *http://hdr.undp.org*.
4. *Djenné Patrimoine* Newsletter Number 21, Autumn 2006; see *www.djenne-patrimoine.asso.fr*.
5. AMUPI: Malian Association for the Unity and the Progress of Islam.
6. The AKTC returned to Djenné in 2010 to undertake a new restoration project of the Mosque, this time to remove much of the accumulated mud on the roof, which posed a big risk to the structure of the Mosque as a whole, owing to its sheer weight.
7. Kola nuts are traditionally given by visitors as gifts to village elders.
8. Personal communication, employee of Cultural Mission, 2005.

Chapter 6

1. See *Africa Research Bulletin* (17235), December 1, 2006–Jan 15, 2007, Blackwell Publishing Lt., for an announcement on a new gold mining venture in Mali in conjunction with an Australian company.
2. Research Diary entry, Wednesday, August 14, 2005.
3. The new Minister of Culture in Mali is Mohamed Al Moctar (2008).
4. *«La Biennale ne sera jamais plus comme avant. Elle va reposer désormais sur quatre considérations autour desquelles le Ministère de la Culture se mobilise et travaille activement : 1 – la culture comme facteur de développement économique; 2 – la culture comme facteur de stabilité du pays; 3 – la culture comme facteur de la préservation des expressions culturelles; 4 – et la culture comme facteur de développement d'un partenariat fécond.» For a full speech transcript see www.maliculture.net.*

Chapter 7

1. *www.unwto.org/regional/africa/menu.htm*
2. *www.unwto.org/regional/africa/menu.htm*

NOTES 221

3. PNUD/UNESCO (*Programme des Nations Unis pour le Développement*), *Rapport de Mission*, July 1997.
4. In 2006 I had been told about the existence of only one female guide working in Dogon Country.
5. Another potential explanation is that some academics who have previously worked in Mali, including undertaking research in Djenné, occasionally return to the town with tourists on an organised lecture tours of the country.
6. High season runs from approximately early December to the end of February; there is also a short "mini-season" in June/July.
7. Personal Communication, employee of Cultural Mission, March 3, 2005.
8. *www.afribone.com/article.php3?id_article=8021,* accessed January 2008.
9. Although some hotels in Djenné source their produce locally, the bigger hotels rely on supplies from Bamako on Mondays, because they fear that the local supply is too inconsistent.

Chapter 8

1. The *Djenné Patrimoine* 2002 event included a photographic exhibition, a guided visit of Djenné-Djeno, and visits to outlying villages. It also included a *soirée culturelle* and a trip on the river by *pirogue* (flat-bottomed boat).
2. *www.tinariwen.com/media.php*
3. The entry price is, however, regarded as too high by many independent guides who, to protect their profit, chose to avoid the *Festival sur le Niger* in favour of free activities.
4. During the *Terra 2008* conference masons from Timbuktu, Ségou, Djenné, and Mopti were invited to erect arches on the grounds surrounding the memorial to Mobido Keita for one of the evening celebrations. At the time, one of the Djenné masons remarked to me that they really should be building the arch at the entrance of Djenné, but they were unable to find the funding to do so.
5. See *www.susan-vogel.com/futureofmud.html* for a film about masons in Djenné, including the 2005 *crépissage* of the Great Mosque.
6. However, many tourists gain access to the Mosque with the help of their guides, who bribe the Mosque guard. I chose never to go into the Mosque, because I believed that if it were known that I been inside, that may have negatively affected my relationship with some people in Djenné.
7. Officially the festival treasurer declared that the festival had raised 4,605,000 CFA (£4,605) from external donors, 544,000 CFA (£544) through the sale of tickets, and 147,000 CFA (£147) through the

artisan hall—a total of 5,296,000 CFA (£5,296) against a hoped-for budget of 12,000,000 (£12,000).

8. This figure is based on the declared number of tickets sold. The real number may well have been much higher.

9. My translation.

Chapter 9

1. See UNESCO link: Culture/World Heritage/Djenné, *http://portal. unesco.org/culture/en/ev.php-URL_ID=29686&URL_DO=DO_ TOPIC&URL_SECTION=201.html*, accessed March 5, 2008.

2. See UNESCO link: Culture/Intangible Heritage/Living World Treasures Programme, *hwww.unesco.org/culture/ich/index.php?pg=00061&lg=EN*, accessed March 5, 2008.

3. UNESCO (2005), Document WHC-05/15.GA/INF.7.

4. Personal communication, June 2005.

5. Personal Communication, December 2005.

6. Personal communication, August 2005.

References

Amselle, J.-L. (1992) "La corruption et le clientelisme au Mali et en Europe de l'Est: Quelques points de comparaison," *Cahiers d'Études Africaines* 32(128): 629-642.
———. (1998) *Mestizo Logics: Anthropology of Identity in Africa and Elsewhere.* Stanford, CA: Stanford University Press.
Arnoldi, M. J. (1988) "Playing the puppets: Innovation and rivalry in Bamana youth theatre of Mali," *The Drama Review* 32(2), 65–82.
———. (1999) "Overcoming a colonial legacy: The new national museum in Mali— 1976 to the present," *Museum Anthropology* 22(3), 28–40.
———. (2006) "Youth festivals and museums: The cultural politics of public memory in postcolonial Mali," *Africa Today* 52(4), 55–75.
———. (2007) "Bamako, Mali: Monuments and modernity in the urban imagination," *Africa Today* 54(2), 3–24.
Asante, M. K. (1987) *The Afrocentric Idea.* Philadelphia: Temple University Press.
Basu, P. (2007) "Palimpsest memoryscapes: Materializing and mediating war and peace in Sierra Leone." In Rowlands, M., and De Jong, F. (Eds.), *Reclaiming Heritage: Alternative Imaginaries of Memory in West Africa*, pp. 231–259. Walnut Creek, CA: Left Coast Press.
Baudrillard, J. (1988) "Simulacra and simulations." In Poster, M. (Ed.), *Jean Baudrillard: Selected Writings.* pp. 166–184. Oxford: Polity Press.
Beck, W. (2006) "Narratives of world heritage in travel guidebooks," *International Journal of Heritage Studies* 12(6), 521–535.
Bedaux, R. M. A., Diaby, B., and Maas, P. (2003) *L'architecture de Djenné, Mali: La Pérennité d'un Patrimoine Mondial.* Leiden: Rijksmuseum voor Volkenkunde.
Bedaux, R. M. A, Diaby, P., Maas, P., and Sidibé, S. (2000) "The restoration of Jenné, Mali: African aesthetics and western paradigms," *Terra 2000*: 8th International Conference on the Study of Earthen Architecture, Torbay, Devon, UK, 2000.
Bedaux, R. M. A., and Van der Waals, J. D. (1994) *Djenné: Une Ville Millénaire au Mali.* Leiden: Rijksmuseum voor Volkenkunke.
Bender, B. (1998) *Stonehenge: Making Space.* Oxford: Berg.
Berque, J. (1996) Preface. In Caillié, R., *Voyage à Tombouctou*, pp. 5-34. Paris: La Découverte.
Blake, J. (2000) "On defining the cultural heritage," *International and Comparative Law Quarterly* 49(1), 61–85.
Bourdieu, P. (1984) *Distinction: A Social Critique of the Judgement of Taste.* London: Routledge & Kegan Paul.

Bourgeois, J.-L. (1987) "The history of the great Mosques of Djenné," *African Arts* 20(3), 54–63, 90–92.

———. (1989) *Spectacular Vernacular: The Adobe Tradition.* New York: Aperture Foundation.

Brenner, L. (2001) "Controling knowledge: Religion, power and schooling in a West African muslim society," *Africa Today* 50(1).

Brenner, L., and Robinson, D. (1980) "Project for the conservation of Malian Arabic manuscripts," *History in Africa* 7, 329–332.

Brunet-Jailly, J. (1999) *Djenné d'Hier à Demain.* Bamako: Editions Donniya.

Butler, B. (2006) "Heritage and the present past." In Tilley, C., Keane, W., Küchler, S., Rowlands, M., and Spyer, P. (Eds.), *Handbook of Material Culture*, pp. 463–479. Thousand Oaks, CA: Sage.

———. (2007) *Return to Alexandria: An Ethnography of Cultural Heritage Revivalism and Museum Memory.* Walnut Creek, CA: Left Coast Press.

Caillié, R. T. (1830) *Travels through Central Africa to Timbuctoo; and across the Great Desert, to Morocco, Performed in the Years 1824–1828.* London: Colburn & Bentley.

Clauzel, J. (1989) *Administrateur de la France d'Outre-mer.* Marseille and Avignon: Jeanne Laffitte and A. Barthélemy.

Cleere, H. (2001) "The world heritage convention in the third world." In Layton, R., Thomas, J., and Stone, P. G. (Eds.), *Destruction and Conservation of Cultural Property*, pp. 99–105. London, New York: Routledge.

Clément, E. (1995) "A view from UNESCO," *African Arts* 28(4), 58.

Clifford, J. (1988) *The Predicament of Culture: Twentieth-Century Ethnography, Literature, and Art.* Cambridge, MA: Harvard University Press.

Clifford, J., and Marcus, G. E. (Eds.) (1986) *Writing Culture: The Poetics and Politics of Ethnography*, Berkeley and Los Angeles: University of California Press.

Cohen, E. (1988) "Traditions in the qualitative sociology of tourism," *Annals of Tourism Research* 15(1), 29–46.

Cohen, W. B. (1971) *Rulers of Empire: The French Colonial Service in Africa.* Stanford, CA: Hoover Press.

Coombes, A. (1994) *Re-inventing Africa: Museums, Material Culture and the Popular Imagination in Late Victorian England. Princeton*, NJ: Yale University Press.

Cuttier, M. (2006) *Portrait du Colonialisme Triomphant: Louis Archinard 1850–1932.* Panazol: Charles Lavauzelle.

Darwin, C. (1859) *On the Origin of Species by Means of Natural Selection, or the Preservation of Favoured Races in the Struggle for Life.* London: John Murray.

De Jong, A. A., and Harts-Broekhuis, J. A. (1985) *Investigations Socio Economiques de la Ville de Djenné et ses Environs, Rapport 7.* Institut de Géographie, Université d'Utrecht.

De Jong, F. (2007) "A masterpiece of masquerading: Contradictions of conservation in intangible heritage." In Rowlands, M., and De Jong, F. (Eds.), *Reclaiming Heritage: Alternative Imaginaries of Memory in West Africa.* Walnut Creek, CA: Left Coast Press.

De Jong, F., and Rowlands, M., Eds. (2007) *Reclaiming Heritage: Alternative Imaginaries of Memory in West Africa*, pp 161–184. Walnut Creek, CA: Left Coast Press.

De Jorio, R. (2003) "Narratives of the nation and democracy in Mali: A view from Modibo Keita's memorial," *Cahiers d'Études Africaines* 172, 827–855.

———. (2006) "Politics of remembering and forgetting: The struggle over colonial monuments in Mali," *Africa Today* 52(4), 78–106.

De Sardan, O. (1999) "A moral economy of corruption in Africa?" *Journal of Modern African Studies* 37(1): 25–52.

Derrida, J. (1996) *Archive Fever: A Freudian Impression.* Chicago: University of Chicago Press.

Desplagnes, L. (1907) *Le Plateau Central Nigérien: Une Mission Archéologique et Ethnographique au Soudan français.* Paris: Emile Larose.

REFERENCES 225

Di Giovine, M. A. (2009) *The Heritage-scape: UNESCO, World Heritage and Tourism.* Lanham, MD: Lexington Books.

Diaby, B. (2000) "Fixed and moveable heritage in Jenné: Problems of conservation and protection." In Ardouin, C. D., and Arinze, E. (Eds.), *Museums and History in West Africa*, pp. 22–28. Oxford: James Curry.

Diakité, D. (1999) "L'Islam à Djenne." In Brunet-Jailly, J. (Ed.), *Djenné d'Hier à Demain*, pp. 45–59. Bamako: Editions Donniya.

Dubois, F. l., and Figaro (1897) *Tombouctou la mystérieuse.* Paris: Flammarion.

Dutt, S. (1995) *The Politicization of the United Nations Specialist Agencies: A Case Study of UNESCO.* Lewiston: Mellen University Press.

Edwards, E. (2001) *Raw Histories: Photographs, Anthropology and Museums.* Oxford: Berg.

Epskamp, K. (2002) "World heritage: Bilateral co-operation between the Netherlands and Mali," *Boekmancahier*, Vol. 14, No. 54, pp. 433–445.

Eribon, D. (1988) "Lévi-Strauss interviewed, Part I," *Anthropology Today* 4(5), 5–8.

Eriksen, T. H. (2001) "Between universalism and relativism: A critique of UNESCO's concept of culture." In Cowan, J. K., Dembour, M.-B., and Wilson, R. A. (Eds.), *Culture and Rights: Anthropological Perspectives*, pp. 127–148. Cambridge: Cambridge University Press.

Fanon, F. (1961) *The Wretched of the Earth.* New York: Grove Weidenfeld.

Ferguson, J. (2006) *Global Shadows: Africa in the Neoliberal World Order.* Durham and London: Duke University Press.

Finn, C. E. (1986) "The rationale for American withdrawal," *Comparative Education Review* 30(1), 140–147.

Fisher, H. (1982) "Review article: Early Arabic sources and the Almoravid conquest of Ghana," *Journal of African History* 23: 549–560.

Fontein, J. (2000) *UNESCO, Heritage and Africa: An Anthropological Critique of World Heritage.* Edinburgh: Centre of African Studies, Edinburgh University.

Forty, A., and Küchler, S. (Eds.) (1999) *The Art of Forgetting.* Oxford: Berg.

Gallais, J. (1967) *Le Delta Intérieur du Niger et ses Bordures: Etudes Morphologiques.* Paris: CNRS.

———. (1994) *"Les hommes dans leur milieu naturel."* In Bedaux, R., and Van der Waals, J. D. (Eds.), *Djenné: Une Ville Millénaire au Mali.* Leiden: Rijksmuseum voor Volkenkunde.

Gardi, B. (1994) "Djenné at the turn of the century: Postcards from the Museum für Völkerkunde Basel," *African Arts* 27(2), 70–75, 95–96.

Gardi, B., Maas, P., and Mommersteeg, G. (1995) *Djenné—Il y a Cent Ans.* Amsterdam: Karthala.

Graham, B. J., Ashworth, G. J,. and Tunbridge, J. E. (2000) *A Geography of Heritage: Power, Culture, and Economy.* London: Arnold.

Greenfield, J. (1995) *The Return of Cultural Treasures, 2nd ed.* Cambridge University Press.

Grosz-Ngaté, M. (1988) "Power and knowledge: The representation of the Mande World in the works of Park, Caillie, Monteil, and Delafosse," *Cahiers d'Études Africaines* 28(111/112): 485–511.

Hall, S. (2005) "Whose heritage? Unsettling the heritage, re-imagining the postnation." In Littler, J., and Naidoo, R. (Eds.), *The Politics of Heritage: The Legacies of "Race,"* pp. 23–35. London: Routledge.

Herzfeld, M. (1991) *A Place in History: Social and Monumental Time in a Cretan Town.* Princeton, NJ: Princeton University Press.

Hitchcock, M. (2005) "Afterword." In Harrison, D., and Hitchcock, M. (Eds.), *The Politics of World Heritage: Negotiating Tourism and Conservation.* Clevedon, NY: Channel View Publication.

Hobsbawm, E. J., and Ranger, T. O. (Eds.) (1983) *The Invention of Tradition.* Cambridge: Cambridge University Press.

Hooper-Greenhill, E. (1992) *Museums and the Shaping of Knowledge*. London: Routledge.

Howard, P. (2003) *Heritage: Management, Interpretation, Identity*. London: Continuum.

HRP (1908) "Review: *Le plateau central Nigérien by Lieutenant Louis Desplagnes*," *Man* 8, 106–107.

Hudgens, J., and Trillo, R. (1999) *West Africa: The Rough Guide*. London: Rough Guides.

Imber, M. (1989) *The USA, ILO, UNESCO, and the IAEA: Politicization and Withdrawal in the Specialized Agencies*. Basingstoke and London: Macmillan.

Imperato, P. J. (1989) *Mali: A Search for Direction*. Dartmouth: Westview Press.

Jansen, J., and Austen, R. (1996) "History, oral transmission, and structure in Ibn Khaldun's chronology of Mali rulers," *History in Africa* 23. 17–28.

Jansen, J., Duintjer, E., and Tamboura, B. (1995) *L'épopée de Sunjara, d'après Lansine Diabate de Kela*. Leiden: CNWS.

Joy, C. (2007) "Enchanting town of mud: Djenné, a World Heritage site in Mali." In Rowlands, M., and De Jong, F. (Eds.), *Reclaiming Heritage: Alternative Imaginaries of Memory in West Africa*, pp. 145–160. Walnut Creek, CA: Left Coast Press.

———. (2010) "Heritage and tourism: Contested discourses in Djenné, a World Heritage Site." In Macleod, D., and Carrier, J. (Eds.), *Tourism, Power and Culture: Anthropological Insights*. Bristol: Channel View Publications.

Joyner, C. C. (1986) "Legal implications of the concept of the common heritage of mankind," *International and Comparative Law Quarterly* 35(1), 190–199.

Kaplan, F. (1994) *Museums and the Making of Ourselves*. Leicester University Press.

Keenan, J. (2009) "Al-Qaeda terrorism in the Sahara? Edwin Dyer's murder and the role of intelligence agencies," *Anthropology Today* 25(4): 14–19.

Konaré, A. (1995) "Towards more efficient international collaboration," *African Arts* 28(4), 27–31.

———. (2000) "Perspectives on history and culture: The case of Mali." In Robinson, D., Bingen, R. J., and Staatz, J. M. (Eds.), *Democracy and Development in Mali*, pp. 15–22. East Lansing: Michigan State University.

Kryza, F., T. (2006) *The Race for Timbuktu: In Search of Africa's City of Gold*. New York: Harper Collins.

Kwint, M., Breward, C., and Aynsley, J. (Eds.) (1999) *Material Memories*. Oxford: Berg.

La Violette, A. (2000) *Ethno-Archaeology in Jenné, Mali: Craft and Status among Smiths, Potters, and Masons*. Oxford: Archaeopress.

Lange, K. E. (2001) "Djenné, West Africa's eternal city, *National Geographic,* June.

Le Vine, V. (2007) "Mali: Accommodation or coexistence?" In Miles, W. S. F. (Ed.), *Political Islam in West Africa: State Society Relations Transformed*, pp. 73–99. Boulder: Lynne Rienner.

Leiris, M. (1934) *L'Afrique Fantôme*. Paris: Librairie Gallimard.

Leprun, S. (1988) *Le Théâtre des Colonies: Scénographie, Acteurs et Discours de l'Imaginaire dans les Expositions 1855–1937*. Paris: Editions L'Harmattan.

Levtzion, N. H. (Ed.) (1981) *Corpus of Early Arabic Sources for West African History*. Cambridge: Cambridge University Press.

Lindholm, C. (2008) *Culture and Authenticity*. Oxford: Blackwell Publishing.

Lowental, D. (1998) *The Heritage Crusade and the Spoils of History*. Cambridge: Cambridge University Press.

Maas, P., and Mommersteeg, G. (1992) *Djenné: Chef-d'Oeuvre Architectural*. Bamako and Amsterdam: Institut des Sciences Humaines and Institut Royal des Tropiques.

MacCannell, D. (1973) *The Tourist: A New Theory of the Leisure Class*. London: Macmillan.

———. (1992) *Empty Meeting Grounds: the Tourist Papers*. London: Routledge.

Magness-Gardiner, B. (2004) "International conventions and cultural heritage protection." In Rowan, Y., and Baram, U. (Eds.), *Marketing Heritage: Archaeology and the Consumption of the Past*, pp. 27–41. Oxford: AltaMira Press.

Manhart, C. (2001) "The Afghan cultural heritage crisis: UNESCO's response to the destruction of statues in Afghanistan," *American Journal of Archaeology* 105(3), 387–388.

REFERENCES

Marchand, T. (2001) "Process over product: Case studies of traditional building practices in Djenné, Mali and San'a', Yemen', *Managing Change: Sustainable Approaches to the Conservation of the Built Environment*, 4th Annual US/ICOMOS International Symposium, Philadelphia, Pennsylvania 2001, pp. 137–159. Getty Conservation Institute.

———. (2003) "A possible explanation for the lack of explanation; or, 'why the master builder can't explain what he knows': Introducing informational atomism against a 'definitional' definition of concepts.'" In Pottier, J., Bicker, A., and Sillitoe, P. (Eds.), *Negotiating Local Knowledge: Power and Identity in Development*. London: Pluto Press.

———. (2006) "Endorsing indigenous knowledge: The role of masons and apprenticeship in sustaining vernacular architecture—the case of Djenné." In Asquith, L., and Vellinga, M. (Eds.), *Vernacular Architecture in the Twenty-First Century*, pp. 46–62. New York: Taylor & Francis.

Marchand, T., Bedaux, R., Diaby, B., and Maas, P. (2003) "Devenir Maitre-Macon a Djenne, rang professionel laborieusement acquis." In *L'Architecture de Djenne, Mali. La Perennite d'un Patrimoine Mondial*: Snoeck.

Mauss, M. (1990) *The Gift: The Form and Reason for Exchange in Archaic Societies*. London: Routledge.

Mbembe, J. A. (2001) *On the Postcolony*. Berkeley and Los Angeles: University of California Press.

McGee, R. J., and Warms, R. L. (2004) *Anthropological Theory: An Introduction History*. New York: McGraw-Hill Education.

McGrath, G. (2005) "Including the outsider: The contribution of guides to integrated heritage tourism management in Cusco, Southern Peru." In Harrison, D., and Hitchcock, M. (Eds.), *The Politics of World Heritage: Negotiating tourism and conservation*, pp. 146–152. Clevedon: Channel View Publication.

McIntosh, R. J. (1998) *The Peoples of the Middle Niger: The Island of Gold*. London: Blackwell.

———. (2005) *Ancient Middle Niger: Urbanism and the Self-Organizing Landscape*. Cambridge: Cambridge University Press.

McIntosh, R. J, Diaby, B. H., and Togola, T. (1997) "Mali's many Shields of its past," *Non-Renewable Resources* 6(4): 111–129.

McIntosh, R. J., Togola, T., and McIntosh, S. K. (1995) "The good collector and the premise of mutual respect among nations," *African Arts* 28(4), 60–69, 110–112.

Meskell, L. (2002) "Negative heritage and past mastering in archaeology," *Anthropological Quarterly* 75(3), 557–574.

Miller, D. (1997) "Consumption and its consequences." In Mackay, H. (Ed.), *Consumption and Everyday Life*, pp. 13–64. London: Sage.

Mommersteeg, G. (2000) "*Le domaine du Marabout: Maitres coraniques et spécialistes magico-religieux a Djenné, Mali,*" *Djenné Patrimoine*, Numéro 8.

Monteil, C. (1903) Soudan français. Monographie de Djenné, cercle et ville. Tulle: Jean Mazeyrie.

———. (1932) *Une Cité Soudanaise: Djenné Métropole du Delta Central du Niger*. Paris: Société d'Editions Géographiques, Maritimes, et Coloniales.

Morton, P. (2000) *Hybrid Modernities: Architecture and Representation at the 1931 Colonial Exposition*. Cambridge, MA: MIT Press.

Mosse, D. (2006) "Anti-social anthropology? Objectivity, objection, and the ethnography of public policy and professional communities," *Journal of the Royal Anthropological Institute* 12, 935–956.

Nash, D. (1996) *Anthropology of Tourism*. Oxford: Pergamon.

Niec, H. (Ed.) (1998) *Cultural Rights and Wrongs*. UNESCO Publishing.

Nora, P. (1989) "Between memory and history: *Les lieux de mémoire,*" *Representations* 26, 7–24.

O'Keefe, P. J. (2004) "World cultural heritage: Obligations to the international community," *International and Comparative Law Quarterly* 53(1), 189–209.

Olaniyan, T. (2003) "What is 'cultural patrimony'?" In Afolabi, N. (Ed.), *Marvels of the African World: African Cultural Patrimony, New World Connections, and Identities*, pp. 23–35. Trenton & Eritrea: Africa World Press.

Oxby, C. (1996) "Tuareg identity crisis." *Anthropology Today* 12(5), 21.

Panella, C. (2002) *Les Terres Cuites de la Discorde*. Leiden: CNWS.

Park, M., and Miller, R. (1907) *Travels of Mungo Park*. London: Dent.

Peers, L. L., and Brown, A. K. (2003) *Museums and Source Communities: A Routledge Reader*. London: Routledge.

Phillips, M. S. (2004) "What is tradition when it is not 'invented'? A historiographical introduction." In Phillips, M. S., and Schochet, G. (Eds.), *Questions of Tradition*, pp. 3–29. University of Toronto Press.

Phillips, R. B., and Steiner, C. B. (Eds). (1999) *Unpacking Culture: Art and Commodity in Colonial and Postcolonial Worlds*. London: University of California Press.

Pottier, J. (2003) "Negotiating local knowledge: An introduction." In Pottier, J., Bicker, A., and Sillitoe, P. (Eds.), *Negotiating Local Knowledge: Power, Identity and Development*. London: Pluto Press.

Price, N. S., Vaccaro, A. M., and Talley, K. (Eds.) (1996) *Historical and Philosophical Issue in the Conservation of Cultural Heritage*. Los Angeles: The Getty Conservation Institute.

Probst, P., and Spittler, G. (Eds.) (2004) Between Resistance and Expansion: Explorations of Local Vitality in Africa. Munster: Lit Verlag.

Prussin, L. (1994) "*Vérité et imaginaire de l'architecture.*" In Bedaux, R., and Van der Waals, J. D. (Eds.), "*Djenné: Une Ville Millénaire au Mali,*" pp. 102–111. Leiden: Rijksmuseum voor Volkenkunde.

Radstone, S. (Ed.) (2000) *Memory and Methodology*. Oxford: Berg.

Ravenhill, P. (1995) "Beyond reaction and denunciation: Appropriate action to the crisis of archaeological pillage," *African Arts* 28(4), 56–57, 110.

Renfrew, C. (2000) *Loot, Legitimacy, and Ownership*. Cambridge: Cambridge University Press.

Riegl, A. (1903) "The modern cult of monuments: Its essence and its development," reprinted in Stanley Price, N., Talley, M. K., and Melucco Vaccaro, A. (Eds.), *Historical and Philosophical Issues in the Conservation of Cultural Heritage* (1996) pp. 69–83. Los Angeles: Getty Conservation Institute.

Robinson, D. (2000) "'French Africans'—Faidherbe, Archinard, and Coppolani: The 'creators' of Senegal, Soudan, and Mauritania." In Robinson, D., Bingen, R. J., and Staatz, J. M. (Eds.), *Democracy and Development in Mali*, pp. 22–40. East Lansing: Michigan State University Press.

Rowlands, M. (1993) "The role of memory in the transmission of culture," *World Archaeology* 25(2), 141–151.

———. (1999) "Remembering to forget: Sublimation as sacrifice in war memorials." In Forty, A., and Kuchler, S. (Eds.), *The Art of Forgetting*, pp. 129–145. Oxford: Berg.

———. (2002) "Heritage and cultural property." In Buchli, V. (Ed.), *The Material Culture Reader*, pp. 105–114. Oxford: Berg.

———. (2003) "*Patrimoine et Modernité à Djenné: Identités nationale et locale.*" In Bedaux, R., Diaby, B., and Maas, P. (Eds.), *L'architecture de Djenné, Mali: La Pérénnité d'un Patrimoine Mondial*. Leiden: Rijksmuseum voor Volkenkunde.

———. (2005) "Value and the cultural transmission of things." In Van Binsbergen, W., and Geschiere, P. (Eds.), *Commodification: Things, Agency, and Identities (The Social Life of Things revisited)*, pp. 267–281. New Brunswick & London: Transaction Publishers.

Rowlands, M., and Bedaux, R. (2001) "The future of Mali's past," *Antiquity* 75, 872–876.

Rowlands, M., and Butler, B. (2007) "Conflict and heritage care: Guest editorial," *Anthropology Today* 23(1), 1–2.

Rowlands, M., and Tilley, C. (2006) "Monuments and memorials." In Tilley, C., Keane, W., Küchler, S., Rowlands, M., and Spyer, P. (Eds.), *Handbook of Material Culture*. Thousand Oaks, CA: Sage.

REFERENCES

Ruskin, J. (1849) "The Seven Lamps of Architecture," reprinted in Stanley Price, N., Talley, M. K., and Melucco Vaccaro, A. (Eds.), *Historical and Philosophical Issues in the Conservation of Cultural Heritage* (1996), pp. 42–43. Los Angeles: Getty Conservation Institute.

Said, E. W. (2003) *Orientalism*. London: Penguin.

Sanankoua, D. B. (1985) "Les écoles 'Coraniques' au Mali: Problèmes actuels," *Canadian Journal of African Studies* 19(2): 359–367.

Samuel, R. (1994) *Theatres of Memory*. London: Verso.

Saouma-Forero, G. (2006) "Africa 2009: A story of African empowerment," *Museum International* 58(1–2), 83–94.

Saul, M. (2006) "Islam and West African anthropology," *Africa Today* 55(1): 2–33.

Schijns, W. (1994) "*L'avenir de l'architecture de terre de Djenné.*" In Bedaux, R.M. A., and van der Waals, J. D. (Eds.), *Djenné, Une Ville Millénaire au Mali*, pp. 169–175. Leiden: Rijksmuseum voor Volkenkunde.

Schmidt, P. R., and McIntosh, R. J. (1996) *Plundering Africa's Past*. London: James Currey.

Schultz, D. (2007a) "From glorious past to the land of origins: Media consumption and changing narratives of cultural belonging in Mali." In Rowlands, M., and De Jong, F. (Eds.), *Reclaiming Heritage: Alternative Imaginaries of Memory in West Africa*, pp. 185–214. Walnut Creek, CA: Left Coast Press.

———. (2007b) "Competing sartorial assertions of femininity and Muslim identity in Mali," *Fashion Theory* 11(2/3), 253–280.

Selwyn, T. (1996) "Introduction." In Selwyn, T. (Ed.), *The Tourist Image: Myths and Myth Making in Tourism*, pp. 1–33. Chichester: John Wiley and Sons.

Sidibé, S. (1995) "The pillage of archaeological sites in Mali," *African Arts* 28(4), 52–55.

Singh, J. 2011. *United Nations Educational. Scientific and Cultrural Organization (UNESCO): Creating Norms for a Complex World*. New York: Routledge.

Singh, K. (1998) "UNESCO and cultural rights." In Niec, H. (Ed.), *Cultural Rights and Wrongs*, pp. 146–160. Paris: UNESCO Publishing.

Smith, L. (2006) *Uses of heritage*. London: Routledge.

Soares, B. F. (2005) "Islam in Mali in the neoliberal era," *African Affairs* 105(418), 77–95.

———. (2005a) *Islam and the Prayer Economy: History and Authority in a Malian Town*. Edinburgh: Edinburgh University Press.

———. (2005b) "Islam in Mali in the neoliberal era," *African Affairs* 105(418): 77–95.

Stanley-Price, N., Talley, M. K., and Melucco Vaccaro, A. (Eds.) (1996) *Historical and Philosophical Issues in the Conservation of Cultural Heritage*. Los Angeles: The Getty Conservation Institute.

Tamari, T. (1991) "The development of caste systems in West Africa," *Journal of African History* 32(2), 221–250.

Tilley, C. (1994) *A Phenomenology of Landscape: Places, Paths, and Monuments*. Oxford: Berg.

———. (1999) Metaphor and Material Culture. Oxford: Blackwell.

Tilley, C., Keane, W., Küchler, S., Rowlands, M., and Spyer, P. (Eds.) (2006) *Handbook of Material Culture*. Thousand Oaks: Sage.

Titchen, S. M. (1996) "On the construction of 'outstanding universal value': Some comments on the implementation of the 1972 UNESCO World Heritage Convention," *Conservation and Management of Archaeological Sites* 1(4), 235–242.

Turtinen, J. (2000) *Globalising heritage—on UNESCO and the transnational construction of a world heritage*. Stockholm: Stockholm Center for Organizational Research.

Tylor, E. B. (1871) *Primitive Culture: Researches into the Development of Mythology, Philosophy, Religion, Art, and Custom, etc.* London: John Murray.

Tythacott, L. (2003) *Surrealism and the Exotic*. London: Routledge.

UNESCO (1999) *Decision Relating to the Implementation of the Yamoussoukro Declaration Concerning the Liberalisation of Access to Air Transport Markets in Africa*. ECA/RCID/ CM.CIVAC/99/RPT: Economic Commission for Africa.

Urry, J. (2002) *The Tourist Gaze*. London: Sage.

Van Beek, W. E. A. (2003) "African tourist encounters: Effects of tourism on two West African societies," *Africa* 73(2), 251–289.

Van der Aa, B. J. M., Groote, P. D., and Huigen, P. P. (2005) "World heritage as NIMBY? The case of the Dutch part of the Wadden Sea." In Harrison, D., and Hitchcock, M. (Eds.), *The Politics of World Heritage: Negotiating Tourism and Conservation*, pp. 11–22. Clevedon: Channel View Publications.

Van Gijn, A. (1994) "*La maison: Structure et organisation de l'espace*." In Bedaux, R., and Van der Waals, J. D. (Eds.), *Djenné: Une Ville Millénaire au Mali*, pp. 95–101. Leiden: Rijksmuseum voor Volkenkunde.

Wall, G., and Black, H. (2005) "Global heritage and local problems." In Harrison, D., and Hitchcock, M. (Eds.), *The Politics of World Heritage: Negotiating Tourism and Conservation*, pp. 156–159. Channel View Publication.

Warikoo, K. (Ed.) (2002) *Bamiyan: Challenge to World Heritage*. New Dehli: Bhavana Books & Prints.

Wooten, S. (1993) "Colonial administration and the ethnography of the family in the French Soudan," *Cahiers d'Études Africaines* 33(131): 419–446.

World Commission on Culture and Development. (1996) *Our Creative Diversity*. Paris: UNESCO.

Wright, S. (1998) "The politicization of 'culture,'" *Anthropology Today* 14(1), 7–15.

Wright, W. (1995) "Bring beauty back to Mali," *African Arts* 28(4), 84–89, 112.

Yalouri, E. (2001) *The Acropolis: Global Fame, Local Claim*. Oxford: Berg.

Yates, F. A. (1966) *Art of Memory*. London: Routledge and Keegan Paul.

Index

Aga Khan Development Network (AKDN), 24
Aga Khan Trust for Culture (AKTC), 22, 23, 33, 48, 120
Algeria, 36, 97, 152
Alpha Oumar Konaré, 34, 54, 56, 89, 97
Al-Qaeda in the Islamic Maghreb (AQIM), 97
amulets (*gris-gris*). 99–104, 107, 125, 142
archaeology, 53–59
Archinard, Louis, 44
architecture, 59–66
artisan associations, 138–41
Association Malienne pour le Soutien de l'Islam (AMSI), 104
authenticity, 48, 135
    artisans, 130, 146
    Colonial Exhibition of 1931, 47
    debate about. 144
    Dutch Housing Restoration project, 143
    Festival du Djennéry, 144
    Festival in the Desert, 182
    Fortier photographs, 20
    jewelry, 141–42, 210
    masons, 66
    tiles on mud buildings, 199
    tourist desire for, 165–68, 176, 197

UNESCO, 143–44
view of *Djennenkés*, 69

Bamako, 25, 33, 44, 55, 59, 65, 67, 68, 97, 98, 100, 115, 129, 137, 141, 151, 160, 168, 172, 173, 174, 184, 189, 194, 207
Bamanankan, 27
Bambara, 26, 27, 102, 150, 184, 194
Biennale de Ségou, 34, 145–46
bogolan (mud-cloth), 115, 129
boubou, 129, 133, 134, 136, 137
Bourgeois, Jean-Louis, 30, 31, 32, 35, 110, 163, 197
Bozo, 26, 27, 28, 29, 44, 113, 184, 191, 194
Brenner, Louis, 96, 99
Brunet-Jailly, Joseph, 34, 35, 66
Burkina Faso, 118, 119, 195

Caillié, René, 41, 42, 43
Centre de Services de Production Audiovisuelle (CESPA), 189
Centre for the Research of Earthen Architecture (CRATerre EAG), 33
Chef du Village, 29, 35, 72, 99, 120, 121, 124, 168, 186, 187, 192, 193, 197, 205
Cheikou Amadou Bari, 25
Clauzel, Jean, 49

231

Cultural Mission, 32–35
    access to archaeological sites, 21,
        56, 57, 58, 164, 176
    declassifying parts of Djenné, 66
    distrust of, 201
    entry to Mosque, 121, 123
    Festival du Djennéry, 190,
        191, 195
    OMATHO, 159
    religious authorities, 105
    staying at, 20
    tiles on mud buildings, 63, 64
Cuttier, Martine, 44

Darwin, Charles, 40
decolonisation, 48–49
Delafosse, Maurice, 50
Desplagnes, Louis, 51
Di Giovine, Michael A., 36
Djenné-Djeno, 18, 22, 53, 56, 57, 58,
    172, 203, 206
    access to, 164
    earliest African city, 52
Djenné Patrimoine, 35, 124, 129,
    130, 144, 179
    authenticity, 199
    Brunet-Jailly, 66
    Cultural Mission, 34
    Dutch Housing Restoration
        project, 69
    Festival du Djennéry, 183, 185,
        195, 197
    garibous, 105
    inventory of artisanat, 144
    riot, 120
    tiles on mud buildings, 64
Dogon, 26, 33, 55, 144, 148, 149,
    157, 168, 169, 170, 171,
    172, 174
Dutch Housing Restoration project,
    66–70

École Coloniale, 48, 49, 50
École du Patrimoine Africain, 23
ethnic groups, 26–29
exhibitions, colonial, 47–48

Ferguson, James, 20, 120
Festival du Djennéry, 179–96
Fortier, Edmond, 31, 45

Gallais, Jean, 27
garibous, 99, 102, 104–5, 106, 109, 119
Goundam, 49
Grandes Familles (prominent families),
    29, 34, 69, 184, 192, 205
Griaule, Marcel, 46
griots, 25, 27

Herzfeld, Michael, 22, 203, 210
history of Djenné, 25
Houghton, Daniel, 41
Howard, Peter, 159

Ibn Khaldun, 25
Imam, 35, 99, 100, 105, 120–24,
    192, 193, 205
intangible cultural heritage, 88–90
International Centre for the Study
    and of the Preservation and
    Restoration of Cultural Property
    (ICCROM), 33, 83
International Council on Monuments
    and Sites (ICOMOS), 33, 80,
    83, 84
Ivory Coast, 36

Keenan, Jeremy, 97

Le Vine, Victor, 96, 97
Leiris, Michel, 46, 80

Maas, Pierre, 27, 59
Maiga family, 29
marabouts (Qur'anic teachers), 28, 96,
    98–107, 119, 123, 192
Marchand, Trevor, 69
Marka, 26, 27
market, Monday, 110–12
Mauritania, 36, 97
Mbembe, Achille, 40
McIntosh, Susan and Roderick, 52,
    53, 55, 57

médersas, 98, 99, 101
Mommersteeg, Geert, 27, 59, 101
Monteil, Charles, 45
Mopti, 63, 66, 121, 122, 129, 136,
    137, 138, 148, 168, 170, 172,
    174, 207
Morgan, Lewis Henry, 40
Mosque
    crépissage (remudding), 22, 24,
        32, 126, 172, 185–87
    history, 30–32
    tourist access, 121, 123, 158, 188
    World Heritage List, 21
Musée des Arts d'Afrique et
    d'Océanie, 54
Musée du Trocadéro, 47

Office de Radiodiffusion Télévision du
    Mali (ORTM), 187, 189
Office Malienne du Tourisme et
    de l'Hôtellerie (OMATHO),
    157–59

Palais du Trocadéro, 44
Park, Mungo, 41
Peace Corps, 54, 110, 118, 153, 180
Peul, 26, 27, 29, 30, 31, 90, 119,
    138, 139, 152, 184, 194
Pondo, 26, 27
population, 26
poverty, 20, 118–20
prayer economy, 99–101

Riegl, Alois, 200, 201
riot in 2006, 120–24
River Niger, 41, 44
Rousseau, Albert, 45
Rowlands, Michael, 204
Ruskin, John, 200

Salafi doctrine, 99
Samori Touré, 44

sanitation, 70–72
Saudi Arabia, 106, 208
Ségou, 41, 48, 136, 149, 168, 172,
    183, 196
Sékou Amadou, 31, 90
Senegal, 42, 44, 49, 77, 104
Sénoussa, 30, 184
Sidibé, Samuel, 55
Soares, Benjamin, 96, 97, 99
Société Malienne d'Exploitation
    de Resources Touristiques
    (SMERT), 151
Songhai, 25, 26, 27, 29, 45, 114, 130
Stonehenge, 204

Tapama Djennépo, 28, 168, 193
Tarikhs, 29, 105
Timbuktu, 26, 29, 33, 40, 45, 48, 55,
    71, 96, 103, 105, 148, 149, 151,
    161, 168, 172, 174, 207
    Essakane Festival, 189
    European explorers, 41–43
    Festival in the Desert, 36, 182
    history linked to that of Djenné, 25
    Islamic centre, 98
    Islamic manuscripts, 57
Togola, Téréba, 55
Touré, Amadou Toumani, 36, 97,
    145, 157
tourists, 165–75
Tuareg, 24, 26, 112, 144, 173, 182
Turtinen, Jan, 76
Tylor, Edward, 40

UNICEF, 20, 26, 105, 110, 118
United Nations World Tourism
    Organisation (UNWTO), 148
USAID, 26

women, 112–15
World Heritage List, 21, 45, 79, 80,
    82, 83, 88, 205

About the Author

Charlotte Joy holds a Ph.D. in Anthropology from University College London. She is completing an ESRC-funded postdoctoral fellowship in Anthropology at the Museum of Archaeology and Anthropology, University of Cambridge, specialising in developing a comparative ethnographic approach to the study of cultural heritage politics and its relation to development issues.

Made in the USA
Middletown, DE
30 January 2018